ILTS
Physical Education (144) Exam
SECRETS

Study Guide
Your Key to Exam Success

ILTS Test Review for the
Illinois Licensure Testing System

Dear Future Exam Success Story:

Congratulations on your purchase of our study guide. Our goal in writing our study guide was to cover the content on the test, as well as provide insight into typical test taking mistakes and how to overcome them.

Standardized tests are a key component of being successful, which only increases the importance of doing well in the high-pressure high-stakes environment of test day. How well you do on this test will have a significant impact on your future, and we have the research and practical advice to help you execute on test day.

The product you're reading now is designed to exploit weaknesses in the test itself, and help you avoid the most common errors test takers frequently make.

How to use this study guide

We don't want to waste your time. Our study guide is fast-paced and fluff-free. We suggest going through it a number of times, as repetition is an important part of learning new information and concepts.

First, read through the study guide completely to get a feel for the content and organization. Read the general success strategies first, and then proceed to the content sections. Each tip has been carefully selected for its effectiveness.

Second, read through the study guide again, and take notes in the margins and highlight those sections where you may have a particular weakness.

Finally, bring the manual with you on test day and study it before the exam begins.

Your success is our success

We would be delighted to hear about your success. Send us an email and tell us your story. Thanks for your business and we wish you continued success.

Sincerely,

Mometrix Test Preparation Team

Need more help? Check out our flashcards at: http://MometrixFlashcards.com/ILTS

Copyright © 2015 by Mometrix Media LLC. All rights reserved.
Written and edited by the Mometrix Exam Secrets Test Prep Team
Printed in the United States of America

TABLE OF CONTENTS

Top 20 Test Taking Tips 1
Health Related Physical Fitness 2
Movement and Skill Acquisition 26
The Role of Physical Education in Promoting Development 61
The Physical Education Program 67
Practice Test 85
    Practice Questions 85
    Answers and Explanations 103
Secret Key #1 - Time is Your Greatest Enemy 123
    Pace Yourself 123
Secret Key #2 - Guessing is not Guesswork 123
    Monkeys Take the Test 123
    $5 Challenge 124
Secret Key #3 - Practice Smarter, Not Harder 125
    Success Strategy 125
Secret Key #4 - Prepare, Don't Procrastinate 125
Secret Key #5 - Test Yourself 126
General Strategies 126
Special Report: How to Overcome Test Anxiety 131
    Lack of Preparation 131
    Physical Signals 131
    Nervousness 132
    Study Steps 134
    Helpful Techniques 135
Additional Bonus Material 139

Top 20 Test Taking Tips

1. Carefully follow all the test registration procedures
2. Know the test directions, duration, topics, question types, how many questions
3. Setup a flexible study schedule at least 3-4 weeks before test day
4. Study during the time of day you are most alert, relaxed, and stress free
5. Maximize your learning style; visual learner use visual study aids, auditory learner use auditory study aids
6. Focus on your weakest knowledge base
7. Find a study partner to review with and help clarify questions
8. Practice, practice, practice
9. Get a good night's sleep; don't try to cram the night before the test
10. Eat a well balanced meal
11. Know the exact physical location of the testing site; drive the route to the site prior to test day
12. Bring a set of ear plugs; the testing center could be noisy
13. Wear comfortable, loose fitting, layered clothing to the testing center; prepare for it to be either cold or hot during the test
14. Bring at least 2 current forms of ID to the testing center
15. Arrive to the test early; be prepared to wait and be patient
16. Eliminate the obviously wrong answer choices, then guess the first remaining choice
17. Pace yourself; don't rush, but keep working and move on if you get stuck
18. Maintain a positive attitude even if the test is going poorly
19. Keep your first answer unless you are positive it is wrong
20. Check your work, don't make a careless mistake

Health Related Physical Fitness

Components of health-related physical fitness

There are five major components of physical fitness that are directly related to health: (1) Cardiorespiratory endurance. This is the ability of the circulatory system, i.e., the heart and blood vessels; and the respiratory system, i.e., the lungs, trachea, bronchi, pharynx, larynx, and diaphragm, to supply the muscles and the rest of the body with oxygen during continuing physical activity over time. (2) Muscular strength. This is the greatest amount of force that any given muscle can generate during a single attempt. (3) Muscular endurance. This is how long a given muscle is able to continue to perform an exercise or activity without becoming fatigued, i.e., becoming unable to perform the movement anymore. (4) Flexibility. This is the ability to move the joints of the body through the full range of motion, e.g., when bending, turning, twisting, stretching, reaching, contracting, extending, etc. (5) Healthy body composition. This refers to the ratio of lean muscle tissue to fatty tissue in the body. The amount of muscle should be greater in proportion to the amount of fat, though there should be at least enough fat to enable normal body functions.

Developing muscular strength, muscular endurance, and cardiorespiratory endurance

Weight training, aka strength/resistance training, can use measured weights; exercise bands, exercise balls or other resistance gear; or one's own body weight. By exercising the musculoskeletal system, resistance training improves neurological control of muscle functions and enlarges muscle fibers. This promotes both muscular strength and muscular endurance—strength by increasing the maximum force a muscle contraction can produce, and endurance by increasing the maximum amount of weight one can lift repeatedly and/or the maximum number of repetitions one can lift the same weight. Cardiorespiratory endurance is not simply aerobic training, as it requires overload, accessing both aerobic and anaerobic energy systems through circuit/interval/other training. Stage training, e.g., a three-stage model, involves: (1) Developing baseline aerobic fitness at 65-75 percent of maximum heart rate, gradually increasing intensity and duration up to 30 minutes two or three times a week. (2) Raising intensity to 65-85 percent of maximum heart rate/14-16 RPE or, in other words, raising the level of intensity from "challenging" to "difficult." Work-to-rest ratios progress from 1:3 to 1:2, then 1:1, gradually increasing interval durations. (3) Short, high-intensity exercises (like sprinting) alternating with active recovery (like jogging), at 65-95 percent of maximum heart rate/17-19 RPE, or boosting the intensity from "difficult" to "impossible." Transitioning from stage (2) to (3) can take 2-3 months or more.

Benefits and characteristics of physical fitness training for developing flexibility

Flexibility not only improves muscular and aerobic training and sports performance and prevents athletic injuries, but also facilitates everyday life activities and prevents age-related mobility loss. Flexibility training releases muscle tension that builds up during workouts and reduces stress in working muscles; balances joint tension, improving posture; and makes muscles more pliable, decreasing injury risk. Stretching exercises should follow each workout, four to seven days weekly. Intensity should create slight muscular tension without causing pain. Instructors should remind learners to continue their breathing patterns throughout stretches. Duration varies according to individual motivation and needs, but generally should be at least 5 to 10 minutes per session. Instructors should design organized workouts to include stretching, as learners most frequently cut this short when pressed for time. Static stretching, done seated, is easy, safe, and (once learned) doable virtually anywhere without equipment or assistance; but limited in efficacy for competitive athletes or increasing flexibility in multiple ranges of motion

(ROMs). Dynamic stretching, done standing, uses reciprocal inhibition of opposing muscles to develop active ROM, gradually increasing in intensity and speed. Best for athletes and as warm-ups for movement-based sports and activities, it should be taught and learned gradually with appropriate movements to prevent trauma from excessive ROM or speed.

NASPE's definition of developmentally appropriate practices and programs

The National Association for Sport and Physical Education (NASPE)'s Council on Physical Education for Children (COPEC) identifies quality PE as both developmentally and instructionally appropriate for the actual children involved. This council defines developmentally appropriate PE practices as acknowledging the changing abilities of children for moving, and as promoting those changes. Developmentally appropriate PE programs are defined as addressing developmental status, body size, age, fitness levels, previous experiences with movement, and other various individual student characteristics. NASPE's COPEC defines instructionally appropriate education as including both research-based and experience-based best known practices in programs that give all children maximal opportunities to learn and succeed. The council identifies the result of a PE program that is both developmentally and instructionally appropriate as a "physically educated" individual. NASPE (1990) defined a physically educated individual as someone who has learned the necessary skills for performing varied physical activities, participates regularly in physical activity, is physically fit, knows the benefits and implications of engaging in physical activities, and values physical activity and what it contributes to healthy lifestyles. NASPE deems appropriate PE programs significant first steps in becoming physically educated.

Developmentally and instructionally appropriate vs. inappropriate practices

Appropriate PE curriculum enhances all students' physical, motor, cognitive, and affective fitness by balancing concepts, skills, games, educational gymnastics, and rhythm and dance experiences with an observable sequence and scope determined by goals and objectives appropriate for all students. Inappropriate curriculum is based on teacher backgrounds, preferences, and interests, e.g., mainly playing large-group or whole-class games without developed learning goals and objectives. Practices inappropriate for developing motor skills and movement concepts limit the number of activities, games, and opportunities for developing basic motor skills and concepts. Appropriate practices frequently offer students meaningful, age-appropriate opportunities to practice locomotor, non-locomotor, and manipulative motor skills, developing confidence in their ability to perform these. Students also develop functional comprehension of body awareness, spatial awareness, effort, relationships, and other movement concepts. Practices inappropriate for promoting cognitive development through PE do not give students opportunities to integrate PE with classroom, art, music, and other school experiences; and do not enable students' learning to move while moving to learn. Appropriate practices design PE activities considering both physical and cognitive development by enabling students to analyze, communicate, question, integrate, apply concepts, and attain multicultural worldviews, thereby integrating PE into the whole educational experience.

Developmentally and instructionally inappropriate vs. appropriate practices

PE practices inappropriate for promoting affective development include teacher exclusion of activities that help students develop social skills, and overlooking opportunities to help children understand emotions they experience from PE participation. Appropriate practices fostering affective development include purposely designing and implementing activities through the school year, enabling students to collaborate, cooperate, and develop emerging social skills and positive self-concepts; and helping every student feel and appreciate joy and satisfaction from participating regularly in physical activity. Inappropriate approaches to fitness concepts include requiring participation in fitness activities without helping students understand why. Appropriate approaches include designing activities that aid students in understanding and valuing significant physical fitness concepts and how these contribute to healthy lifestyles. Inappropriate uses of physical fitness tests include testing twice yearly, only as required by states/districts, or to qualify students for awards; requiring testing without students understanding why or what their results imply; and/or requiring testing without sufficient conditioning or preparation. Appropriate practices include conducting ongoing fitness assessment to help students understand, maintain (or improve), and enjoy physical well-being; sharing results privately with students and parents to develop knowledge, competence, and understanding; and preparing students for tests as part of ongoing PE programs.

Principles of cardiorespiratory endurance

PE teachers should explain to students that cardiorespiratory fitness is considered the most important component of physical fitness because it indicates effective functioning of their hearts, lungs, and blood vessels. They can tell them the heart is a pump with two sides: the right side supplies blood to the lungs, the left sends blood to different body systems. The vascular system provides body tissues with blood, which carries oxygen and carbon dioxide through the bloodstream. Cardiorespiratory fitness lowers risk of cardiovascular disease—America's foremost cause of death. It also reduces body fat and raises energy. PE teachers should encourage students to do all they can to avoid dying from cardiovascular disease, particularly if their families have histories of heart disease and/or diabetes. Cardiovascular disease screening measures total cholesterol, LDL, HDL, and triglycerides, which directly affect heart disease risk. Teachers should have students exercise aerobically, continuously using large muscles, to improve cardiorespiratory fitness, three to five days per week, at 60-85 percent of maximum heart rate, for 20-60 minutes continuously. Good exercises include walking, jogging, cycling, swimming, rowing, in-line skating, spinning, step aerobics, and dancing aerobically to music sustained at the necessary intensity.

Purpose and a philosophy of fitness testing
According to the National Association for Sport and Physical Education (NASPE, 2010) position statement, PE programs not only develop student physical skills and cognitive understanding about physical activity to inform physically active, healthy lifestyles, they also teach students the significance of health-related fitness. NASPE states that, for students to achieve these goals, they must acquire knowledge about health-related fitness components, and a required part of that learning process is the assessment of those components. A philosophy of fitness testing includes that purposeful measurement is a necessary part of quality PE, and fitness education is a component of the PE curriculum conforming to exercise physiology standards. Additionally, assessment and measurement should be integrated with instruction. Moreover, educators should develop plans for applying individual student fitness data to inform their instruction. Cardiorespiratory endurance can be tested in elementary schools using a mile or half-mile run, e.g., the PACER (Progressive Aerobic Cardiovascular Endurance Run) Test. Measurements are number of PACER laps run, and time in minutes taken to complete a mile. Some schools require assessment twice yearly (beginning and end), but require instruction and practice throughout the school year. Baseline and subsequent data enable monitoring student progress.

Safety practices
When exercising to develop greater cardiorespiratory endurance, students need not engage in strenuous activity. Teachers should start them slowly doing activities they enjoy, and supervise them in gradually increasing the intensity of their pace. Activities to improve cardiorespiratory endurance should elevate the heart rate for an extended duration of time, but at a safe level. These include activities like walking, bicycling, or swimming. PE experts say it is impossible to overemphasize the importance of drinking water before, during, and after exercising. Sweating during exercise depletes the body of fluid and electrolytes, which can disrupt heart rhythms, so hydration and rehydration are paramount. It is also

important to pay attention to the heat index—i.e., the effect that higher humidity has of raising the actual temperature to a functionally higher heat—when exercising outdoors, and modify workouts accordingly. Not only does humidity make temperatures effectively higher, it also prevents perspiration from evaporating, which keeps bodies from cooling off efficiently and can result in overheating, heat exhaustion, and heat prostration. Clothing unsuited to the weather can also cause serious health problems.

Flexibility

Flexibility is the ability to move the body freely. It encompasses two parts: range of motion (ROM), which is the extent of direction and distance that one's joints are able to move; and mobility, which is the ability of the muscles to move with restrictions around the joints. By pursuing flexibility training, one realizes benefits including increasing one's range of motion; decreasing one's risks for becoming injured during physical activities by making muscles more pliable, less stiff, and less prone to pulls, tears, ruptures, sprains, etc.; decreasing the soreness of muscles following exercise by keeping muscles more relaxed and looser; and enhancing overall athletic performance by using less energy for body movement through having more flexible muscles and joints. Flexibility not only improves sport performance, it also facilitates activities of daily living like lifting objects or children, squatting down, reaching high shelves, getting out of bed, and turning fully to see behind oneself when backing up or parking a car.

Principles, techniques, and safety practices
Stretching is an equally important part of fitness as strength and aerobic capacity, although some people often overlook it in training programs. Stretching before and after performing other conditioning exercises promotes flexibility and prevents stiffness, soreness, and even injuries. Before stretching, one should always warm-up. Injuries are more likely from stretching cold muscles. One should stretch the whole body, not just selected parts. Each stretch should be held for 15 to 30 seconds or more, but should *not* include bouncing, which can cause injuries. One should stretch until one feels some mild tension in the muscle or the joint, but not actual pain. Pain is a signal to stop whatever one is doing. When resuming, do not stretch as far, as hard, or as quickly; or stretch in a different manner or direction. While stretching, one should never hold one's breath, but should always continue to breathe normally.

Basic full-body stretches
Arms above head, palms up, stretch arms upward: stretches forearms, front upper arms, chest, and upper side muscles. Arms behind back, hands turned inward, stretch arms backward: stretches chest, shoulder, upper arms. Raise arm, bend elbow, place hand on the back. With other arm, grasp opposing elbow, pull upward toward opposite side: stretches outer upper arm, side, and back on raised-arm side. Arms outspread at sides below shoulders, move arms inward, stretching chest, shoulder, front and back arms. Sit with one leg straight, one knee bent upward, lower leg across straightened leg, foot on floor. Turn upper body away from crossed leg, placing hands on floor to side: stretches ribcage, leg, and outer hip. Sit with knees bent outward, as low to floor as possible, feet together, clasping feet with hands: stretches hips, inner thighs. Sit, legs together straight in front, feet flexed. Lean forward, stretching hamstrings. Stand, one hand touching surface; bend opposite knee behind; pull ankle up with same-side hand, stretching quadriceps. Bend from hips/waist; touch toes, stretching backs of legs, lower back. Hands on wall, one foot back, step forward with opposite foot: stretches back lower leg. Perform all one-sided stretches on each side.

Muscular strength vs. muscular endurance

Muscular strength equals how much force one can produce within one effort. Muscular endurance equals how many times one can repeat a movement before muscles become too fatigued to work. As examples, the amount of weight an individual can bench-press signifies that person's muscular strength; the number of times that individual can bench-press that weight repeatedly before fatiguing indicates that person's muscular endurance. The two are not necessarily equal in the same person. Some people can lift enormous amounts of weight, but only a few times, showing high muscular strength but low muscular endurance. Some people can lift a lesser amount of weight, but can repeat it many times, meaning lower muscular strength and higher muscular endurance. Others are high or low in both muscular strength and endurance. People can develop both muscular strength and muscular endurance through strength training, e.g., lifting weights or using resistance, by both executing many repetitions of the same action, gradually increasing the number of repetitions; and also gradually increasing the amount of weight or resistance used. One may build muscular strength and endurance in all muscle groups of the body, or concentrate on specific muscles or muscle groups.

Strength-training routine

Upper body
In lifting weights, one can work each arm individually using dumbbells, or both arms together using barbells. One thing to remember is that training each arm individually can result in slightly different levels of muscular strength and endurance in each arm. To begin workouts for the arms, use a general strength-training routine. Starting with weights of 20 pounds or lower, lift them 12 times; 12 repetitions (reps) equal one set. Do two or three sets of 12 repetitions each. As this becomes easier, start to lift heavier weights in small increments. Also gradually increase the number of sets performed. Increasing the weight builds muscular strength. Increasing the sets builds muscular endurance. One excellent exercise to increase upper-body muscular strength and endurance is doing push-ups. These build the pectoral muscles in the chest, the triceps muscles at the backs of the upper arms, and the deltoid muscles at the fronts of the shoulders. Even a few push-ups can be difficult for people lacking upper-body strength. Perform 10 repetitions, beginning with only one or two sets. Increase by two repetitions per week. Building upper-body strength enables more forceful arm extensions for bench-pressing, swimming, throwing, and more push-ups.

Lower body
Among the best lower-body and leg exercises are squats and lunges. These increase strength and endurance in the gluteus maximus, gluteus medius, gluteus minimus, and tensor fasciae latae muscles of the buttocks; the hamstrings along the backs of the legs; the quadriceps at the fronts of the thighs; and the gastrocnemius and soleus muscles in the calves. Strengthening these muscles improves running speed, power, distance, and stamina. A variation of squatting and lunging is to perform these holding dumbbells in both hands to increase weight resistance. To build muscular strength and endurance in the buttocks and legs, do three to five sets of 10 squats and/or lunges per set every other day. Some trainers recommend engaging in boxing and martial arts as sports that require high intensity and increase muscular strength and endurance. Striking opponents or punching bags with force requires muscular strength; going through 12 rounds in a boxing match requires endurance. While martial arts can involve the hands, arms, legs, and weapons, these sports also require strength and endurance to win. Learning both boxing and martial arts involves combinations of various cardiovascular, strength-training, and mental conditioning activities.

Improving body composition

Body composition is basically the ratio of fatty tissue to non-fatty tissue, especially lean muscle tissue, in the body. For people who are overweight, improving their body composition entails both decreasing their total proportion of body fat and increasing their total proportion of lean muscle tissue. For people who are underweight, it can include both gaining some body fat and also more muscle tissue. For people with normal weights and without excess fatty tissue but lacking muscular development, it involves increasing the proportion of lean muscular tissue in the body. While isolation exercises work only one joint at a time, compound exercises use movements that require articulations of multiple joints at a time. Compound exercises are best for improving body composition. Compound pushing exercises improve upper-body composition through resistance movements of the arms and shoulders. Those using horizontally loaded resistance include push-ups and weighted flat, incline and decline bench-presses, which work the pectorals, triceps, serratus, and lateral deltoid muscles. Exercises using vertically loaded resistance include the shoulder press and military press, which work the anterior deltoid, upper pectoral, and trapezius muscles.

Aerobic exercise
While strength training increases muscle and decreases fat, aerobic training is also effective for decreasing body fat. Visceral fat, surrounding the vital organs and concentrated in the abdomen, is more of a threat to health than subcutaneous fat, found elsewhere just below the skin. Recent research finds that high-intensity exercise reduces more visceral fat than moderate-intensity exercise. The "HIIT" method stands for "high-intensity interval training." High-intensity interval training involves exercising at high intensity and also to develop endurance. It can include running, sprinting, climbing stairs, running up and down stadium steps, or any other aerobic exercise performed at intensity levels of seven out of 10 or above. An example of high-intensity interval training would be running on a track, road, path, or treadmill at 70-95 percent of maximum capacity for 30 seconds to 5 minutes; resting for a duration equal to or greater than the exercise duration; and repeating the interval, for a total of approximately 22 minutes, at least three days of the week.

Safety practices
Before beginning any kind of exercise program, one should discuss it with a doctor or healthcare provider(s) to ensure types and amounts of exercise are safe for one's individual health, and learn whether s/he advises avoiding any particular activities because of specific health conditions (e.g., heart conditions) and/or previous injuries (e.g., not using arm poles while walking on a treadmill following a recent shoulder or upper-back injury). Then one should also have a consultation with a personal trainer who can assess body composition and develop an individualized training program targeting types of conditioning most needed and body parts needing contouring and what kinds, e.g., building muscle, increasing definition, reducing fat, changing shape, etc. Everybody should always warm-up for at least 10-15 minutes first. After warming up properly, they should then perform stretches with all muscle groups and joints to increase flexibility and lower risks for injuries. People should not eat large meals immediately before exercising, but they should eat a small meal 2-3 hours before, or a snack 30-60 minutes before. Drinking water before, during, and after working out is imperative.

Muscular endurance

(1) The continuous tension form of muscular endurance makes demands on the muscles to be under continuing tension for extended durations of time. Some continuous tension activities appropriate for middle school students include tug-of-war, isometric muscle contractions, extremely slow muscle contractions, isolation exercises, compound exercises without lockouts, beginning weight training, and supervised mountain climbing or wall climbing. (2) The repetitive dynamic contraction form of muscular endurance requires repeated muscle contractions over time periods. Some middle-school activities include running, bicycling, swimming, rowing, skating, and weight training involving many repetitions and/or supersets using the same muscle. (3) The prolonged, intense contractions with short rest periods form of muscular endurance involves contractions for longer durations with brief recovery periods between bouts. Some activities include playing football; handball; ice hockey; and weight training that

involves circuit training (going from one exercise or machine to another in a circuit), performing multiple sets of repetitions, and/or performing multiple different exercises to work the same muscle.

Gymnasium or outdoor activities

Grades 4-9
Body core strength provides a foundation for all sports and physical activities. Here are some gym/outdoor activities with core-strengthening exercises for grades 4-6 and 7-9. Equipment includes one basketball, volleyball, soccer ball, or medicine ball per student; jump ropes; folding mats; ribbon sticks, scarves, pom-poms; exercise bands; and masking tape. Have students warm-up first and then choose partners and balls. Teachers review exercises for core strength and stability. Considering any student physical limitations or injuries, teachers offer variations and/or have students suggest variations. Exercises include abdominal crunches with feet on floor, feet raised 90 degrees, and elbow-to-opposite-knee; V-sits (legs and torso form a V); twisting V-sits; same-sided hand-to-heel touch sit-ups; bicycles; hip raises; dolphin kicks; side planks; alternating leg-lowering from 90 degrees; and "superhumans" lying prone, raising opposite arm and leg alternately. Partners alternate: one performs, one gives feedback. Students may roll dice to decide repetition numbers, or repeat to muscle fatigue. Individual students record activities and repetitions they completed. Use these for future reference to monitor progress. Ribbon sticks, scarves, pom-poms and exercise bands can help some students extend their movements. Teachers encourage students to practice their favorite activities every 15 minutes for 30 seconds while watching TV, doing homework, or using computers.

Grades K-6
This creative dance activity for grades K-3 and 4-6 builds endurance and develops spatial awareness and concepts. Equipment needed includes audio player, recorded music, and pathway signs. Teachers review space concepts of direction and pathways, e.g., combining locomotor movements with directions. Teachers call out forward, backward, and sideways directions for students to take while moving around the gym; then combine a locomotor pattern and direction, e.g., walking backward, skipping sideways, galloping forward, etc. Teachers draw these patterns on pathway signs and post on the walls. Teachers point at pathway pictures and have students move using these, first using two body parts and then three, for example, straight, zigzag, small curves, larger curves; small spirals, larger spirals. Teachers lead students around the gym in a large spiral pathway. Have students move in pairs to pathways they choose; have some pairs demonstrate. Have students combine three or more pathways and directions to create "movement stories." Remind them to notice others' movements, shoulder-check while moving backward, and avoid collisions. Have some students demonstrate stories and others identify directions and pathways included. Use music with strong beats during story creation and presentation. For more complexity, have students add shapes (square, rectangular, circular, triangular, figure-eight, or favorite letter, for instance) into stories.

Exercising effective for losing weight

When students who have been inactive want to lose weight and/or become more physically fit, their initial enthusiasm assures their motivation to pursue these goals; however, they must be counseled to moderate their eagerness to obtain results quickly or they will strain their muscles or overwork their entire bodies. Particularly when they are not already conditioned, they must be warned not to begin at high intensity or repeat initial workouts obsessively. These practices cause injuries, derailing fitness efforts early. Students should be taught to begin slowly, paying attention to their bodies' feedback; when they feel ready, they can increase their intensities, speeds, repetitions, and durations gradually, a little at a time. Incorrect form is also a hazard for inexperienced exercisers. They should begin working out in front of mirrors to observe and modify their body positions as needed. Teachers and trainers can help correct form. Students should determine they are using proper form before increasing the speed of their repetitions. Another consideration is not focusing overly on body parts. Students may think exercises to tone and build specific muscles will give them their desired appearance; however, regular exercise combined with healthy nutrition more effectively shape bodies overall.

Physical exercise

Safety during strength training exercises
(1) Never hold your breath, which can cause lightheadedness, dizziness, and fainting. (2) Never lock elbows, knees, or other joints; this produces tremendous stress and can cause injuries. (3) When lifting barbells, always use bar collars. (4) Concentrate on lifting and lowering weights slowly with control to maximize effectiveness and prevent injury. (5) When using free weights, always have a spotter to help prevent injuries and with using correct form. (6) When using free weights, always keep both hands at equal distances from the middle of the bar. Unequal distances can stress and injure one side of the body. (7) Never overly bend or twist the spine; this can cause lower back problems and injuries. (8) While using weights standing up, always keep the knees slightly bent to prevent undue stress on the lower back. (9) When doing leg exercises with weights or resistance, always keep the knees in alignment with the toes to avoid leg injuries. (10) Always replace weights so others will not trip over them. Always place weights on the correct racks so others do not mistakenly pick up the wrong weights.

Biomechanical principles to ensure safety and effectiveness
Using biomechanics correctly ensures safety. For example, lunges with knee aligned over ankle are safe; lunges extending the knee past the ankle are mechanically incorrect and unsafe. Consider individual differences, e.g., a healthy 18-year-old female can safely do a squat-jump, but a 66-year-old female with osteoporosis cannot. Biomechanical changes informing ineffective, inefficient, or unsafe movements include: movement pattern changes, indicating fatigue and compensation with other body parts; body weight shifts, indicating fatigue or excessive difficulty; forward body flexion, indicating fatigue preventing muscles from overcoming gravitational pull; and flexed or bent joints, shortening muscles to be ineffective and inefficient, also indicating fatigued working muscles. According to the force-length curve, muscles generate their greatest force when slightly stretched or just past resting length. To choose safe, effective, and efficient exercises, incorporate walking, cycling, and other natural movement patterns. Repeat the same movements during and between lessons. Design lessons and programs in logical sequences or increments. Minimize degrees of freedom, i.e., number of joints involved. Minimize intersegmental coordination, i.e., different simultaneous arm and leg movements, such as an overhead press plus a squat. Select bilateral exercises for equal, opposite workloads. Distribute forces evenly across the body to minimize impact point. Apply forces horizontally or parallel, not vertically or downward to the body.

Physical fitness and the majority of people

A definition of physical fitness that applies to most people rather than only to professional athletes is being able to actively complete all of one's daily living tasks without becoming overly tired and still having enough energy to pursue leisure activities for enjoyment. Physical activity should include both planned, structured activities, and movement that is integrated into daily life as an essential part of it. Regularly engaging in physical activity and exercise are not only required for being athletic, but for basic well-being and health. To be effective and safe, any comprehensive physical fitness program should incorporate the three major components of (1) aerobic exercise, to promote cardiovascular health, endurance, and to manage weight; (2) resistance training, which decreases risks for lower-back injuries and pain, improves posture, builds strength and muscular endurance, and also manages weight; and (3) flexibility to stretch the muscles and move the joints, which prevents sore muscles, decreases the chances of injury, and maintains and/or improves the range of motion of the joints and the mobility of the muscles.

Durations and intensities of aerobic activity

In fitness plans for most individuals, aerobic activity at a moderate level is recommended to add up to 150 minutes, or 2.5 hours per week. Aerobic activity at a vigorous level is recommended for half that duration, i.e., 75 minutes per week. Individuals may also choose to combine or alternate moderate and vigorous aerobic activities for equivalent durations. During activities at moderate intensities, people are able to speak but unable to sing. During activities at vigorous intensities, people can only utter a few words before needing to pause for breath. Examples of moderate-intensity activities include walking briskly, 3 mph or faster; bicycling at less than 10 mph; playing doubles tennis; doing water aerobics; ballroom dancing, and dancing in general. Examples of vigorous-intensity activities include running, jogging, race-walking; bicycling at more than 10 mph; playing singles tennis; swimming laps; aerobic dancing; doing heavy, continuous gardening that raises the heart rate; hiking with a heavy backpack or uphill; and jumping rope.

Assessing an individual's current physical status

To assess individual current status, define fitness goals, and identify what one is able or willing to do to achieve them, identify the following: current age; indicators of the current body fat, e.g., a "six-pack," a small belly, or a large belly; and an index of current strength, e.g., one can do a few push-ups and pull-ups, at least 10 good push-ups and five good pull-ups, or at least 20 good push-ups and 10 good pull-ups. Define a fitness goal, e.g., wanting people to perceive you (a) are trim and healthy, (b) must work out, or (c) must compete athletically. Define how soon you want or need to accomplish this goal, e.g., in a few months to a year, 1-2 years, or 3-6 years. To define what you are able or willing to do, identify whether you have about 2-4 hours, 5-10 hours, or 11-21 hours weekly to devote to fitness. Nutritionally, are you willing to substitute a few healthy for unhealthy foods, or consistently avoid junk food and eat produce, whole grains, and lean protein? Or eat six small meals daily and follow a strict dietary plan? Individuals should also identify their available exercise equipment and partners.

Health-related fitness

PE programs and teachers instruct students not only in sport skills, but also in the significance of health-related fitness. PE teachers need to help students develop both comprehension cognitively and competence physically to engage in regular physical activity to enable them to follow physically active, healthful lifestyles. To do so, students need to learn about health-related fitness needs, principles, and goals. One required component of this learning process is the assessment of fitness through testing. Some examples of fitness tests often used to assess elementary school student fitness include measuring the number of push-ups, curl-ups, and chin-ups they can do, and how well they can repeat these to a beat, to assess muscular strength and endurance. To assess flexibility, PE teachers may measure how far in inches a student can reach while sitting and how far s/he can stretch. To assess cardiorespiratory endurance and aerobic capacity, a common measure is how many laps a student can run, and the time in minutes it takes a student to run a mile or a half-mile.

Fitness assessment data

Fitness assessment data furnishes students, teachers, parents, and other stakeholders with student fitness feedback. Comparing baseline to subsequent data enables PE teachers to monitor student progress. PE teachers can also use fitness testing data to inform their curriculum development decisions about which program content will best address students' strengths and needs. Students can make use of their own fitness testing data to inform measurable goals they set for personal fitness plans. PE teachers can use fitness testing results to individualize and differentiate their instruction for each student to help them achieve their goals. Fitness assessment data can also be used motivationally: identifying skill improvements and attaining goals give students incentive to live active, healthy lives. When PE teachers conduct authentic fitness assessments, the results inform the context for the curricula and activities they plan. This helps students comprehend the reasons for PE activities, rather than assuming PE is simply playing games. Student motivation for physical activity; understanding of how to evaluate and improve personal fitness levels; self-assessment, data analysis, and development of personal fitness goals and plans are also enabled by using fitness data.

Conducting fitness assessment and reporting the data
According to the National Association for Sport and Physical Education (NASPE), fitness assessment is one of the components of the continual process of enabling students to comprehend, maintain, improve, and enjoy physical fitness that PE teachers should use. PE teachers should physically prepare students in each fitness component and testing protocol of the assessment instruments used to ensure safe participation. Teachers should do everything needed to establish non-threatening, private, encouraging, and educational testing circumstances. For example, they should explain to students what each test is designed to evaluate. They should encourage students to use test results as springboards for personal progress, not to compare themselves with others. Teachers should ensure the privacy of students and parents when sharing test results and not post these publicly to compare. They should use these results as tools to help students and parents develop individual goals and strategies to sustain and improve fitness measures. Teachers should also report student progress regularly to students and parents. Students should be informed immediately after testing of their scores, and use these during instruction throughout the school year. Parents should receive student fitness reports following completed assessments.

Establishing and maintaining personal fitness programs

Statistics show that half of all people who embark upon exercise programs abandon them within only six months of beginning. Therefore, personal trainers recommend assorted techniques to adopt that will increase the likelihood of sticking with an exercise program long enough to make it a permanent lifestyle change and reap its benefits to health and well-being. One technique is to identify the best location for exercising. Students who do not get enough exercise through school PE classes need to choose places best suited for them. Some will find working out at a gym offers fewer distractions and better facilities, equipment, and trainers; others will find exercising at home more convenient. Distantly located gyms decrease the likelihood of attendance. Students should also identify the time(s) with the most convenience and fewest distractions for exercising; and the activities they enjoy most because the more convenient and fun a program is, the more likely they are to continue it. Starting exercise at overly high intensities and/or durations predicts dropout. Those who work out with more experienced partners may also overdo it.

Establishing and monitoring personal fitness goals
Adults and students alike should set fitness goals that lead to long-term changes in lifestyle and are realistic. Goals should include both results and behaviors. For example, jumping 1 inch higher by the next sport season and losing 12 pounds within three months reflect outcome goals. Exercising every weekday at 7:30 p.m. for 20 minutes is a behavioral goal. To set suitable behavioral goals, students should understand the underlying objectives. Students can have far more control over accomplishing behavioral goals than outcome goals, so they should focus on attaining those target behaviors. If they do not meet short-term outcomes by their original goal deadlines, they should not let this discourage them. When they

do accomplish outcome-related goals, students should change their behavioral goals accordingly. If they are not sure they can meet behavior goals consistently, or if they find more effective ways of meeting their objectives, students should re-evaluate their fitness plans.

Maintaining motivation and commitment to personal fitness goals and plans

Planning specific workout times and establishing a routine helps physical activity become a habit. Students can enter these in their smartphone or tablet calendars like appointments; set alarms to remind them when to exercise; and pack workout bags or lay out exercise clothes and gear in advance. If they sometimes don't feel like exercising, they can agree with themselves to do just a short, light workout. Once prepared and warmed up, they will often become motivated for a full session. They should not give up hope if they miss a session, but reevaluate their fitness behavior plans, adjust strategies to prevent future omissions, recommit, analyze past barriers and identify new strategies to surmount them, and make backup plans for unexpected events or situations. Doing a variety of activities and exercises maintains interest. This includes fun activities like playing sports, kayaking; practical ones like walking dogs, yard work, walking to the store; and trying out new activities. Planning activities for the week or month helps. So does changing workouts according to changing interests and moods. Music, TV, and/or reading while walking, jogging, or cycling prevent boredom. Partners provide social support. Pedometers, stop watches, heart monitors, etc., and logging activity in writing or on digital devices help monitor progress.

Interaction between diet, physical activity, and health

Regular physical activity aids in weight control; strengthens the heart, blood vessels, lungs, muscles, bones, and joints; and lowers risks for heart disease, stroke, diabetes, and various cancers. However, physical activity must be combined with good nutrition to be most effective. In fact, improper nutrition can even undermine any benefits of physical activity. For one thing, the body requires fuel to be physically active. People who eat too little and/or eat food that is not nutritious will not have enough energy to exercise. For another, foods high in refined sugars and flours and saturated fats will actually cause fatigue, depriving a person of energy and motivation to be active. In addition, people who want to build muscle cannot do so through strength training alone; they must eat lean proteins to supply the amino acids that are the building blocks of muscle. Foods high in refined sugars and flours and saturated fats are also very high in calories. Exercising, even vigorously for hours, is usually insufficient to burn as many calories as one can easily consume from the junk foods, fast foods, and restaurant foods so prevalent in modern society. Improper nutrition can derail the health benefits of physical activity.

Relationship between physical activity, healthy weight, and general health

To lose weight, you must expend more calories than you consume. In other words, weight loss requires a calorie deficit. Although most people lose weight by reducing the calories they eat, research evidence also finds regularly engaging in physical activity necessary for maintaining that weight loss. This explains why so many people who do not engage in enough regular physical activity regain weight after losing it. Even when people have lost weight, if they are physically active on a regular basis they lower their risk of diabetes and cardiovascular disease beyond the risk reduction afforded by weight loss alone. To put the relationship between diet, exercise, and weight into perspective, consider that a Big Mac from McDonald's has about 550 calories. A person who weighs about 150 pounds would have to run at a speed of 5 mph for an hour to burn that many calories. Few if any people who just ate a Big Mac will want or be able to run that fast for that long. Moreover, its high saturated fat content, refined white flour, etc. all contribute to cardiovascular disease, diabetes, and cancers.

Deficiencies in nutrition and physical activity

According to the Centers for Disease Control and Prevention (CDC), physical inactivity and poor diet are major causes of chronic non-communicable diseases, from which hundreds of thousands of people die every year. In addition to deaths, disabilities caused by strokes, obesity, diabetes, and osteoporosis are the results of improper nutrition and sedentary lifestyles. The Healthy People initiatives have found that almost two-thirds of Americans eat too much saturated fat, three-quarters do not eat enough fruit, and more than half do not eat enough vegetables. People who are inactive physically have nearly twice the probability of developing heart disease as people who are active regularly. This makes physical inactivity approach high blood pressure, high cholesterol, or smoking cigarettes as a risk factor for heart disease. However, physical inactivity is a more prevalent risk factor than any of those others. Sedentary people who are also obese and have high blood pressure, and hence have multiple risk factors, can especially benefit from becoming physically active.

Recommendations for a balanced diet for achieving and/or maintaining a healthy weight

According to the US Centers for Disease Control and Prevention (CDC) and the federal Dietary Guidelines, a healthy diet should place the most emphasis on fruits and vegetables, whole grains, and fat-free or low-fat dairy products. It should also include lean protein sources like beans, fish, eggs, nuts, poultry, and lean meats. It should eliminate or limit trans fats, saturated fats, salt, added sugars, and cholesterol. In addition, a balanced diet should not contain many more or fewer calories than an individual needs every day to function optimally. Eating fresh produce in season, especially produce grown locally, is best. When favorite fruits are out of season or unaffordable, they are available frozen, canned, or dried. One caveat is to avoid canned fruits with heavy, sugar-laden syrups and find those canned in their own juices. If fresh vegetables are unavailable, many are flash-frozen at their peak nutritional value without added sodium or fatty sauces. For canned vegetables, avoid those with added sodium. Some ways to enjoy vegetables more include steaming them; adding different herbs, which provide flavor without salt or fat; sautéing in non-stick pans with a little cooking spray; and trying a new or unfamiliar vegetable every week.

Weight management strategies

The healthiest diets involve balance rather than completely eliminating foods we enjoy. Many people's favorite "comfort foods" happen to have high caloric, sugar, and/or fat content. To lose weight and/or maintain weight loss, it is not necessary to give up these foods entirely, though. One strategy is to indulge in fattening foods, but less often. For example, instead of every day, eat them once a week, or even once a month. Not eating high-calorie foods as frequently reduces overall calories. Another strategy is enjoying fattening foods in smaller portions. For example, if a favorite comfort food is a candy bar, only eat half of it or buy it in a smaller size. Manufacturers offer many miniature, "snack size," or "fun size" candy bars. Sometimes taste and texture provide enough enjoyment rather than amount. Another strategy is comfort food "makeovers." For example, macaroni and cheese can be remade with skim milk instead of whole milk, low-fat cheese, and less butter. Some people incorporate healthier foods to lower calories while adding fiber and nutrients, e.g., cauliflower in macaroni and cheese, puréed spinach or beets in brownies, etc.

<u>Maintaining current weight</u>
Some individuals are not overweight, but will need to plan to avoid gaining weight. Others are overweight, but currently not ready to lose weight. In either case, weight maintenance has the benefits of preventing many chronic diseases, as well as minimizing the need for future weight loss. The number of calories needed to maintain weight varies individually. Variables affecting this include height, weight, gender, age, levels of physical activity, and muscle-to-fat ratio. Muscle tissue burns more calories than

fatty tissue, even at rest. Thus some people have higher basal metabolisms than others; these people can afford to consume more calories without gaining weight. Some of this body composition is natural, some lifestyle-related. More physically active people burn more calories and can eat more than sedentary people. To maintain current weight, it is useful for people to weigh themselves regularly. It is easier to lose a gain of 2-3 pounds discovered sooner than 10 pounds discovered later. If weight creeps up, it helps to self-examine changes in physical activity and eating. People can keep food diaries, activity logs, and use numerous available digital apps for self-monitoring.

Physical fitness and weight management activities

Experts say that, to be healthy, children and teens need to engage in moderate physical activity for around an hour a day, adults around half an hour a day, about five days a week. But most Americans fall far short of these parameters. Increasing the frequency and duration of physical activity improves health even more. People who want to lose weight or maintain their weight loss may need 40-90 minutes of physical activity daily. Modern conveniences plus school and occupational work primarily done seated interfere with physical activity. Lack of financial resources is another obstacle. People living in socioeconomically disadvantaged communities lack not only money, but often also accessible community recreation facilities like safe outdoor parks, indoor recreation centers, facilities, equipment, and clubs or other social groups focusing on physical activities. There are solutions, however. For time, physical activity like walking can be divided into small, 10-minute sessions three times daily. For motivation, family outings, free or low-cost group activities, and walking and exercise partners offer social support.

Encouraging physical activity in communities and families

Research finds people are more likely to engage in physical activities for recreation when they are located near their homes and are free or inexpensive. Even in communities containing beautiful state parks and other natural areas, citizens still prefer recreation that is closest to home and most affordable. People are more likely to exercise regularly when they live within 1 mile of a recreational facility. Another factor affecting physical recreation is safety. People who ride bicycles and walk or jog for recreation often must use public roads and streets, where motor vehicle traffic threatens their safety and discourages their participation. Some communities have obtained funding to create local bike, walking, and/or jogging paths separate and safe from road traffic. Because low-income families are less apt to enjoy access to recreational facilities, experts recommend that establishing free or low-cost facilities in low-income communities would make an appreciable difference in their physical activity levels, improving their health and enjoyment in life.

Enhancing physical activity levels among diverse populations

Experts recommend that local government offices should work together with members of their communities who represent people with disabilities, low incomes, and culturally and ethnically diverse backgrounds. Incorporating the input and insight these community members can contribute, they can collaborate to make organized plans; identify, secure, and prepare or renovate suitable sites; construct community recreation facilities; and staff, operate, and manage them. When families have access to recreational facilities that are close to their homes and provide safe environments, appropriate space and equipment, and beneficial social interaction, they are much more likely to engage in physical activity for recreation, benefiting their physical, mental, and social health and well-being. Some neighborhoods have organized local walking groups and activities in ethnically diverse communities. These combine greater physical activity with safety and social interaction. Residents report greater neighborhood pride and ownership and stronger sense of community. Mexican-American citizens have reported in focus groups that they value family-based physical activities. For culturally competent responses, recreation facilities should organize family exercise programs rather than individually targeting women, men, seniors, youth, etc.

Physical activity addresses stress

One way in which physical activity combats stress is by directly reducing it. Moving at moderate intensity long enough to increase the heart rate, breathe more deeply, work the muscles, and break a light sweat releases endorphins. These hormones, named from the Greek meaning "the morphine within," produce a naturally occurring "high," or sense of euphoria. Endorphins also alleviate physical and mental pain. People feel physically and mentally relaxed after expending energy; working the heart, lungs, and muscles; and perspiring and releasing toxins. Family and friends often observe someone they know well seems and feels much more "mellow" after exercising. Worries and negative attitudes are frequently dissipated by exercise. Another way physical activity affects stress is by improving the ability to cope with it. While some stressors are inherent in life and cannot themselves be eliminated, people's attitudes toward them can change markedly through being physically active. Increased physical strength, stamina, and flexibility afford greater senses of personal competence and empowerment. Increased blood circulation enables clearer thinking, hence more effective problem-solving. Enhanced physical and mental health synergistically improve capacities for dealing with life's challenges.

Physically active lifestyle promotes enjoyment and challenge

Enjoyment: (1) A high school boy never interested in traditional intramural and team sports offered in PE classes sees a brochure on kayaking and decides to enroll in lessons at a local outdoor adventure training company. He finds navigating rapids thrilling and enjoys interacting with nature. (2) Some low-income urban kindergarteners have done unstructured running, jumping, etc., and played simple games like Simon Says at home, but never learned any physically active games with rules. Their teacher introduces them to a variety of games wherein they must walk, run, change directions, link arms, jump, tumble, do extensions; throw, bowl, and fetch balls; touch things, etc., following teacher directions and rules. They enjoy these new experiences. Challenge: (1) A middle school girl can only do a few sit-ups. Her PE teacher assigns 30 sit-ups to alternating pairs. While spotting her partner—a pretty, thinner friend she admires, she sees the effort on her face with each sit-up. She is inspired to complete all 30 during her turn. (2) A high school student has run 500-yard dashes, but never a marathon, and doubts her ability. Her PE teacher encourages her. After training regularly for three months, she successfully completes a full 26-mile race.

Increasing social interaction and decreasing healthcare expenses

Social interaction: (1) Two high school girls have free periods at the end of the day and don't want to wait for the bus. They decide to walk to one of their homes instead. During the 3-mile trip, they enjoy conversing and interacting in the outdoors more than on a noisy, crowded school bus. (2) A boy in elementary school gets good grades but is socially introverted and lacks physical self-confidence. His parents offer to enroll him in Little League baseball. As he learns and succeeds he gains confidence, teammates applaud and encourage him, and he makes new friends. Healthcare expenses: (1) A diabetic child's mother is overprotective about exercise. The school nurse and PE teacher collaborate with her on a plan for regular blood sugar testing during the school day, suitable exercise, and appropriate snacks before and after exercising. As a result, her family doctor reduces the child's insulin dosage. (2) A PE teacher, collaborating with a dietician and school nurse, designs a safe fitness program for an obese high school student. With significant weight loss, his type 2 diabetes symptoms abate. He needs less medication and fewer doctor visits; as a result, his parents' health insurance co-pays decrease.

Helping young people improve their self-concepts and self-esteem

International Council for Sport Science and Physical Education President and professor Margaret Talbot has written that challenging physical activities like sports and dance are powerfully influential for helping youth "learn to be themselves." She finds that, when presented appropriately, such activities teach young people to question assumptions they have held that limit them, and to perceive themselves and their potentials anew. In *Run Like a Girl: How Strong Women Make Happy Lives* (2011), Mina Samuels writes that once she discovered running, she not only gained self-confidence, but she found she was stronger than expected. As a result, she perceived herself differently, as someone with greater potential and a bigger future who could take risks and push herself—not just in sports but other life areas—by competing with herself rather than others, and setting and meeting higher expectations and standards for herself. Psychologists find physical self-worth, sense of autonomy and self-efficacy enhanced through developing competence in sport skills. Studies have found elementary, high school, and Latino students benefit with higher self-esteem from school sports participation and other physical activity.

Enhancment of mental and emotional well-being

Many research studies find improvements in mood, with fewer symptoms of anxiety and depression, resulting from physical activity. Experiments have compared participants with major depression, giving some psychotropic medication and others an aerobic exercise intervention. The exercisers demonstrated more significant improvements and lower relapse rates than those taking the drugs. Other research has shown that walking programs increase positive mood. Six-month resistance training programs have decreased anger, tension, and confusion while elevating moods in participants. Investigators comparing the effects of yoga, dance, or lecture on participants' psychological well-being found significantly lowered negative affect and stress perception in the groups with the physical activities. Large-scale studies with adolescents find correlations between increased leisure-time physical activity and decreased symptoms of depression. In addition, research with 4th-grade Hispanic children from low-income families has found their self-esteem and cardiovascular fitness increased while their depression decreased when they participated in an aerobic intensity physical activity program.

Self-management skills with a physically active lifestyle

Self-assessment skills enable: self-evaluating fitness and interpre-ting results, e.g., choosing and self-administering good fitness assessments; goal-setting and plan-making; and success, new thinking, and learning skills. Self-monitoring skills entail keeping records, enabling viewing one's behavior more objectively and accurately, and gauging progress toward goals. For example, if you cut calories yet aren't losing weight, record-keeping can reveal you are eating more than you thought. Keeping progress records also promotes adhering to fitness plans and programs. These skills sup-ply information and feedback, help change beliefs, aid planning and goal-setting, and raise success probabilities. Goal-setting skills are particularly important for beginners at behavior change. They enable establishing achievable, realistic future objectives. For example, success is more likely for someone wanting to reduce fat with a process goal to eat 200 fewer calories and burn 200 more calories daily than an outcome goal to lose 50 pounds. These skills facilitate planning and feedback, build confidence, change attitudes and beliefs, and increase enjoyment and success. Planning skills enable independently designing fitness programs, reinforcement, self-con-fidence, success, and enjoyment. Performance skills enhance com-petence, self-confidence, attitudes, success, and enjoyment. An ex-ample is learning stress-management and relaxation skills. Balanc-ing attitudes enhances planning; goal-setting; beliefs; and enjoy-ment, e.g., emphasizing exercise's positive aspects, not its negative.

Naturalistic observations vs. structured observations as assessment methods

Naturalistic observations entail unobtrusively observing student performance as it typically occurs in students' usual daily setting, e.g., practice during regular PE classes. While this method has the advantage of seeing realistic instances of typical student behaviors, it has been criticized for allowing the teacher's judgments to be overly subjective. Structured observations provide an alternative solution by applying specific criteria, of which teacher and students are both informed, to evaluate observed performance. This criterion reference has the advantage of shifting observational assessment from more subjective to more objective. Teachers may use a rubric to provide the criteria against which they measure student performance. Structured observations are particularly useful for assessing student motor skills, movement skills, and social skills. Two methods of structured observation are station approach and embedded assessment. In station approach, teachers set up a circuit with several stations, assigning students to individual stations. Some stations involve mini-games, some motor skill practice, some exercising, one the testing station where teachers assess student skills. In embedded assessment, teachers instruct and assess simultaneously, evaluating students' learning while they practice skills—through periodic progress monitoring or end-of-unit summative assessment.

Checklists and record-keeping

Because so many PE activities must be performed physically to demonstrate learning rather than answering questions on written tests, it is natural for teachers to use observation to assess student skill acquisition. When they observe student performance, PE teachers and coaches are typically looking for them to demonstrate skills or skill areas. Checklists lend themselves to observational assessment because they list these skill areas in advance; the teacher or coach needs only check a box reflecting the level of the student's mastery, e.g., yes/no; skilled/talented/athletically gifted; etc. For example, a student checklist for PE class might list student demonstration of: strength and endurance; balance and flexibility; skill in moving through space; interest in a sport or activity the student can pursue on a lifelong basis; ability to follow oral directions in games and sports; age-appropriate, ability-appropriate gross and fine motor skills; and participation in noncompetitive group activities and games. The checklist might also include a space at the bottom for the teacher to write district PE objectives.

A good sport checklist has lines for student name, team, teacher or coach name, and assessment period. Some typical skills to assess via checking Yes or No, with a column at the right for comments, include practice punctuality and participation; positive attitude with teacher/coach and teammates; skills in sport-specific techniques, with lines for the teacher or coach to list these; healthy competitive and aggressive levels for sport participation; and equipment use skills, with lines to write specific pieces of equipment. The checklist can include an additional column for notes or comments. A cheerleading performance checklist can include mastery levels, e.g., Skilled, Talented, or Athletically Gifted, to check for skills like these: energy and enthusiasm; voice inflection and projection; memorization and rhythm of routines; jumping height and technique; tumbling and gymnastics; punctuality, attendance, professional attitude, and cooperation; creativity, e.g., changing or developing cheers, routines, and dances; use of pom-poms, flags, and other show props; choreography and dance skills; and additional sections for recommendations and notes.

Psychomotor, cognitive, and affective domains in PE

The psychomotor, cognitive, and affective domains are interrelated in PE, which makes physical movement meaningful. The psychomotor domain is the performance component whereby students acquire physical skills through environmental exploration. The cognitive domain is the knowledge component whereby students think and relate their experiences to learning. The affective domain is the personal, emotional, and social component whereby students interact with other people, developing a sense of self and others. When students understand why their bodies function as they do through the cognitive domain, they begin to acquire skill competencies through the psychomotor domain, and learn to associate physical activity with positive feelings through the affective domain. In the psychomotor domain, developing competence in motor skill abilities is the essence of PE. In the cognitive domain, students are enabled to become more efficient at moving and at learning through moving, through understanding the principles and concepts of movement. In the affective domain, students develop acceptable personal and social behaviors in physical activity contexts, behaving responsibly as individuals and group members to afford productive learning environments.

When a PE teacher assesses a student in the psychomotor domain, he or she measures student development of health-related fitness and motor skills. For example, when a teacher assesses elementary school student skipping skill, students demonstrate the step-hop pattern; when the teacher assesses older students, they might administer the FITNESSGRAM test battery. When a PE teacher assesses students in the cognitive domain, he or she measures student knowledge about movement concepts, principles, strategies, and tactics. For example, middle school students might be asked to explain verbally a strategy for defending their territory in a sport activity, or to verbalize a "Ready, swing back, step, and follow through" movement skill pattern to use in performing an underhand throw. When a PE teacher assesses students in the affective domain, he or she measures the level to which each student has developed acceptable personal and social behaviors in physical activity settings. As an example, the teacher might have high school students complete written self-reflections about their own performance, write peer performance evaluations of classmates or teammates, or identify, observe, and create (as appropriate) safety rules or guidelines for physical activity participation.

Different types of assessments

While assessment in PE often uses observation of student skill performance, it is not considered assessment unless some written record is made of the observations. When team games are played as part of PE, the game play statistics teachers and coaches record are examples of using event-recording techniques to collect student team performance data. Game statistics, wins and losses, fitness scores, skill assessments, and other daily "snapshots" or performance records are formal. Checklists identifying specific behaviors/skills/performance characteristics according to established criteria are informal, enabling quick evaluations with minimal writing. Rating scales are also informal and brief, identifying the degree or extent to which students perform skills. Rubrics are formal, establishing multidimensional criteria for rating complex skills and behaviors. Student surveys, questionnaires, and interviews are informal, collecting information about how students feel and think about PE. Student logs are formal records of student participation or other characteristics and behaviors over time. Student journals are informal, reflective self-recording tools of student perceptions, attitudes, and feelings about PE experiences. Student projects are formal learning and assessment experiences wherein students investigate, design, construct, and present work. Written tests and worksheets are common formal assessments.

President's Challenge and FITNESSGRAM assessment and feedback methods

The President's Challenge assesses and gives students feedback about their levels of fitness. It tests students using exercises including right-angled pushups, pull-ups, curl-ups, endurance running and walking, the V-sit and reach, and shuttle runs. FITNESSGRAM tests student levels of muscular strength, aerobic capacity, flexibility, endurance, and body composition. The President's Challenge is part of the Presidential President's Council on Fitness, Sports, and Nutrition. It replaces the former Physical Fitness Test established in the 1960s under President Kennedy's initial enactment of the President's Council on

Physical Fitness. It includes an Adult Fitness Test; the Presidential Active Lifestyle Award (PALA) Challenge for integrating physical activity and healthy eating into everyday life; the Presidential Champions Challenge for individuals with more ambitious activity goals; and the Presidential Youth Fitness Program to teach students lifelong fitness and health. Also part of the Presidential Youth Fitness Program, FITNESSGRAM provides educators with choices of varied test items to assess students using Healthy Fitness Zone standards; separate summary, achievement, data sheet, tracking, statistics, information, and summary report forms; and Activity Log and ACTIVITYGRAM modules to report test scores to students and parents. FITNESSGRAM and ACTIVITYGRAM reports are also used in educating students, research studies, and teacher education and preparation.

Use of the FITNESSGRAM
FITNESSGRAM was designed as a part of the U.S. Presidential Youth Fitness Program for lifelong health and fitness. State departments of education frequently designate the FITNESSGRAM as the test for their school district PE departments to use to assess student physical performance. Three main components of fitness evaluated by FITNESSGRAM are (1) aerobic capacity; (2) body composition; and (3) muscle strength, endurance, and flexibility, evaluated through assessment of six corresponding key areas of fitness as subdivisions of these three main components. Student performance on each test for each fitness area is rated as needing improvement, or in a Healthy Fitness Zone (HFZ), which is the desired performance standard. The HFZ is set by the developers of the test to reflect reasonable physical fitness levels that most students are capable of achieving. Individual HFZs vary according to student gender and age. As an example, one state education code defines passing this physical performance test for ninth graders as satisfactorily performing within the HFZ on at least five of the test's six standards.

Considerations for administrators
As a national standardized test battery that education departments administer throughout their states, the FITNESSGRAM must be administered with personnel carefully adhering to its prescribed protocols and regulations to preserve its validity. School district administrators are responsible to know about current regulations and statutes, and assuring all district personnel comply with these. They are also responsible to make sure that all school district staff members are trained correctly in test administration, and are given needed assistance and resources. Specialized training is necessary for administering the FITNESSGRAM test battery, because teachers have to use their judgment to evaluate how students perform physical skills, e.g., push-ups, etc. Educators also have to plan carefully to establish an environment for testing that maintains safety and dignity for every student. State education department officials in states using FITNESSGRAM advise their school district administrators to create fitness testing plans consistent with its test manual and compliant with current regulatory and statutory requirements for administration and results reporting. The FITNESSGRAM test administration manual and PE Resource Guide can be downloaded from websites including the Presidential Youth Fitness Program, Human Kinetics, Cooper Institute, and state education departments using it.

Standardized vs. authentic assessments

A standardized assessment can provide a comparison of the learning a student demonstrates to a national or state average. Standardized tests do this by providing norms, i.e., average scores of samples of students that represent an average of the national or state student population. They can show in what position a student ranks among other students in the country or state. In addition to achievement tests, standardized IQ tests can also show student ability compared to average, high-end, and low-end scores. Subscales on intelligence testing instruments additionally show relative student strengths and weaknesses in various areas, e.g., immediate memory, reading comprehension, vocabulary, manipulating numbers, manipulating shapes, fluid and flexible thinking processes, and crystallized and retained knowledge and information, etc. Authentic assessments can be individualized, whereas standardized assessments cannot. They indicate more about what a student knows and can do in conditions and situations more akin to real life. They can focus more on how a student applies ability and knowledge. They can also reveal more about an individual student's unique qualities than standardized tests of either achievement or IQ can.

Characteristics of a rubric

A rubric specifies certain learning objectives a student should be able to demonstrate, and in what ways. Teachers should first review the rubric with students to inform them of what they are expected to learn. Then they have students use the rubric to guide their learning experiences and work. Finally, they use the rubric to assess whether students have met the learning objective(s). A norm-referenced test compares the student's scores to a previously established norm. For example, standardized tests commonly obtain samples of scores from students they have identified as representative of a given national or state population. They then calculate the average or mean score of these students. Whenever other students take these standardized tests, their scores are then compared to these averages. The test authors or publishers provide statistical computations and tables whereby educators can determine how many standard deviations from the norm a student's score falls, and in what percentile of the population the student's score ranks. Criterion-referenced tests do not compare student scores to a norm, but instead against predetermined criteria of what learning they should demonstrate, determined by test authors, publishers, school districts, individual teachers, etc. They do not determine student rank, but whether or to what degree the student meets lesson, unit, class, course, or subject requirements.

Assessment instruments

Validity
Statistical validity means an instrument measures what it claims and is intended to measure. Some types of validity include external validity, internal validity, content validity, construct validity, face validity, and criterion validity. External validity includes population validity and ecological validity. Population validity is whether a sample population accurately represents the whole population, and whether acceptable sampling methodology is used (e.g., random selection, not convenience sampling). Ecological validity is whether the testing environment or process affects behavior. Internal validity is how strong a causal relationship between variables can be established, as opposed to only correlation. Content validity is how well a measure represents all aspects of the construct measured. Construct validity includes convergent and divergent validity. Convergent validity shows constructs expected to be related are related; divergent validity shows constructs expected to be unrelated are unrelated. A study or instrument with both has high construct validity. Face (representation) validity is general, common-sense, non-objective, non-quantified evaluation based on experience and judgment. Criterion validity is whether an instrument reflects a specific group of abilities. It includes concurrent and predictive validity. Concurrent validity compares an instrument to an established measure; predictive validity tests it over time.

Reliability
Reliability means an instrument gets the same or similar results across repeated administrations. Some types of reliability include test-retest reliability, interrater reliability, internal consistency reliability, and instrument reliability. Test-retest reliability shows test stability when administered repeatedly to the same subjects. Surveys and IQ tests are good test-retest choices because individuals rarely have sudden, pronounced changes in their opinions or IQs within a few months. Educational tests are less applicable, as students learn more over time and will score higher on the second administration. Interrater reliability or interobserver reliability quantifies the amount of agreement between two, or among several, observers or test administrators. This is important in any research requiring different individuals to make qualitative ratings. For example, Olympics judges must be consistent with one another in their scoring systems.

University and school examiners must also adhere to common standards. Internal consistency reliability is whether different items measuring the same construct within a test give the same results or scores. Instrument reliability in physical sciences is whether equipment is calibrated to yield the same measurements every time (within acceptable error margins), and in social sciences, whether an instrument is statistically stable over time.

Principles that inform high-quality, appropriate assessments

Appropriate assessments of high quality should be informed by local, state, and national guidelines or standards so that their results can be used for establishing instructional objectives that are equally appropriate for teachers and students. In addition all educators, including PE teachers, should choose and apply assessment measures that are suitable for ascertaining what kind of progress their students are making toward fulfilling the instructional objectives that they have designated. This applies to both formative and summative assessments, and includes both informal and formal assessment instruments and tools. And therefore, because assessments help PE and other faculty to determine whether and to what to degree they and their students are achieving the instructional objectives they have assigned for their teaching units, PE teachers should also develop evaluation schemes or plans that reflect whether and to what extent those instructional objectives have been accomplished. Although it is true that assessment results do contribute to the grades that teachers give to their students, grades should not be the only results of their evaluation schemes: assessing whether learning goals and objectives have been satisfied is equally important.

Purposes and requirements of assessment measures

Purposes: (1) To gauge student learning; (2) To evaluate and improve instruction; (3) To communicate with students, parents, and administrators and identify curriculum gaps; (4) To evaluate and modify programs; (5) To validate and support programs through consistently providing objective data; and (6) To motivate students to learn through documenting their growth and improvement. Requirements: (1) Validity, by measuring the quantities—skills, behaviors, or performance—it is designed and purports to measure; (2) Reliability, by yielding the same results from measuring the same students over multiple administration at different times; (3) Objectivity, by yielding very similar results regardless of who administers it; (4) Feasibility, by being straightforward, inexpensive to obtain, not taking excessive instructional time, being easy to set up and administer, having instructions who are easy to follow and make reasonable demands on students and administrators, and able to be scored without influencing its objectivity, e.g., if multiple administrators are needed; and (5) Usefulness, by having results that can be applied for progress reporting, program planning, self-assessment, and other valid educational uses.

Traditional approaches to student assessment

Traditional assessment approaches involve teacher-generated written tests and worksheets, including (1) selected-response formats, with questions or items giving alternatives from which students select responses, e.g., multiple choice, true/false, and matching tests/worksheets; (2) Limited open-ended formats wherein questions or items require brief written constructed responses, e.g., open response, short answer, diagram labeling, and fill in the blank. Alternative approaches involve student products, including (1) Audiovisual, made to display or exhibit, e.g., artwork, concept maps, posters, banners, photo exhibits, PowerPoints, videos, iMovies, audio recordings, and sculptures or models of athletes; (2) Written, e.g., research papers, essays, stories, poems, anecdotes, journals, logs, personal fitness plans, checklists, rating scales, brochures, advertisements; teacher, peer, or self-rubrics; performance records, newspapers, constructed magazines, projects, pre-assessment inventories; student surveys, questionnaires, or interviews; editorials, reflection; and (3) Performance tasks, i.e., physical or cognitive behaviors, e.g., officiating a game, playing a game, conducting fitness assessments, giving oral reports, teaching lessons; showcases, debates, skits, role plays, interviews, locomotor, gymnastics, or dance movement sequences; and warmup routines.

Descriptor for student self-monitoring of physical activity

According to the National Association for Sport and Physical Education (NASPE)'s Instructional Framework for Fitness Education in Physical Education (IFFEPE), which parallels NASPE's National Standards for PE, a physical activity descriptor for students is to "Self-monitor physical activity and create an individualized physical activity plan." Benchmarks are, for pre-K/K, setting weekly goals to be active during recess; for grades 1-2, using weekly or monthly activity calendars or planning physical activity participation with family outside school; for grades 3-5, using available technology to set personal fitness goals and self-monitor physical activity, including using logs, journals, stopwatches, pedometers or other assessment tools; for grades 6-8, using online tracking, heart-rate monitors, pedometers, and other available technology to self-monitor physical activity and create physical activity plans incorporating self-management skills, environment, social interaction, and personal preferences; for grades 9-12, using available technology to self-monitor and develop personalized physical activity plans to remediate physical activity level deficits; and for higher education, using available technology to self-monitor and develop short- and long-term personalized personal activity plans to correct physical activity level deficits.

Recording progress using self-assessment

Students can record their own progress by writing in a journal, keeping notes in a notebook, or recording information on index cards and submitting these to the PE teacher throughout teaching and learning. Self-assessment is a practical, quick method for PE teachers to gather information on student progress; relieves teachers of much extra work; engages students in their own evaluation processes; and allows students to communicate what they want to about their progress from their own perspectives. PE teachers can give K-2 students a student log form to complete for self-assessing regular physical fitness activities: The left-hand column lists fitness categories with easy-to-understand self-statements – Cardiovascular endurance, "I have a strong heart"; Muscular strength, "I have strong muscles"; Muscular endurance, "I can do movements over and over again"; and Flexibility, "I can stretch." The right-hand column is blank; students make drawings or cut out and paste in pictures illustrating which activities they do for each category (e.g., running, dancing, lifting things, etc.). This is fun and creative for young students, helps them categorize fitness activities, and gives teachers assessment information.

Methods and considerations for peer assessment

PE teachers must give students clear instructions about peer assessments before letting students conduct them. Students can use rubrics, rating scales, or checklists to obtain the criteria to judge their classmates' or teammates' progress in PE. Students must focus on these criteria to assess peers. This attention to requirements develops their observational skills. PE teachers must teach the observational process for students to make effective peer assessments. For grades 6-8, partners can complete basketball assessment checklists: pairs take turns telling partners what they are looking for in each dribble, pass, or shot, making a check mark or X next to every correctly executed technique and leaving incorrectly done ones blank. Skills can include set shots, balancing the ball, eyes on target, knees bent, limb extension when shooting, follow through, lay-up technique (step with each foot, hop, knee up, aim for backboard), chest and bounce passing technique (fingers spread, step forward, elbows out, push ball, snap, backs of hands facing one another, thumbs down) against a wall, and dribbling technique (head up, use finger pads, dribble below waist, switch hands). One checklist can have two columns on either side of these skills, one for each partner.

Roles of assessment in special education and APE

According to PE Central®, the first step in developing an IEP for a student with disabilities is assessment. Assessment is the interpretation of measures attained via testing, and is focused on identifying the student's individual activity needs. Assessment is also utilized for making placement and program planning decisions. The instruction provided for a student with disabilities, which enables him or her to participate with safety and success in PE classes, depends on a foundation of assessment. Federal IDEA regulations for conducting evaluations require local education agencies (LEAs) to use multiple, varied assessment strategies and tools to collect pertinent information about the student developmentally, functionally, and academically, including information from parents. This information can help to determine whether the student has a disability, and what should be contained in the student's IEP, including supports needed for general education program success. Educators should never use just one assessment or measure as a criterion to determine student disability or educational placement. They should use not only multiple assessment instruments, but moreover technically sound, valid, and reliable instruments. Assessments should include the relative contributions of cognitive and behavioral as well as physiological and developmental factors.

Assessing students with disabilities

Schools must choose and administer assessments without racial or cultural discrimination, and supply and administer assessments in the language and form most likely to give accurate information about the student's developmental, functional, and academic knowledge and abilities. Assessments must be used only for the same purposes for which they have been found valid and reliable. Personnel with adequate knowledge and training must administer each assessment. Administration must adhere to any instructions included by the assessment's producer or publisher. Students should be assessed in all areas where disabilities are suspected. Assessment strategies and tools utilized should supply pertinent information that directly aids educators in defining student educational needs. Results from norm-referenced or criterion-referenced tests should be combined with observational assessments made within the performance environment. Rather than only measure disability, assessments should also measure ability and describe student strengths and needs. Tests measuring physical fitness or motor skill performance should not discriminate based on student disability. Students with verbal learning disabilities need visual demonstrations and cues added to verbal instructions to perform at their ability levels. Formal standardized tests that do not permit students to demonstrate strengths and needs may be inappropriate.

Applying assessment data

Some best practices are to use assessment data to determine if a student requires support for PE, and the amount of support needed for the student to succeed in general PE. Support can include curricular or instructional accommodations. For example, students may be provided with adaptive equipment, adaptive physical education (APE) consultation, direct APE teacher services, peer "buddy" support, and other forms of support. To determine the least restrictive, most appropriate PE placement, educators should consider the following: the results of an ecologically based, comprehensive motor and physical assessment made by a PE teacher qualified in APE and certified by the school's state department of education or other designated accrediting organization; the student's individual psychomotor, cognitive, and affective characteristics that would influence student capability for safely, successfully participating in general PE; and the student's capacity for benefiting from an APE program, which includes such factors as the student's ability to comprehend cause-and-effect relationships, capacity for voluntary movement, ability to interact with other people, and demonstration of the emotional behaviors for benefiting from one-on-one instruction.

Referral process of a student for APE services

Individual school district policies for referral vary. In general, a school must first explore alternative programs and procedures within the general education PE program. If a student has difficulty with regular PE, teachers, parents, and others can refer the student for APE services through the student's teacher or other school personnel at an IEP committee meeting, planning and placement team meeting, or child study conference. General education PE teachers and parents who think a student with a disability would benefit from APE can request referral from the Special Education Director or school principal. Upon written parental consent, qualified personnel conduct formal assessments of the student's motor, fitness, and behavioral skills. A meeting is scheduled to discuss assessment results and determine levels of PE support required. The designated team determines student eligibility for special education services. PE staff can identify, assess, and recommend APE for a student not identified as eligible for special education based on APE guidelines entrance criteria. Students eligible for special education with gross or fine motor skills deficits are referred for PT or OT evaluations, which PE teachers use to develop IEP goals and objectives.

Typical members to be included in a student's PPT or IEP team

Once a teacher, other school personnel, parent, or professional or agency personnel refers a student for evaluation for disability identification and eligibility determination for special education services, the school district convenes a planning and placement team (PPT) or individualized education plan/program (IEP) team. The members of this team typically include the student whenever appropriate; the student's parents; at least one regular education teacher, if the student may be or is placed in regular education; at least one special educator; a person(s) able to interpret evaluations, e.g., a psychometrist, school psychologist, educational specialist, or adapted physical education (APE) teacher; a school district representative who knows the general education curriculum and can allocate resources; and any others with expertise or knowledge pertinent to the student. Student evaluation can include standardized test results; information from parents, teachers, and service providers; formal and informal observations; reviews of school work; Birth to Three System records, etc. The team may design individualized evaluations according to referral concerns. Parents are given written notice of consent for evaluation. Federal regulations require IEPs to be developed for students determined eligible within 60 calendar days after written referrals; state regulations may require them to be developed sooner.

Determining a student's eligibility for APE

A student may be identified for determining APE eligibility under special education services through testing by a physical therapist (PT) or occupational therapist (OT), or be recommended for evaluation by a student intervention team, teacher, parent, etc. Additional indications include these: the student does not perform at his or her ability level in group settings; the student scores below average in two or more parts of the school district's state physical fitness test; the student exhibits social behaviors impeding his or her own or others' learning for more than one-third of class time; or the student scores 1.5 standard deviations (SD) or more below the norm in two or more parts of a designated norm-referenced test. The student should be given a test of gross motor development (TGMD), and if the results are not within normal limits, this is indication for determining eligibility for APE. School personnel should furnish to school PE staff the names of students recommended or identified for APE for the coming school year, plus a copy of each student's TGMD, by the end of the current school year. PE staff should have access to electronic databases for writing IEP goals and objectives for APE.

Movement and Skill Acquisition

Major human body systems

The skeletal system provides the body's structural framework of bones to support it, protects the soft vital organs from harm, collaborates with muscles to produce body movement, stores calcium in the bones, and produces red blood cells in the bone marrow. The integumentary system includes the hair, nails, and especially skin, which is the body's largest sensory organ. It provides tactile sensation, including pain, heat, cold, pressure, and pleasure; regulates loss of blood and other fluids; synthesizes vitamin D; and protects deeper tissues. The muscular system maintains body posture, creates body movements with the support of the bones, generates heat, and consumes energy. The immune system is composed of parts of many other systems, including parts of the lymphatic system, the cardiovascular system, the respiratory system, the gastrointestinal system, etc. It works to protect and defend the body against disease organisms and other foreign elements.

The lymphatic system retrieves fluids that leak from the capillaries (small blood vessels) and contains the white blood cells, hence supporting parts of the immune system. The cardiovascular system transports nutrients containing oxygen and other necessities throughout the bloodstream, transports gaseous wastes for elimination, and supports immune functions. The urinary system regulates balances of fluids, electrolytes, and pH; and removes nitrogenous wastes from the blood. The digestive system breaks foods down into proteins, sugars, amino acids, and other building blocks for the body's metabolic processes, growth, replenishment, and repair. The respiratory system performs gas exchanges by taking in, warming, and moistening environmental air, delivering oxygen, and expelling carbon dioxide. The nervous system provides sensory input, interprets the sensory information, evokes and signals responses, and coordinates muscle functions. The endocrine system secretes hormones that regulate the body's growth, metabolism, and general functionality. The reproductive system produces hormones enabling reproduction and creates, nurtures, and delivers offspring.

The nervous system includes the brain, nerves, and spinal cord. It interprets sensory input, enables thought and emotion, and sends messages to the rest of the body. The circulatory system includes the heart and blood vessels. It delivers blood to and from the lungs and the rest of the body to supply oxygen and remove carbon dioxide. The respiratory system includes the lungs, bronchi, diaphragm, trachea, larynx, and pharynx. It enables us to breathe. The skeletal system includes the bones, cartilage, tendons, and ligaments. It protects the organs, structurally supports the body, and collaborates with the muscles in body movement. The digestive system includes the salivary glands, esophagus, stomach, intestines, liver, gall bladder, pancreas, rectum, and anus. It breaks down and processes food we eat; extracts nutrients to build tissues and supply energy; stores fats, amino acids, etc. for future use; and eliminates waste products. The lymphatic system includes the lymph nodes and vessels. It produces white blood cells for the immune system and transports lymph between the tissues and the bloodstream.

The immune system includes the white blood cells (leukocytes), tonsils, adenoids, thymus, and spleen. It protects the body against organisms and other agents that cause diseases and infections. The muscular system includes all of the many muscles in the body. It enables the body to move with support and cooperation from the skeletal system (bones). In addition to the head, neck, chest, back, arm, hand, leg, and foot muscles, the heart is also a muscle, which pumps blood to and from the lungs and the rest of the body to supply oxygen and remove carbon dioxide. The integumentary system includes the skin, nails, and hair. The skin protects the tissues from injury and fluid loss, provides sensation, and synthesizes vitamin D. The nails protect the fingertips and toes. The hair protects the skin, particularly on the scalp.

The reproductive system includes the ovaries, fallopian tubes, uterus, vagina, and mammary glands in females; and testes, vas deferens, seminal vesicles, prostate, and penis in males. It enables reproduction via the conception, gestation, and delivery of babies. The endocrine system includes the hypothalamus; pituitary, pineal, thyroid, parathyroid, and adrenal glands; and pancreas. It secretes hormones regulating various body functions.

Muscular system

Among cardiac, smooth, and skeletal muscles, skeletal muscles are used in voluntary body movement. They are wrapped in several layers of connective tissue, which join to form tendons attaching to bones. Tendons extend connective tissue around muscles, giving individual muscle fibers support and stability. Ligaments connect bones at joints, and exercise is thought to strengthen ligaments. Tendons and ligaments, combined with muscle and skin elasticity and joint structure, determine flexibility, which can be enhanced through stretching exercises. Type I/red/slow-twitch muscle fibers are needed for endurance activities like long-distance running and cycling, and need more aerobic energy. Type II/white/fast-twitch muscle fibers need less oxygen and are used in short-term, maximum-force exertion like sprinting, jumping, and weight-lifting. Both types are activated in activities needing maximal force production. Lesser force requirements activate slow-twitch fibers first, then fast-twitch if needed. Muscle fibers are always activated in groups called motor units, which include motor neurons. Dumbbell curls use more motor units than picking up a pencil, for example. Resistance and weight training increases muscle fiber size, and strengthens and thickens connective tissues, resulting in larger muscles and greater muscular strength and endurance.

Cardiopulmonary system

The heart's right side receives blood from the veins. When the heart muscle contracts, it pumps blood from its right ventricle, through the pulmonary arteries, to the lungs. This blood acquires fresh oxygen in the lungs from atmospheric air the individual has inhaled, and releases carbon dioxide into pulmonary capillaries. Exhaling expels this CO_2. The freshly oxygenated blood travels through the pulmonary veins, to the heart's left atrium, to the left ventricle. When the left ventricle contracts, it pumps blood through the aorta, the largest artery, to the entire body. The left and right ventricles contract simultaneously, so the cardiopulmonary system functions in a perpetual cycle. Oxygen consumption directly affects cardiorespiratory fitness: heart and lung function determine oxygen transportation to body tissues. The volume of air inhaled and exhaled each minute is pulmonary ventilation, which typically increases when exercising. The differential between oxygen inhaled and exhaled is the measure of oxygen consumption. Its maximum, VO_2max, equals maximal aerobic capacity, frequently regarded as indicating cardiorespiratory fitness. It defines the cardiovascular system's greatest ability to deliver oxygenated blood to working muscles, and how quickly the body can produce adenosine triphosphate (ATP) to supply energy to muscles.

Neural systems

Many areas of the brain, including parts involving motivation, emotions, and memory, are included in the highest level of the motor control hierarchy. In this level, command neurons formulate the intention to move the body and its parts. This message is sent to the hierarchy's middle level in the cerebral cortex's sensorimotor cortex, subcortical nuclei's basal ganglia, cerebellum, and brainstem. The highly interconnected structures in this level determine postures and movements needed to perform an action. Midlevel neurons additionally receive input from receptors in the eyes, vestibular system, skin, joints, and muscles regarding current surroundings and body posture. The middle level uses this complex of data to produce a motor program, which defines the information necessary for performing the activity. It sends this program information along descending pathways, originating in the sensorimotor cortex and brainstem, to the lowest hierarchy level, the motor neurons and interneurons. These determine joint angles and degrees of muscle tension. Continuous monitoring and updating of movements allow for unexpected events. Initial motor programs generate rapid, crude execution of movements. Repeating a movement allows the middle level to supply more accurate information, requiring fewer corrections and enabling learning.

Fundamental processes of physiological life

(1) Organization: Labor is divided at every level of life, each part cooperatively performing its function. Loss of organization, i.e., integrity, causes death, even to a single cell. (2) Metabolism: All the chemical reactions in the body, e.g., breaking substances down to simpler components and releasing energy. (3) Responsiveness: Also known as irritability, detecting changes in external and internal environments and reacting to them—sensing and responding to stimuli. (4) Movement: At the cellular level, molecules move among locations. Blood moves among body parts in the circulatory system. As we breathe, our diaphragms move. Our muscles produce movement through contractility, i.e., ability to shorten. (5) Reproduction: Specifically, transmitting life across generations by creating new organisms. Generally, cellular reproduction means new cell formation to repair or replace old cells and affect growth. (6) Differentiation: How unspecialized cells developmentally become specialized, with distinct structures and functions, e.g., into tissues and organs. (7) Respiration: How oxygen and carbon dioxide are exchanged between cells and the environment, including ventilation, diffusion, and transportation in blood. (8) Digestion: Breaking down foods into simple molecules for absorption and use. (9) Excretion: Removal from the body of digestive and metabolic waste products.

Food calorie

A food calorie, also called a dietary calorie, nutritional calorie, kilogram calorie, or large calorie, equals the approximate amount of energy required to increase the temperature of one kilogram of water by one degree Celsius. (Another calorie term, the gram calorie or small calorie, refers to the approximate amount of energy required to increase the temperature of one gram of water by one degree Celsius. The food calorie/large calorie/kilogram calorie equals 1,000 small calories, or one kilocalorie [Kcal].) Because energy produces heat, we describe "burning" calories. Foods have calories, i.e., potential energy. When we digest food, build and repair body cells, engage in physical activity, and use our brains, we expend energy, or "burn" calories. When people or animals ingest more calories than they expend, surplus calories not used get stored as body fat. Hence overeating results in extra fatty tissue and weight gain. When one expends more calories than one eats, initially the body burns fat for fuel, resulting in weight loss. When no extra fat exists, the body metabolizes muscle for protein and energy, causing muscle wasting. Additional energy expense without sufficient food causes weight loss, emaciation, and ultimately starvation.

Interaction between body systems during physical activity

The skeletal system gives our bodies their structural framework. The bones interact with the muscles to allow our body parts to move when the muscles contract. The skull is a bone that protects the brain, which regulates all body functions including movement. The vertebrae protect the spinal cord in general, including during movement. The joints where bones meet contain sensory receptors that send information about the body's position to the brain. The brain controls the contractions of the muscles to regulate the positions of the bones. The brain interacts with the cardiovascular system to regulate the heart rate and blood pressure, increasing these during physical activity. Baroreceptors in the cardiovascular system send the brain blood pressure information. Receptors in the muscles send the brain body position and movement information. The brain interacts with the respiratory system, controlling breathing rates and monitoring respiratory volume and blood gas levels. The respiratory system provides oxygen to and removes carbon dioxide from blood during breathing, whose rate increases during exercise. The integumentary system's skin receptors send temperature and other sensation information to the brain. The autonomic nervous system controls sweat gland secretions and peripheral blood flow during exercise.

Source of energy for muscular contraction

Adenosine triphosphate (ATP) is a molecule with an adenosine nucleotide attached to three phosphate groups, providing energy for muscular contractions, converted via cellular respiration from food energy. Its energy store is released for muscles to access when the bond is broken between its second and third phosphate groups. When this bond is broken, the third phosphate group is released by itself, reducing the ATP molecule to adenosine diphosphate (ADP) with two phosphate groups. Replacing the third phosphate group, i.e., rephosphorylization, restores ADP into ATP again. The process of cellular respiration that converts food energy to ATP depends largely upon how much oxygen is available. Exercise intensity and duration affect the amounts of oxygen the muscle cells demand and the oxygen supply available to them. Depending on the amount of oxygen available, any one of three exercise energy systems can be accessed selectively: the alactic anaerobic energy system, the lactic anaerobic energy system, or the aerobic energy system.

Alactic anaerobic, lactic anaerobic, and aerobic energy systems

Short-term (10 seconds or less), high-intensity, explosive exercise recruits the alactic (not producing lactic acid) anaerobic (not using oxygen) energy system, e.g., a 100-meter sprint or one weightlifting set. Also called the ATP-PCr (adenosine triphosphate-phosphocreatine) or phosphagen energy system, this is the first accessed for exercise. It uses ATP stored in muscles and then rephosphorylizes the resulting ADP via phosphocreatine. It stops supplying energy when PCr is depleted until muscles have rested and regenerated PCr. High-intensity exercise for up to 90 seconds, e.g., one ice hockey shift or an 800 meter sprint, uses the lactic anaerobic energy system. It functions when the alactic anaerobic system is depleted and the aerobic system cannot handle the exercise intensity's demands. It produces lactic acid as a byproduct in the muscles but does not use oxygen. It directly accesses cellular respiration to convert food energy to supply ATP. Continuous/long-term (beyond 2-5 minutes), lower-intensity aerobic exercise, e.g., running marathons, accesses the aerobic energy system, which depends upon how efficiently oxygen can be sent to and processed by the muscles. It also recruits cellular respiration to get ATP from food energy; however, oxygen is available to the muscles, so no lactic acid is produced.

Exercise science principles

Principle of specificity
The principle of specificity in exercise science means one must exercise the specific body part, muscle(s), or sport movements and techniques that one wants to improve. To strengthen the upper body, one must do exercises targeting the upper body, and the same for the lower body; one will not help the other. Someone who wants to play football must practice the skills specific to this sport; general body conditioning, while it might be a prerequisite, will not improve specific football skills. While core and cardio workouts are necessary to conditioning for improving overall endurance and strength, and the principle of specificity dictates that attaining one's specific goals requires tailoring one's exercise regimen, neither one of these cancels out the other.

Principle of adaptation
The principle of adaptation means the body adapts to exercise, so that with regular practice, certain activities become easier. To continue improving, one must vary one's workouts with different training and/or routines. The body adjusts to demands made of it. Adaptation also means the body adapts to the processes of executing specific tasks.

Principle of overload
The principle of overload means the body only responds beyond its normal level if new stimuli or additional pressures are introduced. Stopping within comfort zones maintains current skill levels, but brings no improvement. This is true for gaining strength, improving athletic ability, or losing weight. To increase what muscles can do, we must require them to function in unaccustomed ways. This is one reason exercise science professionals are helpful: they can push and motivate clients to work past their comfort zones.

Principle of individual differences
The principle of individual differences means not everybody will attain the same results from the same training programs and levels. Every individual has different body chemistry: some must work harder than others for the same results. Another aspect of this principle is that some people are more predisposed to succeed in certain sports or workouts than others, who in turn are more predisposed to other activities. The principle of individual differences indicates the importance of personal training: individuals must tailor their exercise programs for meeting goals at their own paces. Even individuals with stronger talents or skills in a certain activity or sport need to practice it to enable their bodies to adapt.

Principle of progression
The progression principle means, one must progress at a certain, individual rate to get results. While people must push past their comfort zones to improve, pressing oneself overly hard negates natural progression and can cause injury. An appropriate exercise routine is a science. While there is no "one-size-fits-all" formula, there is a formula determining how one should push oneself. The principles of progression and overload balance delicately: progression indicates specific times of being unready for overload, or benefiting from it.

Principle of use/disuse
The principle of use/disuse means one must use muscles to sustain muscular strength—the proverbial "use it or lose it." When we do not practice a sport we want to improve in or use muscles we want to develop, we lose our skills and strength. Anytime we stop exercising or exercise less and notice we are no longer seeing results, this is evidence of the use/disuse principle. With disuse, muscles lose definition; the body compensates for the lack of practice. This is also called the reversibility principle. At times disuse can be valuable: muscle overuse requires healing. Otherwise, moderately high year-round fitness levels are better than seasonal detraining or retraining.

Short-term and long-term effects of physical training upon mental health and cardiovascular health

Motivation to follow and continue physical fitness routines can be supported by both the short-term and long-term effects of exercise on the body, including the brain. For example, training energetically accesses the body's glycogen stores to supply energy. Glycogen depletion then triggers the release of endorphins, hormones that bring feelings of well-being and euphoria (the word endorphin comes from Greek root words meaning "morphine within") in the short term. Additionally, in the long term, exercising regularly can both prevent and relieve depression. Some research studies comparing exercise to antidepressant medications have found exercise equally effective. In addition to the brain, exercise improves cardiovascular health. Physical activity requires the heart rate to increase to deliver oxygenated blood to the muscles. People new to exercising may initially feel dizzy and winded. However, in the short term, exercise increases blood circulation. In the longer term, exercising for a few months can lower one's blood pressure and pulse. Exercising regularly significantly predicts heart health. People who perform cardiovascular (aerobic) exercise consistently lower their long-term risks of heart attacks, strokes, and other cardiovascular disorders.

Effects of individual differences on learning in physical education

Research has shown that situational interest can help motivate students to become engaged in the process of learning. Studies find that teachers can change and arrange task presentation, the structuring of learning experiences, and instructional strategies to enhance student situational interest. Although most research into motivation in physical education is related to theories of achievement goals, these reportedly are not very predictive of motivation or performance. However, researchers find student interest to have greater influence on student learning behavior, as well as on student intentions for future participation. Despite educator recognition of the importance of interest to learning, researchers find teachers still lack clarity in understanding the roles they can play in helping to stimulate and develop students' interest. When individuals interact with the environment, two kinds of interest emerge: situational and individual. Both kinds have two phases. Situational interest has a phase when interest is activated, and an ensuing phase when interest is sustained. Individual interest has a phase when interest emerges, and an ensuing phase when interest is defined.

Individual differences that affect performance

One element of individual differences is age. Some activities are not appropriate for students who have not attained physical maturity. Students also need to understand what their bodies can and cannot do as they pass through different developmental stages and periods. Students of very different ages should not be expected to compete against one another. Age affects strength, aerobic capacity, reaction time, flexibility, and experience. Humans do not attain full strength until about age 20. Humans are most flexible in their teens. Experience, which increases with age, is a crucial element in sports. Another individual difference is somatotype, i.e., body shape. This informs appropriate sport choices. There are three basic somatotypes. (1) Ectomorph: a long, narrow, thin shape with minimal muscle or fat. Good sports for ectomorphs include long-distance running and the high jump. (2) Endomorph: fat, and often pear-shaped, with narrow shoulders and wide hips, with small ankles and wrists but more fat on the torso, arms, and legs. Good sports for endomorphs include shot-putting and wrestling. (3) Mesomorph: muscular, often wedge-shaped, with wide shoulders and narrow hips, strong limbs, and little body fat. Good sports for mesomorphs include gymnastics and swimming.

Differences affecting physical education performance

Individual differences include biological, physiological, and environmental factors affecting performance. For example, muscular tissue composition will influence individual strength, flexibility, and endurance. Individual deficits in rod and cone development in the eyes would inhibit perceptual-motor ability, which could alter reaction times. Children participating more in formal schooling will develop their verbal and reasoning skills further, while children participating more in physical education and/or sports will develop their motor skills further. Development rates across and within individuals vary by maturation and growth differences. Perceptual-motor abilities affecting individual skill performance include: control precision, e.g., hockey-puck handling; rate control, like racecar driving; aiming, e.g., texting; response orientation and choice reaction time, e.g., football quarterbacking; reaction time, e.g., sprinting; manual dexterity, e.g., basketball-dribbling; finger dexterity, e.g., typing; arm-hand steadiness, e.g., performing surgery; and wrist and finger speed, e.g., speed-stacking. Physical proficiencies affecting performance include: explosive strength, e.g., standing long jumps; static strength, e.g., weight-lifting; trunk strength, e.g., pole-vaulting; extent flexibility, e.g., yoga; dynamic flexibility, e.g., squat-thrusts; limb movement speed, e.g., javelin-throwing; static balance; dynamic balance, e.g., gymnastics; object-balancing; multi-limb coordination, e.g., stick-shift driving; gross body coordination, e.g., hurdling; stamina, e.g., marathons; and dynamic strength, e.g.

Positive developmental outcomes of physical education

In the psychomotor domain, effective PE enhances student movement skills for participating in sports and other physical activities, and for being a spectator as well. It affords skills for applying cultural and intellectual pursuits to use leisure time, and skills for preserving the natural environment. In the cognitive domain, effective PE supports higher-order thinking processes through motor activity, enhances academic performance, provides understanding of the human body and knowledge of health and illness and of exercise, enhances understanding of the roles of sports and physical activity in American culture, and supports knowledgeable consumerism with goods and services. In the affective domain, effective PE supports a healthy response to physical activity. It adds to student aesthetic appreciation of beauty. It contributes to student self-esteem and facilitates self-actualization. It helps students direct their lives for setting worthwhile goals. PE reinforces humanistic values. It enables students to use the medium of play for enjoying rich social experiences. PE also informs cooperative play and social interactions. It teaches students fair play, good sportsmanship, and courtesy. Moreover, it supports humanitarian ideals and behaviors.

Health risks associated with physical inactivity

According to Johns Hopkins medical experts, research has definitively proven that a lack of physical activity is a risk factor for cardiovascular disease and other health conditions. People who are less physically fit and less physically active are at higher risk of developing hypertension (high blood pressure). Research shows that even after eliminating the factors of smoking tobacco, drinking alcohol, and eating an unhealthy diet, people who are physically active are still less likely to develop coronary heart disease than people who are physically inactive. Moreover, depression and anxiety can be caused or exacerbated by lack of physical activity. Additionally, scientists think physical inactivity may raise risks for certain cancers. Studies have found obese or overweight people decreased their risks of disease significantly through physical activity. Scientists say lack of physical activity causes many thousands of deaths annually. People tend to become less active as they age. Women are more likely to live sedentary lifestyles than men. White, non-Hispanic adults are more likely to be physically active than Hispanic and black, non-Hispanic adults.

Disease conditions of physical inactivity vs. health benefits of physical activity

Obesity and type 2 diabetes are two common results of physical activity. While obesity contributes greatly to type 2 diabetes, there are also individuals who are not even overweight, but due to their being physically sedentary, combined with poor nutritional habits and other behaviors like smoking tobacco and drinking alcohol, and interacting with genetic predispositions—some of which are much more prevalent within certain racial/ethnic populations—have developed type 2 diabetes as well. Current research studies that find sitting for most of one's waking hours is as harmful to health as habits like smoking. Even when exercising an hour each day, sitting for the rest of the day still has significant negative health impacts. People who drink, smoke, never exercise, spend most of their time sitting, and experience high levels of emotional and/or psychological stress are at much higher risks for hypertension, heart attacks, strokes, type 2 diabetes, some cancers, mental and emotional disorders, poorer quality of life, and earlier mortality. Physical activity can aid weight control, lower risks for heart disease and some cancers, strengthen the muscles and bones, and enhance mental health. While physically active people are not immune to disease, they lower their risks for many illnesses.

Prevention of injuries with physical activity

Research studies show that up to one half of all hip fractures could be prevented by engaging regularly in enough moderate physical activity. Physical activity that bears weight strengthens the bones and prevents them from becoming porous, brittle, and more prone to breaking. Another consideration is that regular physical activity improves coordination, balance, and flexibility. Better coordination, balance, and flexibility can lower a person's likelihood of falling during everyday life activities as well as during sports and recreational physical activities. Stronger bones can prevent fractures in the event of a fall, while improved coordination, balance, and flexibility can avert many falls in the first place. Studies have also proven that people who are physically inactive in general sustain more accidents and injuries than people who are physically active. Children who are physically inactive risk higher stress, anxiety, and lower self-esteem and are likelier to smoke and take drugs. Sedentary workers are absent from work more than active ones.

Contribution to a healthy lifestyle

Because most American students today do not receive PE at the frequencies or durations recommended for optimal health, they must engage in physical activity outside of PE classes and outside of school. To constitute physical activity, brisk walking or other pursuits must use energy by moving the body at a level of intensity sufficient to raise one's body temperature to feel warmer, and to cause one to breathe somewhat deeper than normally. Some students who live close enough can walk to and from school daily. They can play intramural and outdoor sports at school. Outside school, they can vacuum the house, wash the car, cut the grass, do gardening, clean up their rooms, and help their parents with other housework. These combine the benefits of contributing to smooth household and family functions with being more physically active for better health. Students can ride bicycles, go swimming, dance, and take weekend nature walks as more physically active forms of recreation than playing video games or watching TV. Experts recommend that children and teens build up to at least an hour of moderate physical activity most days of the week, while adults should aim for at least a half-hour most days.

Manual skills of reaching and grasping in motor development

Even before birth, fetuses display arm and hand movements—waving arms, making isolated finger movements, and using coordinated arm-hand movements like moving their thumbs to their mouths. Outside the womb, without the buoyancy of amniotic fluid, newborns must contend with gravity. Beginning with jerky extensions and flapping of the arms, they develop successful reaching for objects by 4-5 months. Detailed motion analysis reveals that infants initially problem-solve by moving their hands to targets individually. More sedentary babies must transcend gravity to raise their arms, while more active babies must damp inertia to control spontaneous, continuous arm-flapping. Both only open their hands into fitting shapes after touching objects. By around 8 months, babies can adjust their hand shapes prior to object contact, informing themselves visually about object shapes, sizes, and orientations. While visual information about object properties and locations is critical to adaptive planning of arm and hand movements, babies can reach and grasp as successfully in the dark as in light, so they need not see their arms or hands to guide them—likely because kinesthetics and proprioception work for body parts but not separate objects.

Use of hand-held implements in developmental progress

After babies have mastered the motor actions involved in reaching and grasping objects, they can apply their skills to achieve rewarding results. They learn to differentiate textures: they will bang hard objects against hard surfaces because this makes noise, but will not repeat banging soft objects against soft surfaces as it makes no noise. Infants are observed to test different combinations of objects and surfaces to determine which is noisiest. At 9 months, babies typically can bang on surfaces with spoons, but they take several months longer to develop the fine motor control for using spoons in the complex operation of scooping and bringing food to their mouths. Cognitive developmental psychologist Jean Piaget first described how older babies differentiate their reaching and grasping skills into instrumental actions to attain their goals. For example, around 8 months, babies reach and pull a cloth to move a toy on the cloth closer. Older babies lean forward, holding sticks, to extend their reach for objects. Toddlers rake in out-of-reach objects using canes as tools. They demonstrate comprehension of the tool-target relationship by turning the canes functionally.

Aspects of inter-limb coordination and gait development

Newborns may already have inter-limb coordination, as demonstrated by their crawling, swimming, and stepping reflexes. After developing the locomotion skills of crawling, babies go through several transitional upright stages of pulling up, balancing while standing, and sideways cruising while holding onto furniture for support. These transitional stages culminate in independent walking. From babies' first steps, to toddling, to eventual adult-like walking around elementary school ages, children evidence dramatic gait changes. When babies first begin to walk, their feet are spaced widely apart, with their toes pointed outward. They hold their legs nearly straight, not bending their knees. They typically bend their elbows upward, with the palms of their hands facing the ceiling. They either set each foot down all at once or walk on their toes, instead of rolling the foot from heel to toe as adults do. As their bodies and brains mature, their body proportions change, their balance improves and they gain additional experience, their gait patterns gradually change until by around seven years old, they walk the way adults walk.

Maturational considerations for PE teachers and coaches

Despite common PE class segregation of males from females, some experts find it appropriate to allow adolescents of both genders to participate together in physical activities without body contact that require agility and lower-body strength. Some examples of these include running, ultimate Frisbee, and capture the flag. For activities that need more upper-body strength, PE teachers and coaches should base their assignment of teams on the skill levels of the individual students to prevent them from injuring themselves and one another. Experts also point out the importance of evenly matching sports teams on the basis of levels of maturation and skills. That way, deficits in individual student skill levels are not as obvious, and all students have fun participating. Some examples of suitable activities include individual and/or partners' tennis, badminton, and competitive team activities like flag football. It is important for PE teachers and coaches to monitor student physical activities, and adjust them as needed to assure all students have competitive, positive, and enjoyable experiences.

Basic requirement of coordinating perceptual exploration

Infants need visual information about the characteristics and locations of objects to reach and grasp, as evidenced by their intercepting moving objects, moving their opposite hand to the right place before object arrival. Researchers have observed a basic motor development need is coordination of perceptual exploring and manual skills. Newborns not only bring hands to mouths; when stretching arms out, they also turn their heads to maintain their arm view. As they grow, older babies bring not only fingers, but also objects to their mouths. They coordinate among visual, tactile, and oral exploration; looking at; reaching; grasping; touching; turning; and mouthing objects. Babies also must use balance control, even for simple reaching actions: extending one arm out from the base of support displaces the center of gravity, requiring counterbalancing through opposition. When infants' abdominal and back muscles are not yet strong enough to support them in sitting positions, they use their hands to achieve a "tripod" (three-point) balance. Once they sit independently around 5-6 months, this frees their hands to reach, grasp, and manipulate smaller objects. Within several more months, they can coordinate leaning with reaching to avoid tipping over.

Contribution of perception to motor development in children

The process of absorbing, organizing, and interpreting sensory input—i.e., perception—is multisensory: information from all of the senses contributes to a child's motor behaviors in response to the input received. For example, when infants see a face and hear a voice, they turn their heads. From natural newborn waving and kicking, babies adapt to their environments by developing control over reaching for things; locomotion, i.e., learning to crawl, then walk, then run, etc.; and eventually learning complex skills for sports participation. Developing infant motor behaviors include control over eye movements to gaze at people and things, and control over head movements. As motor competence develops, babies use perceptual information to choose which motor actions to perform. Reciprocally, they get most of this perceptual information through motor movements of their eyes, arms, hands, and legs. According to how slippery, rigid, or sloped a surface is, they will adjust their crawling or walking. Changes in size, weight, muscular strength, and body fat from infancy to toddlerhood present perceptual-motor challenges as they practice various actions.

Kinesthesis and equilibrium

Kinesthesis is the sense of the body parts' positions and movements. Muscles, tendons, and joints contain receptors enabling kinesthesis. We are able to know where all of our body parts are at any time, and in what manner and direction they are moving, through kinesthesis. Equilibrium is our sense of balance. This gives us information regarding where our bodies are in space. For example, we can distinguish whether we are standing up, sitting, or lying down; in an ascending or descending elevator; or riding a roller coaster through our sense of equilibrium. The vestibular system in the inner ear is the sensory system that provides equilibrium. Specifically, the three semicircular canals contain fluid. Whenever our heads move, this fluid moves along with the head. The fluid's movement stimulates hair cells/cilia in the semicircular canals. These receptors send impulses to the brain via nerves. The brain interprets these impulses to understand the movement, giving us feedback about it. Our brains interpret the combined feedback from kinesthesis and equilibrium for orienting ourselves in space.

Relationship of perceptual and motor behaviors

While research has long observed that the developmental domains are interrelated, recent research further reinforces the depth of interdependence among developmental domains, processes, and factors. Some researchers point out that cognition, perception, and motor behavior transpire in the context of culture, social relationships, experience, and emotion, affecting overall brain function and mental and physical health. Others also find perception and motor actions are not independent, but interdependent processes; they characterize these as parts of an action system. Very early strong motivation in infants to pay attention, obtain information, explore, and engage their physical and social environments is evidence that cognitive, perceptual, motor, emotional, and social domains of development are interrelated, demonstrated by visual tracking, head-turning, and reaching. One investigator has observed that infants do not reach for desired objects because of brain programming; rather, they match their movements to their goals and the specific tasks involved. As some define it, behavior equals movement. Psychology is the study of human behavior; perception and motor behaviors inform psychological development. Some researchers find excellent opportunities for studying infants' social cognition by observing how they use social information to guide motor behavior in unfamiliar or physically challenging situations.

Promote motor learning for sports with training

Researchers into education have examined whether learning specific academic subjects could expand students' general attentional and learning skills. Many have concluded the nature of learning is more specific, in that the mind functions in a very detailed manner by adapting to the particular information it experiences. They additionally find that improving any individual mental process seldom improves any other individual one. These conclusions have been applied to the subject of motor learning. Experimental studies have demonstrated that movement is very closely related to sensory stimuli. This indicates that specificity in physical training is necessary for attaining successful outcomes in motor learning. Prevailing scientific evidence shows that, for students to acquire motor skills, the most important factor in practice is practicing the actual target skill itself, rather than related skills or other skills. For functional sport motor skills to become permanent behavior changes, the stimuli presented must duplicate the energy systems and movements used in a designated sport activity. Therefore, researchers conclude actually performing a sport itself is the best training for learning the motor skills involved in that sport.

Teaching individual parts of an athletic skill vs. teaching the skill as a whole

A common consideration in teaching new athletic skills is whether to teach a skill as a whole, or to break it down into its component pieces and teach those individually. Although task analysis has proven valuable for some purposes to education, to acquire specific sport skills, whole training has been found superior to part training for motor learning. For example, in volleyball, to teach spiking the ball, the parts would consist of approach footwork, arm work, jumping, contacting the ball, and recovery. The whole of spiking would be all these elements together. A part of spiking would be contacting the ball alone, or jumping alone, etc. Investigators reviewing the literature could not find even one study showing better results from teaching individual parts of such sport skills, or teaching individual skill parts in progressive sequence. Much additional research corroborates the concept that volleyball and other athletic skills demanding high levels of inter-limb coordination are learned best through teaching and practicing the whole skill rather than the parts, or even progressive parts.

Relationship of sports teaching methods to student learning and experience levels

By studying sports training methods as they are informed by principles of motor learning, researchers have found that, while educators must structure learning environments according to their particular students' skill levels and information-processing abilities, the training methods they use should nevertheless be constant across students. Neuroscience informs that beginners are more limited in their ability to process information. Additionally, motor learning principles dictate a positive correspondence between the relative complexity of the regulatory stimuli educators use and of students' experience, and vice versa. The balance is such that, without enough novelty, motor learning will not take place, while too much novelty will overwhelm student processing capacities. Teachers can control the learning environment to accommodate beginners' lower processing abilities. For example, when teaching volleyball to 3rd-graders, they can limit the content by using a smaller court, fewer players, a lighter ball, and/or a lower net. As students gain playing skills, teachers can introduce more new stimuli, enabling student motor behaviors to progress in complexity.

Significance of posture in classical and contemporary theories of motor development

In both classical and contemporary theories of motor development, the role played by posture is central. In classical theories, which attributed motor skills development to neuromuscular maturation, the gradually increasing erectness of babies' postures as they progressed in overcoming the effects of gravity was demonstration of the growth of control over actions in their cerebral cortices. In contemporary theories involving dynamic systems approaches and perception-action relationships, posture is equally important as action's biomechanical basis. Not only locomotor skills, but manual skills and even raising and turning the head all depend on having a stable postural base. Sitting up, crawling, walking, and every other developmental milestone in posture necessitates learning about new perception-action systems. In learning control over a new postural system, the first step is co-contraction of large muscle groups. This enables focusing attention on the movement's goal-directed aspects by freeing more resources. But movements initiated by co-contraction are energy-inefficient and jerky. With enough practice, babies learn to activate muscles in sequence and take advantage of the forces of inertia and gravity, allowing much lesser exertion of muscular force.

Influences of maturation vs. experience on motor development

While historically, scientists believed that genetically determined growth and development—i.e., maturation—was responsible for motor skill development, more recent research has uncovered evidence that the motor development process is not simply passive in nature, but is also active, as when babies engage in movement and physically explore their environments. As they develop physical abilities through growth and acquire motor skills through independent learning, maturation and experience and their interaction all influence motor development. Earlier motor skills like crawling and walking are more strongly influenced by maturation, though experience also clearly plays a part, as evidenced by babies' learning through experience in early attempts, errors, failures, repetitions, and eventual success. Later, more sophisticated motor skills like playing basketball or juggling are even more influenced by experience, instruction, and social factors as well as genetic predispositions. While early motor skill development follows similar sequences and timing across different cultures, cultural differences do influence the rates at which motor skills develop. For example, babies sit, stand, and walk later in cultures where mothers carry them more, and earlier in cultures where parents train them early in these skills.

Teaching methods for promoting psychomotor learning

Some instructional methods PE teachers can use to promote student psychomotor learning include the task/reciprocal method. In this technique, the teacher uses stations to integrate the students' learning of specific tasks into the learning setup. Another is the command/direct method. In this style, teacher-centered task instruction is utilized: The PE teacher gives students clear explanations of the learning goals, explains the skills to be learned, and then demonstrates these skills for the students. The PE teacher then gives the students time to practice the new skills. During their practice, the PE teacher monitors their progress frequently and regularly. Another instructional method PE teachers can use to promote psychomotor learning is the contingency/contract approach. In this type of instruction, the PE teacher offers specified rewards to students, which are contingent upon their completing the indicated tasks. This behavioral method reinforces psychomotor behaviors, i.e., increases the probability of students' repeating them, by rewarding the behaviors.

Factors that influence the development of children's motor skills

(1) Muscle tone during contraction and at rest varies among children. Hypotonia is low muscle tone, causing floppiness, weakness, and poor balance; hypertonia is high muscle tone, causing stiffness and

difficult movement. Children with Down syndrome may have hypotonia, while those with cerebral palsy often have hypertonia. (2) Strength is relative force of muscular contractions against resistance. Children with weak muscles may have difficulty achieving motor development milestones. (3) Endurance enables children to sustain exertion over time, entailing multiple factors including muscle tone, strength, cardiovascular and pulmonary function, and motivation. Children with low endurance may be able to step up one stair but not climb a whole flight. (4) Balance while stationary and while moving results from vestibular equilibrium interacting with sensory information, including sight, proprioception, muscle tone, and strength. (5) Motor planning coordinates systems controlling perception, movement intensity, speed, and sequencing in the complex and frequently intuitive process of executing steps in physical activities. (6) Sensory integration is interpreting environmental sensory input correctly and responding with appropriate motor activity. Children's response thresholds vary along a continuum among ranges of understimulation, average stimulation, and overstimulation.

Effects of experience on motor patterns

Neurophysiological studies have found the brain has plasticity; i.e., both its structures and functions can be modified by various influences, such as behavioral training and other new learning. Neuroplasticity affords great promise for improving abilities in people with neurological damage or deficits, and those wanting to enhance their cognitive processing skills. Furthermore, some researchers have found specific motor experiences determine the place and character of plasticity in the corticospinal system. For example, training in motor skills stimulates generation of new synapses, enhances synaptic potential, and restructures movement representations in the motor cortex. Training in endurance generates formation of new blood vessels in the motor cortex, but does not change number of synapses or organization of motor maps. Strength training changes activation of spinal motor neurons and generates new synapses in the spinal cord, but does not change motor map organization. All three types of training modify spinal reflexes that rely on each task's specific behavioral requirements. These findings show acquiring skilled movements causes neural circuits in the motor cortex to be reorganized to support producing and refining skilled movement sequences.

Helping students acquire and refine motor skills

Principles of practice, self-assessment, and observational learning
PE teachers not only need to know the process of motor development thoroughly, they moreover need to understand the principles whereby their students learn and transfer new information to progress in learning motor skills and refining them. Instruction and practice are critical: without these, the extent of children's motor skills development is determined only by their natural talents and abilities. But when PE teachers give students structured, frequent practice, their motor skills development improves. In motor skills development, student self-assessment is a tool that can have powerful impact. When PE teachers require students to assess their own abilities and skills, students are encouraged to reflect about their current levels of skill; they become more motivated to advance these levels, and assume control over their development processes. Observational learning is a key principle of PE because students learn motor skills more easily by observing their correct performance demonstrated by teachers than they can by trying to follow verbal directions. It is easier to reproduce physical movements we see than imagine and produce them from what we hear.

Principle of feedback
Input from teachers and coaches is vital for students to learn motor skills. Student motivation and interest are enhanced by positive feedback, while student recognition and correction of errors are enhanced by negative feedback. When students learn motor skills, these are temporarily saved in short-term memory. Positive feedback supports transfer to permanent, long-term memory. It not only encourages, but also

helps students remember all aspects of their performance. Negative feedback is not only corrective, but also motivational: when students and athletes do not improve their technique over time, they lose motivation. Students receive internal feedback through kinesthesia and proprioception. When they produce movements, they receive sensations and information from their muscles, joints, and vestibular (balance) systems. They receive verbal and visual external feedback from teachers and coaches. External feedback that improves internal feedback by enabling students and athletes to establish kinesthetic references for correct movements and techniques is called augmented feedback. Extrinsic feedback includes knowledge of performance, and information about performance and technique. Studies find feedback timing equally important as feedback content. Positive feedback is crucial to beginners for successfully learning skills. Beginners may be bored by negative feedback, but corrections and results are very important to advanced students and athletes.

Helping students develop better spatial awareness and coordination

For students to develop greater spatial awareness and coordination, they need both maturity and plenty of practice. In their lessons, PE teachers should concentrate on activities that require vision, hearing, and/or touch; that are sequential in nature; and that children enjoy performing. It is very beneficial to students for PE teachers to discuss the specific steps for performing fundamental skills with them. For example, running; hitting and catching a ball; dribbling a basketball, making a basket; and setting a volleyball are all skills and activities that PE teachers can break down into incremental steps and teach them one step at a time. Instructional strategies that are recommended include first introducing a skill to students; having the students practice the skill using a variety of equipment and in a variety of settings; modifying games to incorporate practice of the requisite skills; implementing lead-up games containing these practice modifications; and then, after enough practice, giving students the opportunity to use the skills they have learned and practiced in the contexts of real games.

Spatial awareness
Spatial awareness involves consciousness of and decisions about changes in objects' positions within three-dimensional space. The sequence of developing spatial awareness has two phases: (1) recognizing object locations in space relative to one's own body; and (2) locating multiple objects in space relative to each other, independently of one's body. PE teachers can apply the concept of spatial awareness to class activities by instructing students to move toward and away from, behind and in front of, over and under, next to, inside, and outside various objects. They can provide hoops, balls, boxes, etc. as objects in various sizes and shapes. These activities develop spatial awareness, particularly in younger children or students with spatial awareness deficits. PE teachers can assess student body awareness by observing them play Simon Says; asking them to touch their body parts; make straight, twisted, and round shapes with their bodies; and fit them into variously-sized spaces. They can enhance body awareness by having children touch one body part to another, twist their necks, nod heads, wiggle noses, open mouths, close eyes, shrug shoulders, bend elbows, clap hands, snap fingers, bend knees, stamp feet, and wiggle toes.

Effort awareness

Effort awareness refers to an individual's knowledge of time, force, and balance and how these are related to physical movements and athletic activities. According to the findings of research studies, movement concepts are interrelated and interactive with the concepts of space, direction, and speed. When students understand these concepts, they will be able to move so as to avoid collisions with other people and/or objects, and they will have self-confidence in their ability to move effectively. In order to understand a sport and perform it successfully, a student or athlete must incorporate the movement concepts of vision, space, direction, and speed. For example, when a student plays basketball or soccer, s/he has to determine what the appropriate amount or distance of personal space is among players. In addition, these movement concepts are all connected with one another. For example, a student playing a sport has to coordinate speed and direction in order to change or maintain his or her pathway without losing speed. This consists of the abilities to perform ably within space and to change one's motion.

Helping students develop body awareness and spatial awareness

To help students develop body awareness, PE teachers can instruct them to touch or point to their various body parts, form their bodies into different shapes, and to fit their bodies into differently sized and shaped spaces. These can both assess and develop body awareness. To assess and develop spatial awareness, PE teachers can provide differently sized and shaped objects like boxes, balls, hoops, etc. and have students move around, over, under, into, out of, in front of, in back of, and toward and away from them. To help students develop understanding of force, PE teachers can place targets at varying distances and have students throw beanbags, balls, or other objects at the targets. They can prompt students to notice how much force they must use to reach nearer vs. farther targets, and discuss use of relatively too much and too little force. Another exercise is to have spotters (carefully) positioned behind each student, and have students forcefully throw or otherwise propel wind-resistant objects like swim fins away from them to observe how this forces their bodies backward. This can also be done in swimming pools.

Instructional activities to help students gain understanding and control of the spatial concepts

PE teachers can help students develop their understanding of the spatial concept of direction by instructing them to move to the left, to the right, forward, backward, up, down, and diagonally in space. They can prompt students to be aware of their own kinesthetic feedback that tells them in which directions they are moving. Activities that develop rotation skills also help children's awareness and control of the directions in which they are turning. Locomotor "car" activities for children that involve taking turns walking in pairs, one behind the other with hands on the front child's shoulders, can include having the front child "steer," changing walking directions. This develops the front child's skill in controlling direction, and the back child's skill in following directional changes. Rotation activities for middle childhood using equipment can involve exploring moving in various directions. Students learning to fall sideways should practice doing this in both directions. PE teachers can direct students to notice the high, middle, or low levels of their bodies or body parts during movements. When teaching how to land safely from falls by rolling sideways, PE teachers can have students practice with falling from different levels.

Helping students develop understanding and control of the movement concepts of pathway, energy, time, speed, and force

PE teachers can help students develop understanding and control of pathways of movement through space by having them walk and run in a circle, a zigzag pattern, a serpentine pattern, etc. They can also help students develop concepts of planes in space by having them move along circular, vertical, or horizontal pathways. To help students understand different types of energy required in different activities, they can have them perform short-term, high-intensity activities like lifting weights and sprinting, and explain these use fast-twitch/type II/"white" muscle fibers; and longer-duration, lower-intensity activities like distance running and bicycling, and explain these use slow-twitch/type I/"red" muscle fibers. The latter require more aerobic/oxygen-using energy whereas the former do not use oxygen and cannot be repeated once muscles fatigue until rested and replenished. PE teachers can have students run or perform other movements at different speeds to understand the roles of time and speed in movement, and have them practice increasing and decreasing the rates of their movements to gain control over speed. They can teach students how force, time, and speed interact during running as they must modify their stance time and peak force/impact time to change running speeds.

Torque

Torque is the rotational version of force. In other words, torque represents how much a given force can make something or someone rotate or turn. Large torque is strong rotation; small torque is weak rotation. In the US/English system, the unit of torque measurement is the foot-pound; in the SI system, it is the Newton-meter (Nm). With torque represented as T, force as F, and the perpendicular (right-angle) distance from the force's action line as $\perp d$, the formula for measuring torque is $T = F \perp d$. A practical example to illustrate how torque operates is to imagine two skaters on ice. One skater has longer arms and the other has shorter arms. Each skater's body is equal to a rotational axis. If both skaters extend their arms horizontally and a third person pushes on each skater's arm, this will cause the skaters to rotate. Each skater's arm length equals the quantity $\perp d$, i.e., distance between the axis (skater's body) and force. Equal force will make the longer-armed skater rotate faster because the longer arm creates greater torque.

Biomechanical summation of forces

Summation of forces is to attain maximal force with any movement that uses multiple muscles in a manner that enables generating the maximum force possible. Thus the total amount of force is a sum of the total individual muscles when these are added together. The general principle of the order of use is that larger, stronger muscle groups in the center of the body initiate power, and smaller muscles in the extremities are used for coordination and finer movements. The largest, heaviest body parts are slowest and move first; smaller body parts are faster and move last. Force is both simultaneous and sequential. To attain maximal force, use as many body parts as possible. Sequential force, e.g., of body, then arm, then forearm, must be well-timed: if these follow too early or late in the sequence, they are ineffective. For example, the summation events in kicking a football are: body weight is transferred forward with the abdominals leading, the hip moves forward, the leg trailing, abdominals and quadriceps move the thigh forward, quadriceps and calf muscles straighten the lower leg, and calf muscles snap the foot.

Center of gravity

The center of gravity is the point at which a single force, of magnitude mg, meaning the weight of the system or body, would have to be applied to a rigid system or body in order to achieve an exact balance of the rotational and translational effects of the gravitational forces that act on the parts of the system or body. Put another way, the center of gravity is the point at which the weight of a system or body can be considered as acting. Although there is a minuscule difference between the center of gravity and the center of mass, they can be considered as the same for all practical applications. Therefore, center of mass is considered a synonym for center of gravity; however, center of pressure is not a synonym. In terms of the human body, its center of gravity is not fixed at any certain location in the anatomy. The location of the human body's center of gravity changes in accordance with the positions of the various body parts. The symbols used for center of gravity are C of G or COG.

Kinetics and running

Most sports require running speed—to outrun opponents in races, as a running start to develop enough takeoff velocity for jumping distance or height, to get to a base before being tagged, to evade tacklers, etc. Although speed-walkers can attain high speeds via an unusual gait that drops the hip with each step, running typically has faster speeds than walking. Kinetics is the part of biomechanics involving the study of movement and the forces that produce movement. The definition of running is a gait that includes an aerial phase when no body parts contact the ground or floor, with no external forces on the body (excluding gravity and wind resistance). Runners must modify the stance phase (when contacting the ground) to change speeds. A force plate measures running forces according to Newton's third law of motion (for every action there is an equal and opposite reaction): foot force produces a downward, backward force vector; the ground produces an upward, forward force. The force plate measures this ground reaction force (GRF). Faster running requires shorter stance time plus higher peak forces. Force = impulse / impact time; impulse is relatively constant. Bent knees extend impact time, reducing joint forces and injuries.

Biomechanics concepts and principles

The concept of force-motion states that, when we produce or change movement, unbalanced forces act upon our bodies or objects we manipulate. Force-time states that substantial changes in motion are produced over time, not immediately. Inertia defines the property all objects have of resisting changes in states of motion. Range of motion is the overall extent of motion a person uses in a movement, described through angular or linear movement of the body parts. Balance is an individual's capacity for controlling his or her body position in relation to a base of support. The coordination continuum means the goal or purpose of a movement determines the most effective timing of segmental movements or muscle actions. For example, people extend their hips, knees, and ankles concurrently to lift a heavy object but use more sequential movements in the kinematic chain, from legs to trunk to arms, in overarm throwing. Segmental interaction means that forces operating in a system of rigid, lined bodies are transferable through joints and links. Optimal projection means there is a best range of angles of projection for given goals or purposes in most human throwing and propelling of projectiles.

Applying biomechanical principles

When PE teachers instruct students how to apply biomechanical principles, students learn to produce and control force in ways that make their movements safer and more effective. For example, on the topic of effects upon objects, PE teachers can instruct students in applying the concept of force relative to how objects move in space. Learning objectives could include calculating and showing how the movements of projectiles are affected by the application of force; explaining and demonstrating how absorbing force increases their control over objects in sports activities, like collecting a soccer ball, bunting a softball, or catching a football; and explaining and demonstrating how efficient movement reduces the likelihood of injuries during various sports activities. For example, in soccer, kicking the ball using the instep rather than the toes can prevent injuries. On the topic of balance, PE teachers can instruct students in analyzing the concept of balance during complex movement patterns. As an example, a general learning objective could be for students to explore how their center of gravity affects their balance and performance during various movement activities.

Locomotor skills

Among motor skills, one major category is locomotor skills. Locomotor skills are movements wherein we use our legs and feet to move our bodies from one location to another. The basic locomotor skills children develop, in the approximate order they usually learn them, are: walking; running; hopping; jumping; skipping; galloping; sliding, i.e., galloping sideways; and leaping. Most normally developing children typically learn to walk around the age of 1 year. They usually have learned to run, hop, and jump by the age of 2 years. They begin to learn how to gallop, skip, slide, and leap around the age of 3 years. Young children will need to be provided with plenty of opportunities for practicing, though most of them find practicing fun during early childhood. They also will need their parents to provide them with some instruction to acquire the basic locomotor skills, which they do not necessarily just learn on their own.

Tips parents can give to young children to help them master basic locomotor skills

Here are some tips for parents to help their young children master the basic locomotor skills. Walking: Tell children to walk with straight, smooth steps and swing their arms in opposition to their feet. Have them practice different walks, e.g., on tiptoe, low with bent knees, fast and slow, robotic and liquid, etc. Galloping: Tell children to use one foot as "leader" and the other as "follower," alternating sides. Jumping: Have children keep their feet together, pushing and landing with both feet. Have them try jumping rope; see how high they can jump, how many times in a row, and how quietly they can land. Hopping: Have children see how quickly and slowly they can hop, and whether either side is harder. Side-sliding: Tell children to spread their arms, lead with one foot, and rise in the middle. Leaping: Have children lead with one foot and leap over an object, landing with the other foot. Skipping: Tell children to march, raising one knee high and hopping on the other foot—step/hop, step/hop, alternating sides.

Critical fundamental motor skills for children to learn in elementary school

Some fundamental motor skills critical to learn in elementary school include running, jumping vertically, leaping, dodging, kicking, overhand throwing, catching, ball bouncing, punting, forehand striking, and two-handed side-arm striking. Some examples of the overhand throw as applied in advanced form in specific sports include baseball and softball pitching, tennis and badminton serving, throwing a javelin, volleyball passing, and basketball shoulder passes. Some examples of the two-handed side-arm strike as applied in advanced sports-specific forms include swinging a golf club, hockey stick, or baseball bat; forehand drives in tennis, badminton, disc golf, squash, or table tennis (ping pong); and cut shots in volleyball, golf, or pool. Running, vertical jumping, kicking, and catching should be introduced in kindergarten. Running, vertical jumping, and catching should be mastered in 2nd grade, kicking in 3rd grade. Overhand throwing, ball bouncing, leaping, and dodging should be introduced in 1st grade. Ball bouncing, leaping, and dodging should be mastered in 3rd grade, overhand throwing in 4th grade. Punting, forehand striking, and two-handed side-arm striking should be introduced in 2nd grade. Punting should be mastered in 4th grade, forehand and two-hand side-arm strikes in 5th.

Non-locomotor skills vs. locomotor skills

Whereas locomotor skills involve moving from one location to another using the legs and feet, non-locomotor skills are motor skills that do not involve moving among locations. Non-locomotor skills involve little or no shifting of the base of support, and do not cause changes in position. Lifting a weight and squeezing a ball are examples of non-locomotor skills. Some other common movements that involve non-locomotor skills are balancing, swaying, turning, twisting, and swinging. Bending is movement around a joint between two body parts. Dodging is sharply avoiding a person or object, e.g., by leaning away or ducking. Stretching is extending or hyperextending the joints to straighten or lengthen the body parts. Twisting rotates the body or body parts around an axis having a stationary base. Turning is moving the body through space in a circle, releasing the base of support. Swinging involves circular or pendular movements below an axis of the body or body parts. Swaying is like swinging, but above an axis. Pushing is applying force against a person or object to move one's body away or move the person or object away. Pulling is exerting force to move people or objects closer to one's body.

Teaching and learning various non-locomotor skills

In grade 1, teachers introduce non-locomotor skills like bending, twisting, curling, and swaying involving a broad range of joints by discussing weight transfer, arm-leg opposition, and other mechanics involved. Teachers have students imitate elephants swaying and trees swaying in wind. Teachers assign small groups to develop warm-up routines using these skills, identify joints used, and name each movement. In grade 2, teachers introduce and demonstrate the motions, pair students to perform warm-up and cool-down activities requiring two people using these movements, and have students identify joints and major muscle groups involved and identify exercises targeting each joint in a warm-up routine. In grade 3, teachers introduce and demonstrate the skills, work on building student comprehension of principles of improving flexibility, discuss which joints can move, and list exercises targeting each joint in a fitness routine. Teachers design a fitness routine for students to improve range of motion in specified joints, connecting the different movements; and pair students to perform these and improvise exercise that equally stretch opposing muscles in specified joints. Teachers have individual students create and lead warm-up and fitness routines in class.

In grade 4, teachers review non-locomotor skills and discuss their importance in physical activities, including bending in tucked, pike, squat, forward, and backward positions; stretching before physical activity, including identifying muscle groups to stretch in warm-up and cool-down; static balancing, with 1-part to 4-part bases and in gymnastic routines; and dynamic balancing, including turning in dance and games and flopping from sitting, kneeling, and standing positions. Teachers guide paired students in mat exercises, have them create routines targeting multiple muscle groups, and have all students perform these. In grade 5, teachers review; have students develop skills further through individual and group activities; perform bends, stretches, and rolls on mats; and create warm-up and cool-down routines, and lead the class in performing these. Teachers invite a physical therapist or other professional to discuss stretching and injuries caused by improper stretching. In grade 6, teachers review; have students explore non-locomotor movements on mats, pointing out specific movements discovered; assign pairs or small groups to create warm-up routines, recording and displaying activities and muscle groups included on posters; assign homework of short reports with diagrams explaining the relationship of stretching and injury prevention; and emphasize more independent student movement development.

Manipulative or object control skills

Manipulative or object control skills are the category of motor skills that involve using objects. They include both fine motor skills, as in buttoning buttons, zipping zippers, fastening and unfastening clasps, twist ties, etc.; using crayons, pencils, pens, and other writing, drawing, and painting implements; using spoons, forks, and other eating utensils; and gross motor skills, as in swinging a baseball bat, a tennis racket, a jai alai cesta, a jump rope, a golf club, a bow and arrow, etc. The actions included in manipulative skills include pushing, pulling, lifting, swinging, striking, throwing, catching, kicking, rolling a ball, volleying, bouncing, and dribbling. A consideration to keep in mind when young children are first learning manipulative skills is not to expect them to be perfectly accurate, for example hitting a target, throwing directly to another player in a game, or catching a ball thrown to them. Children must first master the throwing, catching, hitting, kicking, or other action before they can develop accuracy as well. It can help to have children practice the movements and techniques with imaginary objects to begin, and then progress to real objects.

Manipulative movement activities involving throwing

Teachers can put hoops on the ground or hang them from door frames or trees with rope for young children to practice throwing things through them. Parents can develop throwing skills at home by having children throw rolled socks into laundry hampers or baskets. When they succeed, have them take one step further back for the next throw. Teachers and parents can use pillows or cushions to set up courses (with or without children's participation), placing empty boxes, wastebaskets, buckets, etc. as "golf holes." Have children take turns throwing beanbags into the holes. Children can crumple paper into "snowballs"; adults tape these up and give baskets of them to two groups of children. Mark a line between groups with rope, tape, or chalk. On a signal, children throw "snowballs" over the line for 30 seconds, see who has the fewest snowballs left, switch teams, and repeat. Have children clean up by throwing snowballs into baskets. Adults can cut centers out of empty plastic food tubs to make rings, and have children try to toss rings over plastic bottles. Have children try to toss coins onto paper or plastic plates on the floor or ground. Let children throw a ball trying to knock a stuffed animal off a stool.

Older children can practice throwing for accuracy or distance. Here are some activities to practice throwing for distance. 1) "Force Back": Students face one another in pairs, throwing a ball toward the other as far as they can. The thrower's partner catches or retrieves the ball, throwing it back from where it landed. 2) "Three Court Ball": Assign students to two equally-numbered teams. Each team has one-third of a court and a tennis ball. Students try to throw the ball into the middle third of the court and have it bounce over the other team's goal line. 3) "Scatterball": Use a baseball diamond or any field with several bases arranged in a diamond, circle, square, or other enclosed shape. Divide students into two teams: throwers and fielders. Throwers take turns, one at a time, throwing balls as far away as they can. Then each thrower runs around bases until told to stop. The fielders catch or retrieve the balls thrown and collect them in a basket, bucket, or other receptacle. Switch teams and repeat. The team scoring the most runs wins. Students can also practice catching by throwing and bouncing balls or beanbags in pairs, groups, and teams.

Locomotor, non-locomotor, and manipulative skills

Baseball, basketball, and football
Baseball requires locomotor skills for players to run to the bases after a hit, and to run to catch fly balls. It requires non-locomotor skills as players twist their bodies to field the ball, catch the ball, and when batting; lean backward or forward to field balls, lean or bend down to catch low or rolling ground balls; reach out to tag runners out before they reach a base; and go through the movement sequence of pitching that involves leaning back, twisting, raising one leg, etc. Catchers also move their bodies while squatting to catch pitches without changing their base of support. Baseball additionally involves manipulative skills for pitching, catching, fielding, and batting. Basketball involves the locomotor skills of running and jumping; the non-locomotor skills of leaning, stretching, and bending; and the manipulative skills of dribbling, passing, catching, and throwing the ball. Football involves the locomotor skills of running, and sometimes jumping over other players; non-locomotor skills of bending in the huddle and twisting when dodging tackles; and manipulative skills of holding, passing (throwing), intercepting, and receiving (catching) the ball.

Tennis, volleyball, and golf
Tennis involves the locomotor skills of running, walking, and jumping over the net at the end of a match. It uses the non-locomotor skills of bending to pick up a ball, stretching and twisting to prepare for a serve; and stretching, bending, leaning, and twisting and reaching to return the ball in a volley. It uses manipulative skills for swinging the racket to hit the ball when serving and returning. Volleyball uses the locomotor skills of walking to take and rotate positions, and running to reach the ball; the non-locomotor skills of stretching, reaching, twisting, and bending to reach the ball in high and low positions; and the manipulative skills of serving the ball using the fist, spiking the ball from above with the palms of the hands, and hitting the ball from below with the fists. Golf uses the locomotor skill of walking; the non-locomotor skills of twisting and turning to swing, and bending to retrieve the ball from the cup, green, trap, etc.; and the manipulative skills of swinging the club to hit the ball, retrieving the ball by hand, and writing down scores.

Volleying
Fourth-graders should run and change direction dribbling a basketball or kicking a soccer ball. Fifth-graders should integrate skills by changing speeds and directions to evade defenders while dribbling a

basketball, running with a football, or kicking a soccer ball; or consistently and strategically moving to open spaces to receive passes in small-sided games. Sixth-graders should run and leap over consecutive cones or other obstacles without stopping. Kindergarteners should be able to volley beach balls or balloons to themselves five successive times and hit balls or balloons up 9-12 inches continuously with different body parts. First-graders should be able to vary their striking force and volley 6-10 times upward, alternating left and right palms. Second-graders should be able to volley with partners using both hands, and volley underhand while walking forward c. 20 feet. Third-graders should make and catch forearm passes to themselves, and volley to partners using overhead passes. Fourth-graders should serve underhand or overhand with correct form, and consistently volley using forearm passes to themselves. Fifth-graders should serve underhand, overhand, pass overhead, and forearm pass; show correct overhead volleying form against a wall; and consistently serve volleyballs over nets 6 feet high or walls from 15 feet away. Sixth-graders should return volleyballs with forearm passes at least 6 feet high.

Softball vs. baseball

A variation of baseball, softball uses a smaller infield and a larger ball. Two main rule differences from baseball are that, in softball, pitching must be underhand; and regulation softball games have seven innings rather than nine as baseball does. Softballs are 11-12 inches in circumference, which is 3 inches bigger than baseballs. Infields have bases 60 feet apart, not 90 feet apart as they are in baseball. Two types of softball are slow-pitch and fast-pitch. Slow-pitch, the kind most often played, has 10 players per team. Slow-pitch softball sometimes uses a ball larger than the usual 12 inches. Slow-pitch softball requires the pitcher to throw the ball in an arcing path. It also does not allow bunting the ball or stealing bases as baseball does. Fast-pitch softball has nine players per team, the same as baseball. As its name indicates, it requires faster pitching than slow-pitch softball. Fast-pitch softball also permits bunting and stealing as baseball does. In both slow-pitch and fast-pitch softball, an underhand pitch is required. Pitching distances required are from 46 or 43 feet for men, 39 feet for women, and 35 feet for girls. This contrasts with baseball's 60.5 foot pitching distance.

Soccer

Soccer fields are rectangular, with a goal at each end. Soccer teams have 11 players, who score by kicking the ball into the opposing team's goal. Some competition rules stipulate a minimum number of players per team, commonly seven. Only goalkeepers are allowed to touch the ball with their arms and/or hands while it is in play, and only in their penalty areas in front of the goals. Goal posts are 8 yards apart. Outfielders are allowed to contact the ball with their heads and/or torsos in addition to their feet. Whichever team scores more goals by the end of the soccer game is the winner. For tied scores, a draw is declared; there is a penalty shootout; or extra time is designated, depending on the format of the competition. Soccer has 17 official game laws. Soccer balls are 27-28 inches around, weigh 14-16 ounces, and are inflated to pressures of 8.5-15.6 pounds per square inch (at sea level). Adult pitching distances are 110-120 yards long and 70-80 yards wide internationally, 100-130 yards long and 45-90 yards wide non-internationally. Soccer/association football's highest governing body is FIFA (Fédération Internationale de Football Association), which organizes the World Cup every four years.

Tennis

Tennis is played with rackets strung with cord hitting a small, felt-covered, hollow rubber ball over/around a net in the center of the court to the opponent's side. Courts are clay, grass, asphalt, concrete, or acrylic, and sometimes carpeted indoors. Nets are 3 feet high in the center, and 3 feet 6 inches high at the posts. The object is preventing opponents from returning the ball within bounds. Returning the ball within bounds earns a point. Tennis is played by opposing single players or doubles (teams of two). One player, behind the baseline between sideline and center mark, serves the ball. Receiver(s) can be anywhere on their side of the court. Legal services must clear the net without touching and go diagonally into the opposing service box. A "let," a serve hitting the net before landing in the service box, is void and retaken. Serves falling wide or long of the service box or not clearing the net are faults. Touching the baseline or extension of the center mark with one's foot before hitting the ball is a foot fault. Two consecutive service faults (double faults) give receiver(s) the point. Legal returns hit the ball before two bounces. Players and teams cannot hit the ball twice consecutively. During rallies, legal returns can hit the net.

Track and field

Track and field is a sport that encompasses a number of different competitive athletic activities that involve running, jumping, and throwing skills. Among running events, it includes sprinting (short, fast running contests), middle- and long-distance races, hurdling (jumping over barriers while running), and relay races. Included among jumping events are the long jump (a horizontal distance jumping contest), high jump (a vertical height jumping contest), triple jump, and pole vault (clearing a high bar by propelling one's body with a pole). Throwing events include the shot put (swinging and flinging a small, heavy iron shot for the maximum distance), javelin (throwing a long, spear-like projectile for distance), discus (throwing a flat, disc-shaped projectile for distance), and hammer throw (throwing a hammer-like projectile for distance). Track and field also includes events that combine multiple sports into a single contest, such as the heptathlon combining seven events, the decathlon combining ten events, and others. Athletes win running events with the fastest time, and jumping and throwing events with the longest heights or distances. Major track and field competition activities include the International Association of Athletics Federations (IAAF) governing body's World Championship, and the Olympics.

Volleyball

Volleyball teams have six players, scoring points by grounding the ball on the opposing team's court, and extensive rules. Serves are from behind the court's rear boundary line with the hand/arm, over a net. The receiving team must keep the ball airborne within their court and return it to the serving team's court. Players can touch the ball up to three times; one player cannot touch the ball twice consecutively.* Grounding the ball on the opposite court is a "kill," winning the rally for that team, which gets a point and the serve beginning the next rally. A team loses a rally by committing a fault. Faults include: catching and throwing the ball, *double hit, four consecutive ball contacts by one team, making the ball touch the floor outside the opposite court or without clearing the net first, touching the net (a net foul), and crossing the boundary line while serving (a foot fault). Common volleyball techniques include spiking and blocking (both requiring vertical jumping skill), setting, passing, offensive and defensive roles, and specialized player positions.

Manipulative movement skills

<u>Dribbling and shooting</u>
Kindergarteners should be able to twirl a hula hoop and roll it on the floor. They should be able to drop a ball and catch it at the peak of its bounce. They should be able to dribble a ball continuously with their dominant hand. First-graders should be able to juggle two scarves, pass beanbags hand to hand between their legs in a figure 8, and dribble a ball with their dominant hand while moving. Second-graders should be able to dribble a ball around stationary objects, and dribble a ball with both left and right hands while standing in place without losing control. Third-graders should be able to circle a hula hoop around the waist without using the hands; juggle three scarves or plastic bags in a cascading pattern; and dribble a

basketball in a figure-8 pathway, alternating dribbling hands, to the opposite sides of cones set 10 inches apart.

For dribbling and shooting, 4th-graders should be able to demonstrate a bank shot with a basketball, and dribble the ball around obstacles with good ball control while changing directions at a jogging speed. Fifth-graders should be able to juggle small objects like beanbags, tennis balls, etc. in a cascade pattern; dribble a basketball with good control while changing speeds and directions around defensive opposing players who must walk and not use their hands; and demonstrate a basketball layup using the opposing foot on takeoff while moving continuously throughout. Sixth-graders should be able to shoot a basketball from anywhere on the court behind the second hash mark*, demonstrating good form. *PE teachers may want to vary the distance they use to assess this skill. Sixth-graders should also be able to demonstrate good skills for handling basketballs. For throwing and catching, kindergarteners should throw and catch beanbags to themselves and catch teacher-thrown (7-9 inches) foam balls from 5 feet. First-graders should roll a tennis ball and scoop up a slowly rolled tennis ball in their hands; throw small, soft balls with hand-foot opposition; and consistently catch big (4-9 inches) balls self-tossed above the head.

Throwing, catching, and rolling skills
Second-graders should catch small, soft tennis/yarn balls at peak, self-tossed above the head; throw balls 7 inches and larger against walls from roughly 8 feet away and catch them before they bounce; and underhand-toss small balls with correct form and accuracy to targets or partners from 15 feet. Third-graders should demonstrate correct form in a two-handed overhead/soccer throw, pass balls to slowly-moving partners using chest and bounce passes, catch balls while slowly traveling, and overhand-throw small balls using correct form to partners and targets from at least 20 feet. Fourth-graders should throw and catch footballs, Frisbees, and other sport-specific balls or objects with correct form; consistently scoop up rolled balls with hands using mature form (knuckles on ground, pinkies together), moving laterally to get ahead of the ball; and play "keep-away" and other small-sided, low-level throwing-catching games. Fifth-graders should throw and catch footballs, basketballs, and other sport-specific balls within skill combinations, e.g., catching, dribbling, and passing to moving teammates; and throw lead passes including chest bounce, overhand, and underhand to moving teammates with mature form and accuracy. Sixth-graders should accurately throw and catch footballs, basketballs, and other sport balls to and from partners in dynamic situations with mature form, and advance balls down playing areas passing back and forth in small-sided games.

Striking sport balls or objects with implements
1) Kindergarteners: Balance beanbags or objects on rackets and paddles while walking; hit balls off batting tees using implements. 2) First-graders: Strike beach balls or balloons forward using short implements while walking 20 feet without letting them hit the floor; strike four times without their hitting the floor using short, light implements (e.g., lollipops). 3) Second-graders: Bounce, then strike balls at walls or targets; strike beach balls or balloons with implements over low nets to partners without their touching the ground or floor; consistently strike balls upward with only one bounce. 4) Third-graders: Successfully hit balls or objects from close-proximity "soft tosses"; bounce and strike small foam tennis balls with soft, controlled forehand across the gym or into large areas; use long-handled implements to strike objects on the floor or ground to targets. 5) Fourth-graders: Successfully hit self-tossed objects with one bounce; volley or rally objects using implements over nets and low barriers; receive teacher hockey passes and shoot to targets from about 10 feet. 6) Fifth-graders: Successfully strike underhand teacher-pitched (3-5 inches) whiffle or foam balls; repeatedly hit balls forehand or backhand against walls at close range; bounce and hit small foam balls with soft, controlled backhand into large areas; dribble and shoot at goals with continuous action using long-handled implements. 7) Sixth-graders: Successfully strike underhand-teacher-pitched softballs; serve balls without bouncing consistently at target areas; and give-and-go using long-handled implements.

Kicking

1) Kindergarteners: Dribble a soccer ball slowly with both feet while walking; approach stationary balls and kick with high follow-through without stopping; kick stationary balls with any foot part with high leg backswing and follow-through. 2) First-graders: Dribble medium/large balls with either foot, walking/jogging; kicking balls with solid contact, high follow-through; approaching stationary balls, kick without stopping with high follow-through. 3) Second-graders: Dribble balls using both feet, jogging; trap balls when stopping; show correct form kicking balls using insteps; kick slowly-rolled balls to kickers with solid contact and high follow-through. 4) Third-graders: Dribble soccer balls using feet insides/outsides, running at varying speeds; pass balls to partners or targets using inside-foot kicks somewhat accurately and consistently; punt balls, with or without a bounce, using correct form, 15 feet or more most times. 5) Fourth-graders: Dribble around stationary opponents or objects without object contact or ball loss; trap teammate-rolled balls; dribble and instep-kick moving balls at large goals. 6) Fifth-graders: Dribble around lightly resistant, moving opponents; punt soccer balls and/or footballs 30 feet or more with two- or three-step approaches; make lead passes while dribbling with inside-foot kicks to moving teammates. 7) Sixth-graders: Change speeds and directions to evade opponents while dribbling soccer balls; trap balls from different speeds and heights; show competency with soccer dribbling and inside-foot passes in "keep-away" games.

Requirements for recreational activities

For people to engage in recreational activities, they must have free time when they are not occupied with working, activities of daily living, sleeping, or social obligations. Historically, people had less leisure time than they do today: they needed more time to survive physically and economically. With industrialization, higher standards of living, longer life expectancies, and more commercially offered recreational activities, people now have more leisure time available. Although some perspectives see leisure as spare time, others see it as an essential part of civilization and personal development because it enables people to reflect on the realities and values they overlook during daily life activities. Leisure is viewed as both a reward in and of itself and a reward for work, or even the purpose of work. Today, leisure has come to be seen as reflecting a nation's character and values: the United Nations Universal Declaration of Human Rights considers leisure a human right. Recreational activities are pursued for purposes of pleasure, healthy lifestyles, social interaction, competition, physical and mental rehabilitation, and other therapeutic and preventive medical purposes.

PE competencies

Grades 1-2

1) Body awareness: demonstrate body movements (flexion, extension, rotation) and shapes. Walk, run, skip, and slide. Stop at boundaries with control. Quickly, safely change direction without falling. Throw underhand, roll, and dribble a ball. Identify walking, running, galloping, skipping, hopping, jumping, leaping, and sliding. 2) Space concepts: Demonstrate directions, pathways, levels, and ranges during activities; perform locomotor skills while changing these; apply them in simple activities or games (moving to dodge tagging, etc.). 3) Movement quality: Understand and apply energy and force, time, flow, balance concepts to psychomotor skills, e.g., starting and stopping without falling; bending knees to lower center of gravity; showing understanding of hard and soft, tense and relaxed force variations; controlling personal force, e.g., in tagging, striking; demonstrating fast and slow movement; moving to simple beats and rhythms; following simple, teacher-led rhythmic movements; combining jumping and turning, bouncing and catching; showing smooth transitions between dance or rhythmic movements. 4) Health-related fitness elements: Begin identifying physiological exercise effects like faster breathing and heart rate; define the four health-related fitness components in their own words. Additional competencies

include movement-related problem-solving skills, awareness of personal responsibility for individual wellness, self-confidence and success, safe behavior for self and others, and appropriate social interactions.

Grades 3-6
1) Grades 3-4: Describe movements identifying body parts and actions. Identify basic muscle groups and movements. Show awareness of body part relationships (opposition, unison, sequence). Demonstrate leaping, alternating leading foot. Apply space concepts in movements with others. Balance on various equipment with control. Show an understanding of static and dynamic balance. Show comprehension of how bodies create and absorb force. Choose forces appropriate to tasks. Control personal and manipulative force, like dribbling while walking and running. Demonstrate slow, medium, and fast movement. Move with tempo changes. Incorporate various equipment into rhythmic patterns and movements. Combine up to three movements with or without equipment, e.g., jump-roping routines. Demonstrate smooth transitions among sequential motor skills, like running to jumping. Solve movement challenges combining concepts of force, time, and balance, e.g., gymnastics routines. Define, apply, and assess the four health-related fitness components. 2) Grades 5-6: Identify specific muscle groups and movements. Combine body movements and shapes. Identify major skills in beginning gymnastics, dance, and sports. Recognize similar skills in different activities. Perform movement sequences. Adjust force for tasks projecting objects, using various equipment. Adjust body movements for speed changes. Combine movement concepts and motor skills in series.

Grades 7-8
Give partners and groups constructive feedback; solve more complex problems with larger groups in simple movement challenges. Describe body movements using more advanced terminology. Show an understanding of body part relationships in performing more complex skills. Identify major skills involved in more complex gymnastics, dance, sports, and/or related activities. Recognize similarities in the use of space in tactics, dance, gymnastics and other advanced activities. Perform more complex movement sequences like low/high ropes exercises. Keep time to music while performing steps and patterns in a variety of dance styles. Adjust movements with partners or groups to a beat. Combine speed, force, directions, levels, and pathways in a dance routine, a sport tactic like dribbling against a defender, or other complex series of movement concepts and motor skills. Demonstrate mature form in various basic skills; adjust skills to more complex situations, e.g., throwing and hitting to different locations. Assess personal performance on Fitnessgram or other nationally accepted instrument. Monitor heart and respiratory rate, perceived exertion, recovery rate during and following activity. Understand basic FITT principles. Play by rules, show appropriate sports conduct, officiate small-group games, appropriately assume leader-follower roles, cooperate with others, show appreciation for appropriate feedback, interact with others from diverse backgrounds.

Grades 9-12
Recognize personal strengths and weaknesses and develop strategies accordingly. Give partners and groups critical, specific feedback to improve skills and efficiency. Describe body movements using advanced terminology. Identify similar skills in different activities, like volleyball spikes and tennis/badminton smashes. Apply space concepts applicably in varied activities, e.g., dance or gymnastic floor routines and set plays and other tactics in sports games. Recognize similar uses of space among different advanced activities. Apply balance skills in various activities like yoga, skiing, Tae Bo, and volleyball. Demonstrate competency choosing and performing skills in several new activities, e.g., territorial team sports, wall and net sports, target sports, run-scoring games, rhythmic activities, and outdoor adventure or recreation activities. Choose, perform, and apply knowledge and skills proficiently in two different kinds of sports or physical activities. Regularly participate in physical activities to attain and maintain personal activity goals. Assess, refine, maintain comprehensive personal fitness plans based

on nationally accepted assessment. Adjust activities according to knowledge of physiological effects. Analyze characteristics of sports and activities. Persevere to achieve higher performance levels. Anticipate and correct potentially dangerous outcomes (spotting, refereeing, and belaying). Evaluate competition by quality, not results. Show self-discipline and self-direction. Respect feedback and revise actions. Develop leading and following skills. Include diverse others. Help others.

People with disabilities

Barriers to participating in sports
Depending whether an individual has acquired a disability later in life or has had it from birth, some individuals will not have had experiences with sports early in life. This presents one obstacle to sports participation later and throughout life. Another common problem for people with disabilities is people in their communities, schools, and organizations lacking awareness and understanding of how to include persons having disabilities in sports events they organize and manage. Limited community resources, programs, and opportunities to acquire training, participate, and compete affect people with disabilities. This limitation sometimes results from the aforementioned lack of awareness and understanding about inclusion methods; and sometimes also exists despite community awareness, understanding, and desire, e.g., when funding and support are still missing. Lack of accessible gyms, buildings, and other facilities is another barrier. Dearth of accessible transportation interferes with attending sports events to participate. Social and psychological barriers include parent, teacher, coach, and even disabled people's attitudes and beliefs toward disability and sports participation. Inadequate access to information and resources is another obstacle.

Opportunities for athletes
Associations and organizations in the world devoted to accommodating athletes with disabilities have grown markedly from the 1970s until now. Many of these are international groups. People with disabilities in some nations also have more opportunities now than in the past for participation in PE in schools, community associations, clubs, and casual recreational activities. In the arena of competitive sports, opportunities include disability-specific and sport-specific world championships; the Parapan American Games and other regional tournaments featuring multiple sports; certain Olympics Games events designated for athletes with disabilities; similar such events in the Commonwealth Games; and additionally, some athletes with disabilities compete against non-disabled athletes in some mainstream competitions. Internationally, 18 or more games now exist for athletes with disabilities. Among the three biggest international competitions, the Special Olympics offer year-round opportunities for training and competition to people with intellectual disabilities at every level; the Paralympic Games include intellectual disabilities, cerebral palsy, spinal cord injuries, amputations, visual impairments, and other disabilities; and the Deaflympics offer competitions for deaf and hard-of-hearing athletes.

Benefits of sports competition
Research evidence in recent decades shows that quality of life and functional abilities are improved for people with disabilities by participating in sports and other physical activity. Studies have found that physical well-being and health are enhanced across disability groups by participation in physical activity and sports. General affect, as well as physical fitness, are seen to improve through sports and physical activity in psychiatric patients diagnosed with anxiety and depressive disorders. Research studies have also established correlations between physical and sports activity and increased self-esteem, social awareness, and self-confidence in people with disabilities, which can contribute to their empowerment. Also in recent decades, a major focus has developed on including and integrating people with disabilities into mainstream sports. This has resulted in many new opportunities for them to compete or participate. Disability sports participation also contributes on a global scale to national identity and nation-building. After natural and man-made disasters, sports participation helps to rehabilitate people with disabilities.

Physical benefits of recreational activities

Participating in recreation can enhance an individual's physical health and wellness. This is especially true of participating in outdoor recreational activities. According to the findings of research studies, people who are often active in recreation offered at state parks are found to make fewer visits to the doctor, to have lower body mass indexes (BMIs, i.e., the ratio of their weight to their height), and lower systolic (the top or first number) blood pressure than people who are not active in such recreational parks activities. Moreover, a State Parks report from California (2005) has shown that recreational activities outdoors constitute some of the best opportunities for people to increase the amounts of exercise that they get. In addition, another research study (2001) has found that the amounts of physical activity in which people participate in their communities are directly influenced by how many recreational facilities are available in their area.

Effects of recreational activity during leisure time

The relationship between physical and mental health is reciprocal: Not only does physical wellness promote better mental health, but mental wellness also can have an impact on physical well-being. When people participate in physical, recreational, and leisure activities, it gives them a sense of control over how they spend their time. This is important to busy people who often feel overwhelmed by all of the obligations they must meet. It also offers relief from those required duties in the form of having fun instead of only doing things they have to do. Leisure activities give people opportunities to achieve balance in their lives. Recreational activities help individuals manage stress more effectively, and they decrease symptoms of depression. Parents benefit their children by participating in leisure activities as they model healthy ways of managing emotions and addressing stress for them. One State Parks report (California, 2005) found that simply remembering a past outdoor recreation can elevate one's mood.

Relationship between leisure physical recreation and quality of life

Research studies investigating the effects of leisure recreation have found that quality of life is improved by finding balance in life, and one important way people can find such balance is by allocating some of their time for leisure and recreation. In addition, physical recreation is especially related to enhancing self-esteem. People who participate regularly in recreational activities are more likely to report greater satisfaction with their lives. Greater life satisfaction is implicated significantly in better mental health. Better mental health is in turn associated with better physical health. As overwhelming evidence of this, in a 2000 study by the American Recreation Coalition, 90 percent of respondents who regularly engaged in recreational activities reported satisfaction with their physical fitness and health. A sharp contrast was the 60 percent of respondents not regularly engaging in recreational activities, who reported dissatisfaction with their fitness and health. Such benefits make recreational therapy (RT) important in rehabilitation programs. The American Therapeutic Recreation Association highlights RT benefits to recovering addicts, psychiatric patients, seniors, and children including better body function, improved cognitive function, stress management, and accelerated healing from medical conditions.

Rhythmic movement activity

Elements of rhythm
The elements of rhythm include beat, duration, tempo, accent, meter, phrase, rhythms, and polyrhythms. Beat is the underlying pulse that can be heard and counted in music, percussion, and rhythmic movements like tapping toes, clapping hands, snapping fingers, dribbling basketballs, etc. Duration is the length or span of time covered by a beat. Tempo is the speed or pace at which music and rhythmic

movement proceeds, from slow to fast and everything in between. Accent is additional emphasis on one or more beats. Meter is the rhythmic organization/time signature of music. For example, the 4/4 time signature means there are four beats to each measure and the quarter note gets one count. The 6/8 time signature means there are six beats to each measure and the eighth note gets one count. Just as a phrase in language is a combination of words, a musical phrase is a combination of beats, which can be longer than a single measure. Rhythms are combinations of beats, which may be equal in duration/interval ("1, 2, 3, 4") or uneven, mixing fast and slow beats and/or different durations. Polyrhythms are multiple rhythms played simultaneously in layers.

Motor patterns
"Brain Dance" (A.G. Gilbert, 2006), done to music from *Christy Lane's Authentic African and Caribbean Rhythms* (2000) is a warm-up activity for completing the eight motor patterns on the beat in sequence. (1) Breath: Move arms up and down, coordinating with inhaling and exhaling. (2) Tactile: To "wake up proprioceptors," i.e., raise awareness and sensation of location in space and body movement, brush, squeeze, tap, and slap body areas and muscles. (3) Core-distal: Bring all body parts close to center, and then extend outward. (4) Head-tail: Bring head and tailbone closer front and back; flex, extend, and laterally flex the spine, e.g., rounding, arching, and side-to-side "snake" movements. (5) Upper-lower halves: Move only the upper body and arms bilaterally first, then move only the lower body and legs bilaterally. (6) Body-side (left/right halves): Move the left arm and leg together, then move the right arm and leg together. (7) Cross-lateral (diagonal body division): Make movements in opposition, e.g., lifting the left knee, touching it with the right hand and vice versa, crossing the midline. (8) Vestibular (inner ear): Disrupt and restore balance by moving off-balance and then stopping, using movements like rocking, spinning, etc.

Integrating non-locomotor and locomotor movements
The "hip-hop" activity (Cardinal, 2013) gives students practice in changing duration among regular time, half-time, and double-time, plus emphasis on beat and phrasing. Recommended musical selections are Pachelbel's *Canon in D* and Jay Sean's *Do You Remember*. Teachers lead students in tapping two fingers together to music, lightly so as not to influence classmates or overwhelm the music, first in half-time, then regular time, and then double-time. Students then repeat each step individually for practice. Then they repeat tapping while marching in place (non-locomotor), then while walking (locomotor) with full motion through each beat's duration—first at half-time; then when the teacher says "Hip," speeding up to regular time; when the teacher cues "Hop," slowing down to half-time; when the teacher says "Hip-hip," speeding up two levels to double-time; and when the teacher says "Hop-hop," slowing down two levels to half-time. Each is performed for two 8-counts, rotating from half-time to regular time to double-time, back to half-time, etc., including full range of arm movements. Tapping-and-walking combinations begin with just walking half-time, then walking regular time while tapping half-time, then walking double-time while tapping regular time, then walking half-time while tapping double-time, etc.

An activity (Cardinal, 2013) that emphasizes accent and phrasing involves bouncing pinky balls on different beats within a measure or phrase, first while standing (non-locomotor and manipulative) and then while walking (locomotor, non-locomotor, and manipulative). Teachers instruct students to stand and bounce balls on the "1" of each 4-count phrase, then on the "2," then on the "3," then on the "4," practicing repeatedly before changing beats. After enough practice, teachers have students do this while walking. They can then give them different combinations of bouncing with walking, such as step, bounce, step, bounce; bounce, step, bounce, step; step, step, bounce; bounce, bounce, step; etc. Teachers can give students music with a 4/4 time signature and then change to 3/4 (waltz) time music, 2/4 time, etc. The most challenging transition is from the "4" to the "1" count without stopping while walking through space. Recommended music includes: *Beer Barrel/Pennsylvania Polka* from *Christy Lane's Let's Do Ballroom* for 2/4 time; *Edelweiss* from the same source for 3/4 time; *Mad World* by Tears for Fears or the cover by

Michael Andrews & Gary Jules for slower 4/4 time; and *Viva la Vida* by Coldplay or *I Gotta Feeling* by The Black Eyed Peas for faster 4/4 time.

Dance

Creative movement and dance

According to the National Association for the Education of Young Children (NAEYC – Dow, 2010), within the art form of creative movement, the words "dance" and "movement" are interchangeable. The human body is this art form's medium. The basic elements of dance/creative movement are: (1) the body, its parts and range of motion; (2) space; (3) time; and (4) energy. Teachers can vary these elements when teaching children, e.g., by assigning variations in body part movements like marching while touching knees; clapping; holding arms up high, with one knee straight and one bent, on tiptoes; lying on the back with legs/feet in the air; etc. They can assign spatial variations, e.g., marching high, low, backward, turning, or in a square; temporal variations, e.g., marching in slow motion or as fast as possible, for a designated number of steps and then freezing; etc. Energy variations include marching as if stomping through mud, as if stuck in quicksand, as if barefoot on hot blacktop, without making any sound, etc.

Techniques taught and learned in various forms of dance

Ballet is the foundation for all other Western dance forms, so students taught ballet will be well equipped to learn other forms. The development of core strength, which is essential; the five foot positions; and many steps, turns, and jumps from ballet are shared by jazz, modern/contemporary, tap, and ballroom dance. Some additional techniques not taught in classical ballet include: pelvic rotations and ribcage isolations in jazz dance; torso contractions and extensions in modern/contemporary dance; loosening the ankles in tap, as well as "spanking" and other tap-specific foot movements; specific frames, holds, and other postures in the Viennese Waltz and quickstep in ballroom dance; specific turns, steps, and other movements in the cha-cha, samba, rhumba, pasodoble, and other Latin ballroom dances; and general techniques in ballroom dance bearing weight and leading more on the heels than the toes, and movement down, into the floor instead of up, away from it as in ballet.

Safety and injury prevention

Thorough warm-ups and cool-downs are critical. Warm-ups must have cardiovascular elements increasing body temperature, heart and breathing rates, blood circulation to muscles, muscle tone, joint flexibility, reaction speed, mental alertness, and motivation to move; and move major muscle groups and angular, gliding, and rotational joints, including internal and external hip rotations. Cool-downs lower body temperature, slow breathing and mind, deeply stretch muscles, reward the body for its exertions, and should be followed by recovery periods. Thorough warm-ups and stretching can prevent delayed-onset muscle soreness, cramps, sprains, and tendonitis. Avoiding muscle fatigue prevents inflammation and cramping. Hydration and keeping dietary electrolytes balanced also prevents cramps. Dance spaces should have clean and sprung wood floors, high ceilings, no obstacles, good lighting and ventilation, access to water, separate male/female changing rooms, and wheelchair and telephone access. If only concrete flooring is available, high-impact jumping and running must be avoided to prevent stress fractures. Teacher first aid training and kits are necessary. Student footwear must be appropriate to floor surfaces (slippery, dirty, etc.). Teaching and learning correct body alignment also prevents (or at least limits) injuries and promotes proper dance technique, more effective mechanical functioning, and more energy-efficient movement. Pilates, Feldenkrais, ideokinesis, and yoga improve alignment.

Types of music

Classical ballet commonly employs classical music. Many classical compositions were written expressly for the purpose of accompanying ballets. For example, Tchaikovsky was well-known for composing ballet music, including *The Nutcracker, Swan Lake, Romeo and Juliet,* and *The Sleeping Beauty.* Modern classical composer Igor Stravinsky collaborated with choreographer Michel Fokine for Sergei Diaghilev's Ballets Russes production of *The Firebird* (1910). Cincinnati Ballet choreographer Adam Hougland created an opera ballet to Mozart's masterpiece *Requiem Mass in D Minor.* In ballroom dance, the Viennese waltz was/is traditionally performed to waltzes by classical Viennese composers like Johann Strauss; however, today's creative choreographers also use diverse contemporary music in 3/4 time, e.g., on TV's *Dancing with the Stars.* Latin ballroom dances traditionally used music specifically for each dance, e.g., rhumba, samba, cha-cha, pasodoble, tango, etc., but *DWTS* also uses other music with appropriate tempi and rhythms. Jazz and tap dances have often been choreographed to/for Broadway show tunes, but can use any compatible music. Contemporary dance choreography frequently interprets song lyrics or expresses lyrical or evocative music. Hip-hop music most often accompanies hip-hop dance.

<u>Benefits of participating in dance activities</u>
Dancing increases aerobic fitness, cardiopulmonary and cardiovascular fitness, endurance, muscular strength, muscular endurance, muscle tone, and motor fitness. It strengthens the bones through bearing weight and decreases risk of osteoporosis. It aids in managing a healthy weight. Dancing improves a person's flexibility, agility, and coordination. It enhances spatial awareness, balance, and sense of direction. People who learn to dance enjoy greater physical self-confidence, overall self-confidence, and self-esteem. Dancing improves mental functioning. It promotes better well-being, in general and psychologically. Because of the social interactions inherent in learning to dance, and dancing in classes, groups, and with partners, dance also improves social skills. Serious dancers become very physically fit; even those more casually involved in dance will get more physical activity, improving their health and well-being. Dance can be pursued competitively or socially. Inclement weather does not interfere with dance as it does with outdoor sports. Today there are many places to take dance classes or lessons, including dance studios, dance schools, fitness clubs, colleges and universities, university extensions, dance halls, community recreation centers, etc.

Gymnastics

<u>Types of apparatuses used in gymnastics</u>
Low parallel bars are 7 feet long, 15 inches high, and 18 inches wide for practicing hand balances. Standard parallel bars are adjustable hand rails, made of fine-grained wood, on uprights connected by oval-shaped pressed steel rails. Rails go under upright and are completely secured inside the base. Bars adjust from 3 feet and 9 inches to 5 feet and 3 inches high and from 15 to 18 inches wide. Mats are thick pads covered with canvas or other material, filled with 2 inches of kapok/felt, made in various lengths, widths, and grades, to protect gymnasts when landing or falling. A side horse is a cylindrical body with an approximately 14-inch diameter, covered in leather/other material, mounted on steel legs/base, with two pommels, i.e., handles, on top near the middle. Horse height is adjustable from 36 to 57 inches. A spring board is an inclined board about 6 feet by 22 inches, over a fulcrum about half its length. It is lightweight, usually made of ash, shod with robber, and with its upper end carpeted in cork. It is used to spring off from for tumbling, horse and buck vaulting, and to parallel bars.

<u>Educational gymnastics vs. Olympic-style gymnastics</u>
Olympic gymnastics are better learned outside school hours. Educational gymnastics have different, non-competitive purposes: to teach children to increase their skills for controlling and maneuvering their bodies effectively against gravity's force, on the floor and on apparatus, through learning experiences. It integrates movement concepts, e.g., body and space awareness, force and effort, movement qualities and relationships. It also integrates with skill themes, e.g., balancing, transferring weight, traveling, jumping, and landing. Children must experience these in isolation and/or in dance or game contexts before experiencing them incorporated into gymnastics. Under traveling, some introductory themes include travelling independently and safely, to/from and on/off apparatus, changing direction/level, on

feet/hands, together/apart, and in shapes. Under weight-bearing, included are getting on/off apart, weight on hands, balancing on different surfaces and body parts, balancing and rolling, landing and rolling, changing feet relationships with weight on hands, and while balancing. In weight transfer, included are log/side rolling, forward rolls, jumping and landing, and back safety rolls. Under relationship, included are individual sequences; partner sequences together, apart, or side-by-side; and symmetrical and asymmetrical movements.

Tumbling terminology and stunts

Tumbling is a series of acrobatic, controlled large-muscle movements including flips, springs, rolls, falls, dives, twists, etc. Tumbling stunts can be on the mat, deck, or ground; semi-aerial, i.e., from the feet to the hands to the feet; or aerial, i.e., from the feet through the air to the feet going forward, backward, or sideways. Mat stunts include chest rolls, from a hand balance onto the chest; dives—from a running start, leaping into the air, ending on the chest, back arched, rolling downward; rockers on the stomach, back arched; forward/backward rolls, and sideward shoulder rolls. Semi-aerial stunts include front/back walkovers; barrel rolls; cartwheels; cradle rocks to back and shoulders; egg rolls/fish flops, backward to short head balance to shoulders forward, rolling down to chest, stomach, to standing; round offs, changing forward to backward momentum via inward half-turning; front, back, leaping, or one-arm handsprings; headsprings; and shoulder/neck springs. Aerial stunts include brandy/Baroni, a handless roundoff; somersault/side somersault/front flip with half-twist/back somersault; spotter, landing on the takeoff spot; cutaway, landing behind it; gainer—backward somersault landing ahead of the takeoff spot; layout; tuck; whipback; bounders; alternates; and Rudolph (brandy with full twist). There are others for doubles and triples.

Intermediate movement themes

Here are some intermediate themes for grades 4-7 educational gymnastics lessons. For traveling: moving into and out of balance, and jumping with turns. For weight bearing: balancing while curling, stretching, twisting, or otherwise changing body shapes; partner balances; counter-tension (away); platform balance; and counter-balance (together). For body shape: the body shape in flight. For relationship: partner matching and copying, small group sequences, and using the partner as an obstacle to move over and/or through. For traveling into and out of balance, there are five steps in a learning experience. (1) Run and jump onto a vaulting surface. (2) Run, placing hands on the apparatus, and land on the same spot. (3) Repeat (2), but add a roll upon landing. Practice roll progressions for the backward safety roll. (4) Change the relationship of the feet while performing various vaults into the air; move into a balance. (5) Hold the balance; then move into another balance. Refinements for these steps are: (1) Move into a balance. (2) Take off with feet, and raise the hips as high as possible. (3) Use a curved surface area; tuck tightly. (4) Spread, cross, or bend the knees. (5) Make the sequence parts flow.

Benefits to children of learning tumbling and gymnastics

Learning tumbling and gymnastics skills and routines contributes significantly to children's development in many domains—not only in sport-specific skills, but additionally in academic performance and personality, psychological, and social development. Students meeting challenges in gymnastics, e.g., learning skills for performing on balance beams and parallel bars, gain self-confidence in their own abilities, which extends to school subjects and other life areas. Younger children think concretely, not abstractly; their lives are more physical than mental. The superior body movement and coordination they develop through tumbling and gymnastics give them much of their self-confidence. Children lacking natural talent to be "star" athletes in other sports benefit from success in tumbling and gymnastics as teachers can control the challenges and progress they experience. Students learn to overcome fears and to perform in front of others. The training required in gymnastics builds determination and a hard work ethic; its controlled environment and rules teach discipline. Physical strength and flexibility from gymnastics benefit student athletes playing football, basketball, baseball, and other sports. Athletes typically need more flexibility—which also prevents many injuries. Listening, following directions, taking turns, politeness, and respecting others are social skills learned in gymnastics.

Cooperative games

In cooperative games and activities, students must work together to discover solutions to different challenges presented by the activities. Examples include activities to develop communication skills, teamwork skills, and problem-solving skills. One cooperative PE game activity for developing communication and teamwork skills is "Caterpillar Riot": Teams of 5 or 6 students stand in line, each wearing a hoop; hoops should touch. Each team is a "caterpillar." The goal is to collect as many objects from the floor as possible by moving the caterpillar forward. To advance, the rear player in each line steps into the hoop of the player ahead, picks up his or her empty hoop, and passes it to the front of the line. The front player puts the hoop down, stepping into it. Each player moves forward into the next hoop. Only the front player may pick up objects; other players must carry objects collected. When all objects are collected, the game ends. Builds include a preparatory race, advancing caterpillars without collecting objects; playing the full version; adding a time limit to the full version; and playing blindfolded.

One game PE teachers can have a whole class of children play is Astronaut, which involves running and dodging movement patterns and skills. It develops endurance, locomotor skills, non-locomotor skills, and group cooperation. The only equipment is one balloon per child. Teaching tips: The game is best played in a large, grassy area. Include short rest periods for young children, who tire quickly. Do not let children keep balloons afterward. To play, select four children as astronauts. The rest are Martians. Each astronaut has an air supply, i.e., an inflated balloon. On the teacher's signal, the Martians chase the astronauts, trying to destroy their air supplies by popping the balloons. Once all four balloons are popped, start over with four different astronauts. Repeat until all children have been astronauts. One variation is to add flags: once a Martian pulls an astronaut's flag, s/he must surrender the balloon to that Martian.

<u>Communication, teamwork, and synchronization</u>
To play "Toxic Waste": The equipment used includes ringette rings, foam balls, jump ropes, cones, and optional blindfolds. Teams of four students each have one foam ball sitting on top of a ringette ring with four jump ropes tied to it. The goal is for students to move the "toxic waste" foam ball from one end of the gym to the other without touching the ringette ring's ball, so students must utilize the ropes. If the ball falls, whichever team dropped it must return to the starting line and start over. After students play the original game, the teacher can add a build wherein one student on each team is blindfolded. After each round, the teacher blindfolds one more player, continuing until all players are blindfolded. One safety rule is that blindfolded students must walk, not run. After playing, the teacher can initiate student discussion by asking them questions such as, "To succeed in moving the toxic waste to the other side, how did you have to coordinate your movements as a team?" "What were the communication challenges in the game?" "How was your communication affected by having one or more players on your team blindfolded?"

<u>Competitive team games</u>
Four-Corner Cage Ball involves kicking and crab-walking movements, and develops striking skills, arm and shoulder strength, and teamwork skills. Equipment is four cones and one cage ball. Divide the class into four teams, each forming one side of a square marked by cones. Number off each team; children must remember their numbers. Place a cage ball in the middle of the square. Call a number. All children with that number crab-walk to the cage ball; their goal is to kick the ball over the heads of another team. Other players, also crab-walking, can only block the ball using their feet. Any team having the ball kicked over their heads gets a point. Start again, calling new numbers. The object is NOT getting points. Teaching tips: With this competitive game, children may become excited, forget the rules, and block the ball with their hands. Teams can be given points for doing this if not for safety. For safety, no hard shoes or boots are

allowed, and children should remove glasses. If outdoors on grass, carefully check first for debris. If running out of time without everybody getting a turn, extend boundaries as needed; call two or three numbers at once.

Outdoor adventure activities

Some exciting, fascinating, rewarding outdoor adventure activities include mountain-climbing; rafting; canoeing; kayaking; whitewater paddleboarding; sailing; driving powerboats; slacklining; rope-climbing; exploring mines; exploring caves; walking long-distance footpaths; backpacking; hiking; running; jungle treks; expeditions through primary rainforests; nature hikes and walks; exploring wild areas in four-wheel drive vehicles; and orienteering, which involves navigating a wilderness environment with a compass and a map, while also racing against others to reach a destination first. Some outdoor adventure enthusiasts pursue these interests close to home, which is most convenient and affordable, while others travel to other countries and exotic locations. Some altruistically-minded adventurers combine adventure expeditions to other lands with team community service projects when they arrive. Others find adventure experiences inspire photography, drawing, painting, writing music, writing literature, other artistic pursuits, or scientific/practical inventions. People unfamiliar with and interested in adventure can learn from experienced, credentialed instructors in the outdoor industry—as adventure school faculty or independent freelancers—many with websites advertising their services. In addition to teaching techniques and safety practices, instructors also mentor, motivate, and encourage learners; build their confidence and self-esteem; and foster their skills for teamwork, decision-making, and problem-solving.

<u>Behavioral and administrative types of courses</u>
Some of the courses offered in the area of outdoor adventure include leadership, group dynamics, risk management, conflict management, expedition planning, execution, and evaluation. Classes are offered in specific activities, e.g., backpacking techniques for beginners; slacklining techniques, including choosing the correct trees and avoiding damage to the trees used; learning to set up a line; and learning to stand and balance on a line before learning to walk on it. Multi-pitch climbing techniques include anchoring skills with gear anchors and multidirectional anchors, anchor builds, rappelling techniques, belaying directly off of anchors from above, belay station rope management, belay transfers, efficiently changing leaders, self-rescue techniques, and other hands-on learning. Some outdoor adventure schools and instructors use sports like paddleboarding in whitewater rapids while standing up as facilitation techniques for therapeutic recreation. They advocate these activities for being experienced in natural environments, including elements of perceived or actual danger, and providing challenges to participants. Beginning courses in kayaking techniques teach the basic strokes, e.g., the forward stroke, forward sweep stroke, and low brace stroke, starting in calm lakes. Once learners can paddle in straight lines, they can learn how to turn using the paddle as a rudder and use steering strokes.

<u>Obtaining information on safety and risk management</u>
The *Outward Bound Wilderness First-Aid Book* (Isaac, 1998) is a manual of standard operating practices for risk management and safety in outdoor adventure recreation and education programs. Other outdoor education organizations offer similar books. Additional good resources include government education departments and recreation agencies, which have published outdoor activity risk management guidelines in many countries. Research studies published by various organizations provide data and narratives regarding risk management and incidents. For example, *Adventure Program Risk Management Report, Volume I* (1995) was issued by the Association for Experiential Education. The American Camping Association (ACA) and other outdoor associations have published guidelines, articles, and manuals describing risk management in rope challenge courses and many other specific adventure activities. Adventure Incorporated and others offer risk management specialists as consultants. The National Outdoor Leadership School organizes an annual Wilderness Risk Manager's Conference in America. Every

developed nation offers outdoor and adventure risk management and first aid training courses, listed at www.outdoored.com. Professional Outdoor Education listservs also extensively discuss safety and risk management practices.

Benefits of outdoor adventure and education
Outdoor learning in nature affords background benefits of increasing physical, mental, and spiritual health; personal and social communication skills; sensory, aesthetic, and spiritual awareness; sensitivity to one's own well-being; and the ability to exercise personal control. Outdoor learning in the natural environment can also have planned benefits when providers or educators determine or negotiate these. For example, through structured, well-planned, hands-on learning experiences, teachers and providers help students to develop their own self-esteem, take personal responsibility, cooperate with others, and respect others' needs. They help them develop better appreciation of the world and its peoples, which allows them to expand their personal horizons. They teach them to understand why people must establish and maintain sustainable relationships with the environment. They improve students' practical teamwork and problem-solving skills. And they foster knowledgeable, positive student responses regarding personal well-being and health. Outdoor learning allows bonus benefits as well through incidental learning and greater than expected value, which highly supportive learning atmospheres enable. Wider benefits include greater sustainability and other benefits for families, schools, sponsors, society, and future generations, who are all stakeholders in outdoor learning success.

Primary equipment in football, baseball, and hockey games

Football players need heavy shoulder, chest, and elbow pads to protect them from body contact injuries. Helmets are imperative to prevent head and brain injuries from collisions and blows. Recently the NFL began requiring players to wear knee and shin guards; PE teachers should have students follow this practice. Baseball does not require body contact through hitting or tackling like football. However, because it involves swinging hard bats and hitting and throwing balls which become projectiles, baseball players must wear helmets to protect against head injury. When traumatic brain injuries do not occur, getting "beaned" by a baseball is still extremely painful—even when wearing a helmet, let alone to an unprotected head. Being accidentally hit by a baseball bat can also seriously injure a student. Hockey players use angled wooden sticks, which can cause injuries. Ice hockey uses a small, dense, hard rubber puck, which can be very injurious if striking a player. Helmets, neck guards, shoulder and chest pads, elbow and forearm pads, and shin guards are included in hockey, plus heel guards on skates in ice hockey. Mouth guards are recommended in football and hockey to protect players from lost and broken teeth.

Students with disabilities

Modifying creative movement and dance activities
According to experts (cf. Dow, 2013), all children can participate in most movement activities when they are modified. Each child can approach movement according to his or her individual abilities, experiences, and imagination. For instance, if a teacher gives children a greeting activity involving their waving various body parts, they can instruct children with physical disabilities to move their fingers, toes, eyelids, or tongues. When leading children in a jumping activity, if the class includes children in wheelchairs, teachers can instruct them to move their heads, shoulders, arms, and/or fingers instead of their legs. If the teacher is instructing children to form the shapes of alphabet letters with their bodies, s/he can guide children with physical disabilities to use their fingers or arms rather than their entire bodies. Children who are unable to do this can point to or hold up a picture or large shape of each letter to participate actively. Children of all/most ability levels can participate in dance stories by exploring and elaborating on characters and events in stories, poems, books, or songs through creative movement, including facial expressions.

Modifying educational gymnastics

Some gymnastics educators state that inclusion is not difficult because coaching practices should not really change: in providing opportunities according to individual student needs, program competencies and strategies can be preserved while maintaining awareness of disabilities. Educators have effected cultural changes by informing coaches at national championships that inclusion tools, tips, and other resources would become available. They find it necessary to raise awareness of and communicate social messages about inclusion before teaching technical elements of coaching students with disabilities. They advocate developing disability action plans. Some agencies and organizations offer funding to support such plans' strategies. Following awareness and education, educators identify the next step as requiring teacher or coach accreditation processes to incorporate mandatory training in inclusion management. They point out that high-performance coaches do this routinely when they assign unevenly-numbered teams and small-sided games and focus on developing specific tactics, techniques, and skills. An inclusive approach, they say, involves the same practices, but simply done for different purposes. Some experts use the TREE acronym and principle for modifying and challenging sports players according to individual ability: Teaching style, Rules and regulations, Equipment, and Environment.

Modifying curriculum and instruction in group or cooperative PE activities

To provide inclusive PE environments, modifications are needed to make learning environments safe and meaningful for every student, enable all students' successfully learning appropriate PE skills, and eliminate mismatches between lesson content and student skill levels. To be appropriate, modifications must not make settings or activities unsafe for non-disabled students; not ruin activities or games by precluding fun; not overburden regular PE teachers; and enable safe, meaningful, and successful disabled student participation. Curriculum modifications include: (1) multilevel selections of different learning objectives in the same domain, (2) objectives from different domains overlapping in the same activity, and (3) different alternative activities. Part (1) includes modifying tasks and equipment, e.g., for limited strength, speed, endurance, balance, or coordination; extending skill stations, e.g., holding basketball on lap tray, dropping ball to floor, slapping ball three consecutive times, dribbling while stationary or walking, or dribbling while jogging and or guarded; modifying instruction, e.g., in class format, teaching style, cues and signals, instruction and participation duration, setting, distracters, motivation level, direct instruction, movement exploration, and strategies intervention model. Part (2) includes cooperative learning; class-wide peer tutoring; teaching locomotor skills plus walking, dribbling, and 3-point shooting in a basketball game. Part (3) includes pull-out activities; concurrent multiple activities; and pocket-reference IEP objectives and RPE modifications, arrangements, and activities.

Aspects of inclusion for participants

Experts identify the building-blocks of adventure PE programs as the core values of adventure education, which include: emphasizing non-competitive activities; participants' sense of accomplishment from successfully completing a specifically designed activity sequence; trust and cooperation fostered among co-participants; the communication participants exchange to attain their goals; the ability to implement activities at individual participant levels; the combination of enhancing strength, coordination, flexibility, and endurance while having fun; and the fact that activities require participants to cooperate with nature, promoting better appreciation and respect for the natural environment. Adaptations include allowing longer times to complete tasks, slowing activity paces, demonstrating activities visually and verbally, employing peer partner assistance, simplifying steps, modifying body positions, removing obstacles and distractions, increasing participation time by using stations, providing ramps, shortening course or activity distance, and using signing gestures along with verbal instructions. Special and regular education teachers must collaborate creatively to assess needs and find appropriate curriculum adaptations that both enable individual success and attain the school's/organization's and individual student's learning goals.

The Role of Physical Education in Promoting Development

Behaviors developed through participating in sports, games, fitness and other PE activities

Students in grades 5-6 should show self-confidence by identifying PE activities that are personally challenging to them, identifying the skills they need to develop and/or refine personally to succeed, and choosing and practicing specific skills they need to improve. They should demonstrate safety for themselves and others and apply the appropriate etiquette in specific sports and activities, e.g., taking turns; avoiding personal fouls, like body contact in basketball; avoiding excessive force to the point of injury in football tackling and blocking; helping up fallen opponents; not teasing teammates or classmates for being out of condition; not celebrating opponent mistakes; not arguing with every call made by referees, umpires, or teachers; not insulting others; not denying fouls; avoiding inappropriate language; and shaking hands after contests. They should follow and help establish rules and procedures, show responsibility for their own actions and the capacity for receiving and providing honest feedback, show willingness to engage with others of different socioeconomic levels, contribute to positive group dynamics, and show cooperation by encouraging and supporting classmates and teammates with different skill levels and abilities.

Personal and interpersonal behaviors

Grade 7-8 students should demonstrate personal responsibility for their individual wellness by acquiring and identifying knowledge about the connections among exercise, nutrition, and fitness, and apply this knowledge in selecting activities for improving and maintaining their fitness goals. They should participate in lifelong and leisure sport or dance activities in and out of school to show they recognize the importance of physical activity to personal wellness. They should further their individual self-confidence and success through identifying how personal performance is affected by attitude, energy, and effort; set personal goals for attaining higher performance levels in challenging and new activities; and show positive attitudes about developing personal skills. They should show positive and supportive behavior to demonstrate safety for self and others. Appropriate social interactions demonstrating responsibility include: playing by the rules and not taking advantage of classmates or teammates; practicing proper sports conduct, e.g., accepting teacher, coach, and referee decisions without argument; and officiating in small-group games. Additional appropriate social behaviors and interactions include: showing appreciation for applicable feedback, being willing to work with others from diverse backgrounds, being able to adopt leader and follower roles as indicated, and cooperating with others within task activity structures.

Behavioral and social skills

High school students should show recognition of personal responsibility for individual wellness by demonstrating they understand how personal traits, styles, preferences, and performance change throughout life, and applying this understanding to continually evolving fitness plans. They should also further their achievement and maintenance of personal fitness goals through regular participation in suitable physical activities. To further their self-confidence and individual success, they should be able to analyze the characteristics of the physical and sports activities they personally find challenging, rewarding, and enjoyable, e.g., they are high-risk, competitive, individual, group, socially interactive, aesthetically satisfying, etc. They should also challenge themselves in developing higher or new skill levels, and demonstrate perseverance in pursuing higher performance. By participating in related activities like spotting, refereeing, and belaying, they should demonstrate their ability to anticipate and correct consequences from physical activities that are potentially dangerous. Appropriate social interactions include: showing responsibility through sportsmanlike conduct; preventing dangerous outcomes; using quality of play, not results, to evaluate competition; displaying self-discipline and self-direction; revising their actions to show respect for feedback; exhibiting strategies to include diverse others in physical activities; recognizing and developing their leading and following abilities in group activities; and showing cooperation by helping others participate.

Promoting the development of leadership and teamwork

When students must play a game or sport as team members rather than individuals, a team captain is often designated. This student must take responsibility for things like choosing team members; planning and organizing plays; developing tactics; providing motivation to team members; encouraging team solidarity; and getting team members to cooperate, collaborate, and function as a unit rather than a collection of individuals. Learning to perform these duties successfully will develop student leadership skills. Teamwork is also essential in sports. Purposes and benefits of team sports include winning contests, attaining shared goals, preparing for jobs and wider society, learning to build confidence and manage emotions, learning about oneself and others, and surviving and flourishing in large classes and schools. The power of numbers enables teams to accomplish things individuals cannot. When team members conflict with and/or work against one another, a team thus divided will more likely lose. Supporting each other and working together enables a team to win. Team members must accept their team roles, the team itself, its ground rules, and the individuality of their teammates.

Developing positive social behaviors for cooperation and fairness

In virtually all sports, fair play is a universal standard. Thus when students learn sports in PE classes and activities, they are held to the same standards that adult athletes are to behave fairly by following the established rules of the game; not cheating by breaking or circumventing those rules; and treating their peers fairly by not taking advantage of their weaknesses, unfairly exploiting their strengths, or making fun of their shortcomings or difficulties. Sports have structures and rules to promote fairness. Playing sports can help young students learn to be more fair in their behavior, for example, by not choosing team members preferentially out of friendship or enmity; not rejecting students because they have disabilities or are shorter, slower, weaker, or have less experience; and not excluding students from diverse cultural, ethnic, or socioeconomic backgrounds. When students play team sports or games in PE, they must develop and refine skills for cooperating with others. When they respect and listen to others, help others participate, and work jointly as a team, they develop cooperative skills that will enhance their social interactions outside of PE activities in their schools, families, communities, current and/or future jobs, and everyday lives.

Learning to be considerate of others

When students learn to play individual and team competitive sports, the meaning of competition is better construed as striving for excellence than exhibiting adversarial hostility. While individualistic American culture places great emphasis on competition in contrast to collectivist cultures' emphasis on cooperation, American sports also emphasize good sportsmanship and fair play. In this spirit, students should view other teams and individual competitors as worthy opponents rather than enemies, and the object of play as a challenge to exceed opponents' strategies and performance rather than a mission to destroy them or pound them into the ground. Good sportsmanship includes being a good winner by respecting opponents' efforts and acknowledging the competition they offer, and being a good loser by giving winners the credit they deserve for superior strategy and performance. Consideration promotes mutual respect and enabling healthy competition rather than antisocial or destructive behavior. Another element of sportsmanlike conduct is helping others, e.g., helping up an opposing player that has been knocked down. Supporting teammates teaches students to be supportive in friendships and workplace, family, and intimate relationships.

Promoting student respect for peers

PE experts assert the importance of teaching not only information, skills, and strategies, but equally teaching effective skills and objectives. Without these, they say students, despite having the knowledge and skills, may not want to participate in PE activities. Values, attitudes, feelings, and interpersonal behaviors affect student motivation. Hence, the National Association for Sport and Physical Education's (NASPE) National PE Standards include "responsible personal and social behavior that respects self and others in physical activity settings" (2004). As role models, PE teachers should never show favoritism among students or marginalize students with lesser motor skills. They should also not limit the health benefits of PE activities for students with either lower or higher skills, but provide challenges to all levels. When designing PE activities and curriculum, teachers should deliberately include ways to teach respect for self and others, cooperation, teamwork, skills, and techniques. As examples, students can practice teamwork along with meeting individual and group goals during modified game play; students can learn to value safety for themselves and classmates while learning or practicing educational gymnastics skills and routines.

Elements of peer acceptance

Children and teenagers judge their own competence in large part through social comparison to their peers and evaluations from those peers. Moreover, students' beliefs of self-worth, approaches to motivation, participatory behaviors, and emotional experiences are all influenced by their peers. One type of relationship that researchers have investigated relative to student behavioral and psychosocial results in sports and physical activities is peer acceptance. This represents the extent to which members of a peer group like or embrace an individual, varying from rejection to popularity. Research has consistently revealed strong relationships between students' degrees of perceived physical competence and their degrees of peer acceptance. For instance, teens and children find competence in sports an important factor in peer group popularity and status. Investigators have found that students who are perceived as physically skilled by both themselves and their teachers were also rated as liked by their peers by both themselves and their teachers.

Practicing inclusion of their peers

A common requirement in many PE standards is for students, particularly at the high school level, to demonstrate positive social interactions by including diverse types of students with them in their PE activities. Student diversity includes disability. Students with disabilities, especially physical disabilities, have historically been excluded from many PE activities because they could not participate in typical ways. However, modern federal laws mandate including students with disabilities in all aspects of education. One way students can include disabled peers is for PE teachers to instruct them to be peer facilitators, enabling them both to assist and participate. For example, non-disabled students can use hand-over-hand assistance to enable students with upper-body or limb disabilities to hit balls with bats and racquets; hit balloons with noodles; throw Frisbees at bowling pins; hit balls off tees at bowling pins; hit hockey pucks with hockey sticks; drive wheelchairs while dribbling balls with hockey sticks attached to the chairs; or catch whiffle balls, sponge balls, or beanbags in boxes. There are also many modified games wherein non-disabled students and those in wheelchairs or lacking upper-body control can participate together, and activities that include students with intellectual disabilities.

Developing understanding and appreciation of diversity

Experienced PE teachers have observed that students and teachers alike often suffer from unrealistically stereotypical views of diverse students. This is detrimental even when the stereotype appears positive. For example, many Americans view Asian-Americans as the "model minority" for being intelligent, academically successful, quiet, well-behaved, and hardworking. However, not every Asian-American is intellectually gifted, an excellent student, a model of good behavior, or even an English speaker. Making stereotyped assumptions can hurt such students by depriving them of needed behavioral and academic support. When teachers ask students the first thing they think of when they name Asian-Americans, students say "smart"; when they name African-Americans, students say "good athletes." Yet not every African-American person is athletic. Even in their own culture, some African-American students excelling academically may be stereotyped as "acting white." Educators call for the necessity for teachers to examine and challenge their own stereotypical beliefs, and understand their own diversity, in order to teach students to do the same.

Cultural implications involved in teaching PE activities

PE teachers need to realize some cultural differences they will encounter when teaching diverse students. For example, Hispanic students tend to learn kinesthetically. While this is a natural fit with PE activities, some Anglo-American teachers who introduce new activities using verbal information may need to adjust instruction to begin with movements, which Latino students need to engage in learning. Hispanic and Asian students not raised in America are likely to avoid eye contact with teachers, and teachers should not demand it. Latino students may not be expressing agreement when they nod; their silence may not indicate understanding or agreement, but confusion or embarrassment. For all English language learners (ELLs), teachers should include visual aids in demonstrations and employ peer facilitators to bridge language barriers. American teachers accustomed to encouraging competition must realize Latin, Asian, Native American, and other collectivist cultures frown on competing and value cooperating, and should accordingly deemphasize aggressive competition. Knowing what teachers expect of them makes Asian students more comfortable, as do cooperative learning environments; positive reinforcement benefits them. Culturally, they communicate nonverbally, e.g., leaning forward or backward; they rely on this more when they are ELLs.

Benefits of diverse students to PE team sports and activities

PE classes and teams incorporating students from heterogeneous sources benefit from a wider variety of contributions than those with narrowly homogeneous origins. For example, although American teachers and students might view the non-competitive cultural values of the collectivist traditions in which Hispanic, Native American, and Asian students have been raised as detrimental to winning in competitive team sports, this is not the only way to view them. Because they value cooperation for the good of the group, subsuming individual identity in favor of group identification, and helping others to promote collective harmony, students from these cultures can actually make better team players than some highly individualistic American students who behave more like high-profile athletes than they do like equal team members. Students from collectivist cultures are also more likely to engage in respectful sportsmanship than compete in overly aggressive ways. Deferring individual accomplishments and attention for being important parts of a group make them valuable contributors to team solidarity and success.

How diverse cultures value and view physical activity

Asian cultures often have a holistic view of physical activity and sports. They value the connection between mind and body, and practice various sports and disciplines to develop spiritual awareness as well as physical skills. Yoga, tai chi, and the many martial arts are examples of Asian traditions combining physical and spiritual discipline this way. PE teachers should realize that Asian students previously accustomed to these traditions may view playing sports or games in PE for fun as irrelevant and spiritually unsatisfying, view playing them for aggressive competition as against their values of cooperation and group harmony, and view competing in sports for individual attention and fame as inappropriate. American cultural groups also view physical activity and fitness differently. For example, research finds that, compared to white girls, African-American girls are less physically active; tolerate, accept, prefer, and are more satisfied with larger body sizes or weights; and do not view celebrities as physical role models. The time and expense of hair and nail maintenance, lack of urban neighborhood safety, and school and extracurricular time constraints also limit their participation in structured physical activities.

Physical activities afford opportunities for personal challenges and satisfaction

Although mainstream American culture emphasizes competition in sports, students need not always compete to excel in PE activities. The concept of a "personal best" can be even more consistent with individual excellence, as it does not depend on comparisons or differences with other students and teams. Also, social psychologists studying achievement motivation have found students with a higher internal locus of control—i.e., they attribute their successes and failures to their own internal factors, not external influences—are more likely to maintain motivation to achieve more constantly across time, settings, and situations than those with a more external locus of control—i.e., they attribute their successes or failures to the help or interference of people, things, and events outside themselves. Students who strive to run faster than their last or current time, farther than their last or current distance; lift more weight or complete more repetitions; jump higher; and even in team sports, score more points than before, etc., compete with themselves, not others. Thus changes or differences in opponents will not affect their motivation or efforts. Also, in contrast with being on a losing team, students who achieve their own personal physical activity goals experience satisfaction regardless of what others do.

Competition and achievement in physical activities

When children are young and in earlier motor development stages, they may learn, practice, and enjoy running, jumping, hopping, skipping, balancing, etc., individually or in groups, but not competitively. As they grow, though, they will be exposed both in and out of school to running races to see who finishes first, experiencing their first taste of competition. Soon they will learn to play games and sports in PE classes. Individual activities include comparisons like who can hang from a high bar the longest, jump the highest and farthest, or make the most baskets, as well as run the fastest. While competitive themes pervade both individual and team activities, when students begin learning team sports, the inherent object is for one team to win by scoring more points, gaining more yards, making more runs or goals, etc. While some students may already have met "personal best" goals, if they find all their peers exceed them in certain activities, competition can motivate them to increase their standards and efforts accordingly. Because American education also compares academic achievement against national averages, PE competition and achievement can inform and transfer to other school subjects.

Positive social interactions and healthy alternatives to risky behaviors

When younger children are first taught to play organized games with peers, they must learn to follow rules; take turns; share; cooperate with others; and refrain from hitting, kicking, biting, punching, and other antisocial behaviors. These are novel experiences to many youngsters. The structure and rules of organized games are ideal contexts to teach them to control aggressive behaviors; and to reinforce the pro-social, unselfish, helpful, and cooperative behaviors young children also naturally display at times. By participating in games, sports, dance, etc., older students learn not to reject, ignore, insult, tease, taunt, assault, or take advantage of peers; to offer helping hands when they need them; include peers with different backgrounds and abilities in physical activities; detect when and how to assume leader or follower roles; and include, invite, and help other students participate. When students improve their physical fitness, they gain self-esteem and physical well-being that often discourages incompatible habits like overeating, smoking, drinking, and taking drugs. Spending time being physically active leaves less unoccupied time for dangerous pursuits. Students interact socially through sharing sports, games, and dance instead of substance abuse or other risky behaviors.

The Physical Education Program

Legal aspects of equipment and class organization

Because class sizes are generally increasing and PE classes are often large, supervision is harder, accidents likelier, and PE lawsuits are increasing. Teachers risk liability because they are recognized as certified professionals with high-responsibility, high-profile roles. Their training should meet national standards. Teachers and coaches are liable for acts of omission, e.g., not supervising PE activities, and acts of commission, e.g., endangering or threatening students with harm. In lawsuits, levels of negligence are decided according to the roles teachers or coaches played in preventing injurious conditions in adequately or inadequately providing post-injury care, and by professional standards compliance or noncompliance. To be judged negligent, four parts are required: duty, breach of duty, cause, and damage. Common areas of negligence in PE include supervision, instruction, classroom environments, first aid emergencies, and transportation. Guidelines to prevent negligence claims include using common sense, being informed of colleagues' best-practice guidelines, and following practices and procedures given in texts and in national organizations' guidelines. PE teachers should continually, actively supervise throughout activities, ascertain whether students are safely and properly executing them, and encourage peer supervision in addition to teacher supervision.

Insufficient or improper advance instruction directly informs teacher liability. Also, teachers should not let students lacking judgment of their personal capability perform movements. Safety instructions should be stated simply. Instruction in procedures and protocols for equipment setup, use, and takedown is a must. In classroom environments, teachers must watch out for potential dangers. Environmental conditions can vary day to day. Teachers should space students to mitigate problems. PE equipment should only be used as designed to be used. Regarding emergencies, students risk injury more when moving than still. PE teachers are expected to give injured students appropriate help, e.g., first aid treatment before medical access. They should be trained and currently certified in first aid. First aid procedures should be included in class objectives, permanently displayed school-wide, and developed among school personnel. Teachers should know of pre-existing student conditions. They should write detailed reports of any incidents, including prevention measures. Transportation outside school risks liability: teachers should get written parental consent, and always follow school policies, practices, and procedures.

PE teacher or coach liability

In classrooms, student movement is limited; however, in PE classes, movement is the primary activity. Additionally, PE teachers and coaches contend with movement by many students simultaneously. Baseballs, softballs, footballs, tennis balls, discus, shot puts, javelins, and other projectiles can injure students, and baseball bats, tennis racquets, golf clubs, and other implements propel projectiles at high speeds, further increasing injury risks. Also, PE facilities are bigger than classrooms, and include both indoor and outdoor spaces, so PE teachers must cover and supervise greater physical areas—with different characteristics—than classroom teachers. Another factor is that PE includes swimming. This introduces water, in swimming pools and showers, presenting additional danger and injury risk in the forms of drowning in pools and slipping and falling in showers. PE teachers should never allow students and athletes to be alone without faculty supervision in these facilities. Teachers and coaches should be first in and last out of pools. Another injury and liability source is personal vehicles owned by teachers or coaches that are used for transport to activities outside school. In some states, statutes cap teacher liability limits within public school duties; however, coaching AAU programs/midget football/Little League, etc., outside school are unprotected by these caps.

<u>Maintain student safety and limit teacher liability for personal injuries</u>
Experts advise supervising students between classes, intervening in student altercations or fights, monitoring and supervising the athletic and PE complexes' multiple entrances and exits, and collaboratively developing plans with co-workers for the latter. PE teachers and coaches should lock gyms and pools between classes (particularly when gym equipment is set up), not give students keys, and always check gyms and pools for athletes and students before locking doors. Equipment where students and athletes could fall should always have sufficient mats under it—the more dangerous, the thicker the matting. Legal experts with PE coaching and teaching experience opine only the basic vaulting and tumbling skills of gymnastics should be taught in PE class, and with individual spotters in these. Falls are more likely since most average students lack the strength to support their bodies or hang using their arms. Falls from inverted positions risk spinal damage, paralysis, and even death. Experts warn teachers and coaches never to use trampolines in PE class, and if they are used in gymnastics, cheerleading, or other extracurricular events, to ensure their insurance covers trampolines and trampoline accidents—it often does not, or charges prohibitive premiums for coverage.

<u>Practices to limit the chances of student injuries and coach or teacher liability</u>
Experts with both PE and legal experience caution PE teachers and coaches to remember that if basic rules are not followed in sports like softball, these seemingly innocent activities can become dangerous. For example, teachers must instruct students to call for fly balls; students who do not should back away from those who do. With 30+ students on a fielding team instead of 9 in a regulation or non-class game, collisions are far more likely. Serious injuries are more probable from head-to-head/smaller-to-bigger student collisions. All sports have safety rules to observe. PE teachers and coaches must check slip-resistant surfaces for wear or inadequacy, particularly in water's presence; inspect facilities monthly, and report any repair or maintenance issues to school administrations and maintenance departments; procure and use eye protection when reasonable; use applicable safety equipment for each sport or activity; prevent non-participating students from getting in harm's way; follow physician instructions in any students' doctor excuses; review safety rules with students before every new activity and sport; never punish or discipline students with strenuous exercise; confer with school nurses regarding any student medical conditions causing strenuous activity intolerance; and avoid student physical contact, except for safety reasons.

State departments of education and family life education

In some states, family life education elements are included in health and physical education classes required for graduation or diplomas. For middle and high schools, health and PE core curriculum content standards in some states include content regarding human sexuality and relationships. Education departments provide for parents who object to this content based on their cultural, religious, or moral beliefs by incorporating a policy that their children may be excused from those parts of the courses if parents furnish the schools with a signed statement that this content conflicts with their personal beliefs. In these cases, the schools provide excused students with alternative instructional content and activities that they determine are in alignment with their state's PE core curriculum content standards and their local health education curricula. Parents' written statements must explain to school principals or administrators how the content conflicts with their beliefs. Once administrators clarify school programs with parents, students may be excused, but must complete agreed-upon, assigned activities; e.g., taking a course in nutrition and foods, a PE class, or an independent study project, in place of a human sexuality course, to meet core curriculum content standards for comprehensive health and PE.

Sensitivity to diverse cultural and religious beliefs

Although the standards set by state education departments for comprehensive health and PE afford a structure for their local school districts to follow, each school district is also responsible for maintaining a balance between aligning its curriculum with the state standards and also taking into account and fulfilling the diverse needs of its student population. In many American states, conditions of constant change in demographic profiles are increasingly the norm these days. With such continual flux, it is not realistic to expect any one teacher to know about all of the cultural beliefs, traditions, and expectations of every group represented in his or her school. As a result, school districts have the duty of collaborating with their community-based cultural and religious organizations to build cultural and religious sensitivity as a continuing endeavor. Some states have established networks to help school districts to find and access organizations specializing in expertise related to this subject. As an example, the state of New Jersey's Department of Health and Senior Services has developed a Network for Cultural Competence, with a website where educators can locate and contact groups with resources promoting cultural knowledge and responsiveness.

Designing PE curriculum

The National Association for Sport and Physical Education (NASPE, 2009) has indicated the increasing importance for PE teacher preparation to include cultural diversity in pedagogy. While research into general education offers more plentiful instances of cultural relevance, some investigators point out its comparative dearth in physical education. Some authors recommend methods for establishing equitable PE practices relative to race, social class, gender, and sexuality. Some focus more on evidence of versions of unintentional racism in PE. However, less research is available into culturally relevant physical education (CRPE). Past studies have shown that teacher practices did not become more culturally sensitive as a result of taking courses in multicultural education. Others cite factors like communicating with students having limited English-language proficiency (LEP), the local relevance of various physical activities, and curricula including diverse representations and languages as challenges to PE teachers in attempting to design urban PE curricula that are culturally relevant.

Fitness education

Fitness education is a part of a total PE program, directed toward helping students gain information and higher-level comprehension of both the processes of physical activity habits and health lifestyle, and the products of good health, wellness, and health-related physical fitness. The Fitness Education Project team formed by the National Association for Sport and Physical Education (NASPE), after reviewing current literature and consulting with nationwide professionals with expertise in pedagogy and content specialties, PE district curriculum materials, and state and national PE standards to gain insights, produced a comprehensive Instructional Framework for Fitness Education in Physical Education (IFFEPE). This document's purpose is to guide educators in designing and providing fitness education by informing them as to what students should know, understand, and be able to do at each grade level from Pre-K through college. The IFFEPE's authors developed it based on the assumption that all students, regardless of age, gender, ethnicity, or cultural background, can attain healthy levels of physical fitness through engaging regularly in moderate to vigorous physical activity.

NASPE

The National Association for Sport and Physical Education (NASPE) created a Fitness Education Project and a team dedicated to it. This team studied the current research into fitness education and conferred with experts in fitness education content, instruction, curriculum, and standards across the country.

Based on the information they acquired, the team developed a comprehensive Instructional Framework for Fitness Education in Physical Education (IFFEPE). This resource is a set of materials to help students by guiding PE teachers and others in designing current, coherent, sequenced, integrated fitness education curriculum and instruction. Full or partial lessons from the IFFEPE can be incorporated in established PE curricula to meet grade-level fitness content. Its benchmarks enable measurement of values, knowledge, and skills requisite to competence, development of courses or curricula, or curricular inclusion of applicable domains. IFFEPE content is holistic, treating all areas as important to include in fitness education. It is designed for all students, and allows educators plenty of the creativity and instructional innovation fitness education requires. PE teachers, fitness leaders, administrators, and curriculum coordinators can use it to identify desired fitness education learning experience results, and to tailor content to meet diverse student needs on program, local, or state levels.

APE

Under the federal Individuals with Disabilities Education Act (IDEA), students with qualifying disabilities receive special education and related services and have IEPs (individualized education programs). Special education includes PE. If a student's disability requires adaptations to participate in PE, the student must receive APE. While therapeutic recreation (TR), physical therapy (PT), and occupational therapy (OT) are related services, PE and APE are not related services, but instead are direct educational services according to federal law. APE is aligned with PE in terms of curriculum purposes. In defining APE, the IDEA includes motor fitness, physical fitness, fundamental motor patterns and motor skills, individual and group games and sports, lifetime sports, aquatics skills, and dance skills. These are the same skills as in PE, but individualized in design to meet the unique needs of students with disabilities. Student difficulties with physical mobility, functional independence, or motor performance that impede participating and benefiting from PE should receive APE. PT, OT, and TR may additionally be recommended for some students, but are not substitutes for or interchangeable with APE.

Benefits of APE
The federal Individuals with Disabilities Education Act (IDEA) mandates a free and appropriate public education (FAPE) to students who are eligible for special education services in the least restrictive environment (LRE) possible. This includes physical education services. Students who cannot participate in or benefit from regular PE services because they have limitations in functional activities, motor activities, or physical mobility are therefore required to be given APE services, which are adapted to enable them to participate in and benefit from PE. Some of the benefits of APE to these students include developing functional, developmentally appropriate motor skills in young children that enable them to play and participate in educational environments with non-disabled peers; promoting an active lifestyle that incorporates physical activity; developing basic motor skills needed to participate with peers in sports and games; improving the self-image and self-esteem of students; gaining skills that increase mobility, physical independence, self-help, self-sufficiency, and independent living; and reducing health-related complications.

Improvement for students with disabilities
Historically, students with disabilities have often been excused from PE classes or assigned timekeeper, scorekeeper, or other sedentary roles. This reinforced assumptions that persons with disabilities must be physically passive and contributed to obesity and shorter lifespans for disabled individuals. The APE goal of over 50 percent moderate-to-vigorous physical activity (>50 percent MVPA) equals the regular PE goal. Alternative activities should not be sedentary. Educators should collaborate with students, parents, administrators, other professionals, and community members to develop active APE programs. APE can modify PE activities to enable students with disabilities to engage successfully in games, rhythms, exercises, and sports. Mainstreamed students can participate in APE within regular PE classes or in self-

contained classrooms. Teachers can provide individualized PE instruction within group settings. Teaching, skills, and activities should be differentiated for each student's unique capabilities as much as possible. Students with disabilities may practice and demonstrate functional physical fitness through alternative means. For example, a non-ambulatory student could demonstrate sufficient upper-body strength for throwing a basketball at an eight-foot-high basket, or a student with limited motor, physical, and cognitive skills could demonstrate sufficient aerobic endurance for playing a modified soccer game for 10 minutes before having to stop and rest.

Importance of FMS to child development

Fundamental movement skills (FMS) are significant to children's motor development, influencing physical, cognitive, and social growth. FMS are building blocks for games, dancing, sports, and other physical activities, as well as for lifelong interest in, motivation for, participation in, and enjoyment of active lifestyles. FMS have three categories: locomotor; manipulative; and stability, including rotation and balance. Rotation activities for young children include: Spinning, in both directions, eyes closed; slowly is equally good. Standing, bending, looking between legs; touching hands and head to the floor; waving to friends and throwing beanbags into hoops through legs; walking backwards looking through legs. Spinning inside a chalk circle or hoop lifted, while rotating the hoop. Pencil rolling: rolling on the floor with arms above the head, keeping fingers on a line, co-rolling with hands joined, or holding onto scarves. Lying stomach-down on slowly rotating office chairs. Novelty spinning on or in blankets, towels, cardboard boxes, or wash baskets in various directions. Sausage rolls: roll up children in blankets, sheets, or parachutes, and then unroll. Wheelbarrows: hand-walking with legs held, head lower than body (vestibular stimulation). Lying stomach-down on cylinders or exercise balls. Self-pulling or spinning on scooter boards using arms or ropes. Twirling to music while holding scarves.

Activities to develop rotation skills

Older children can do rotation activities like these: On a vinyl or wood floor, spaced freely, have them spin around on their stomachs; on their bottoms, with or without using hands; on their backs; and standing. Ask what happens when they extend their legs and tuck their bodies. To improve rotation speed, provide smoother surfaces. Observe balance and change of focus. On grass, mats, or pads, have children rock forward, backward, shoulders to feet and back, from back to one foot, and up to standing. Ask what shapes they can create by rocking. Observe for slight spinal curve for protection. Using rolled mats or cylinders shorter across than children's leg lengths, have them sit cross-legged, feet together, tilt side to side, then rock, then come up into sitting position; sitting astride cylinders, rock side to side; challenge them to see how long they can stay on. Observe for neutral head position and controlled movement. Using equipment (ribbon balls or tennis balls in stockings or hoops, etc.) and music, teachers and students suggest individual and peer-led exploration and experimentation. Vary music speeds, body positions, and rotation planes. Explore different directions and heights with one piece of equipment. Design short movement sequences individually or in groups. Observe for loose grip, wrist action with small, fast movements, and arm action for large, slow movements.

Activities involving walking and running

Children younger than five years of age
Musical Hoops: Give children hoops, have them dance to music and use varied locomotions, and jump into the nearest hoop when the music stops. Remove hoops each time until children must squeeze into hoops together. Whistle Stop: Children walk around, avoiding touching others; they freeze in place upon a whistle-blow. Change locomotion every time. Movement A-to-B: Have children take small or giant steps, run, turn while walking, walk heel to toe, jump, hop, tiptoe, crawl, roll, etc., between two points. Traffic

Lights: Children imitate cars. Large red, green, and yellow cardboard circles are "lights." They run fast near green, walk slowly near yellow, stop instantly and jog in place near red. Cars: Children walk around in pairs, one child behind with hands on the front child's shoulders. The front child "steers," changing directions; they take turns. Motor Bikes: Children run or walk around, with feet shoulder-width apart and knees slightly bent; on a whistle-blow or other signal, they must stop, jump, and land as quietly as possible, holding their landings for three seconds. Tail Chase: With "tail" scarves tucked into their waistbands or pockets, children try to catch one another's tails, protecting their own tails while moving. When children catch others' tails, they give them back and keep playing. Vary locomotion, e.g., by jumping, to increase difficulty.

<u>Children 5-12 years of age</u>
As a favorite warmup, groups of four to five can play Follow the Leader. Regularly change the locomotor skill and leader. Another popular game is Stuck in the Mud. Teachers can vary locomotor skills; for example, the student can free the tagger "stuck in the mud" by running twice around the tagger and high-fiving him or her. Teachers can also vary the traveling locomotor skills used. Buzz Off is played like Stuck in the Mud, except when a player is tagged, he or she stands still, scratching as if bitten by an insect. To release the tagged player, two other players go to him or her, pass their hands over him or her, and say "Buzz off." In Blob Tag, two students holding hands try to tag others while remaining connected. Whenever they tag someone, that student joins the "blob." Once they have a "blob" of four, they break into two pairs and keep tagging until all students are joined in "blobs." In Fast Cars, students stand in a circle; each is given a car name (e.g., Toyota 1, Honda 1, Toyota 2, Honda 2, etc.). Whenever the teacher calls out a car name, students race around the circle and "park" in their original positions.

Manipulative movement activities involving throwing

<u>Children under five years of age</u>
Teachers can hang hoops from door frames or trees with rope for young children to practice throwing things through them, as well as put hoops on the floor or ground. Parents can develop throwing skills at home by having children throw rolled socks into laundry hampers or baskets. When they succeed, have them take one step further back for the next throw. Teachers and parents can use pillows and cushions to set up courses (with or without children's participation), placing empty boxes, wastebaskets, buckets, etc., as "golf holes." Have children take turns throwing beanbags into holes. Children can crumple paper into "snowballs"; adults then tape these up and give baskets of them to two groups of children. Mark a line between groups with rope, tape, or chalk. On a signal, children throw "snowballs" over the line for 30 seconds; see who has the fewest snowballs left, then switch teams and repeat. Have children clean up by throwing snowballs into baskets. Adults can cut centers out of empty plastic food tubs to make rings; have children try to toss the rings over plastic bottles. Have children try to toss coins onto paper or plastic plates on the floor or ground. Let children throw a ball trying to knock a stuffed animal off a stool.

<u>Children 5-12 years of age</u>
Older children can practice throwing for accuracy or distance. Some activities to practice throwing for distance include: "Force Back" – Students face one another in pairs, throwing a ball toward the other as far as they can. The thrower's partner catches or retrieves the ball, throwing it back from where it landed. "Three Court Ball" – Assign students to two equally numbered teams. Each team has one-third of a court and a tennis ball. Students try to throw the ball into the middle third of the court and have it bounce over the other team's goal line. "Scatterball" – Use a baseball diamond or any field with several bases arranged in a diamond, circle, square, or some other shape. Divide students into two teams: throwers and fielders. Throwers take turns, one at a time, throwing balls as far away as they can. Then each thrower runs around bases until told to stop. The fielders catch or retrieve the balls thrown and collect them in a

basket, bucket, etc. Switch teams and repeat. The team scoring the most runs wins. Students can also practice catching by throwing and bouncing balls or beanbags in pairs, groups, and teams.

Application of movement principles to landing

Impact when landing should be distributed across the greatest possible distance, area, or both; and joints should be bent when landing from jumps, for absorbing force. Learning cues for landing on the feet include landing with feet apart and knees bent. Children should land in a toes-ball of foot-heel sequence, and wriggle toes, pull in stomachs, tuck bottoms under, stretch arms in front, hold heads up, look straight ahead, and hold the landing three seconds. To land prone on hands or arms, they should hold arms shoulder-width apart, bend elbows, keep hands flat, spread fingers, hold heads up, keep bodies straight, and pull in stomachs to prevent back arching. Three phases of learning are: Discovery – children explore, show no stable support base, land flat-footed, and show little "give" in the knees. Development – children land from various distances or heights, realize the importance of shock absorption, show stable support base, land more consistently in toes-ball of foot-heel order, bend knees after heels touch ground, and rotate forward upon landing. Consolidation – Children show control and confidence landing in unpredictable or changing circumstances, show a wide support base, make controlled landings safely, and absorb shock through "give" in the hips, knees, and ankles.

Learning how to fall sideways and land on hands

This involves the movement concept or skill of rolling sideways for safely landing after falling from various levels. First, students fall from kneeling sideways, rocking onto their arm, side, and shoulder. They should try this in both directions. Then they roll sideways down a wedge to practice falling down a slope. Then, while moving, they fall, roll sideways, and then stand up and keep moving. This begins with walking, increasing the speed gradually to jogging, then running, and then with dodging. Students can pair up, shake hands in front support position, and then try to pull each other off balance. In "Tip the Spider," one partner in a pair on all fours is the spider. The other partner tips the spider onto his or her side by pushing on his or her closer shoulder while pulling on his or her opposite hand. Teachers should look for straight arms, hands facing inward to body, and even, soft surfaces. They can ask students when they might use this kind of landing, and what they must do to land safely when falling sideways.

Descriptive vs. prescriptive feedback

One way to differentiate descriptive feedback from prescriptive feedback is that in descriptive feedback, the teacher tells the student what he or she observed the student doing incorrectly; in prescriptive feedback, the teacher tells the student what the student needs to do to correct the error the teacher observed. For example, with a basketball jump shot, if the teacher says, "You didn't follow through," this could suffice for a more advanced player who knows how to perform a follow-through correctly but just forgot or has not yet developed full automaticity with it. However, with a less experienced player who has not yet learned how to follow through or may not understand how to correct what he or she did, the above descriptive feedback example is not enough. Prescriptive feedback would involve specific correction instructions, e.g., "Flex your wrist harder when you let the ball go." This tells the student what to do to correct the jump shot. In order to give effective prescriptive feedback, PE teachers must know what the student did incorrectly (i.e., did not follow through) and provide a problem solution to correct it (i.e., flex the wrist harder upon releasing the ball).

Optimizing skill development with feedback

Experts advise "When in doubt, be quiet" (Wrisberg, Human Kinetics). When athletes have internal feedback, external feedback is unnecessary. Studies find solicited feedback more beneficial than unsolicited feedback, and students can improve skills with comparatively little external feedback, requesting it less than 10 percent of the time in one study. Most requests are early in learning new skills. Athletes and students more likely want feedback with more technically difficult skills. Also, external feedback should not duplicate internal feedback; it should fill a need in the absence of internal feedback, e.g., when a student asks why he or she keeps making the same error. When teachers and coaches have developed good communication with students and athletes, they should be able to tell whether or not they need feedback; and students and athletes are more likely to request it when needed. Because problem solving is part of all learning, teachers and coaches help most by giving feedback about sources of pertinent internal feedback, like directing them to focus on body parts, positions, movements, and relationships. Early in practicing technique, program feedback has priority; later, when students and athletes have mastered basics, parameter feedback has priority. Letting students and athletes request feedback affords them more independent learning, and assures their motivation to hear the teacher's or coach's instruction.

Experts advise keeping feedback simple, yet not simplistic. It should give students and athletes the most useful information pertaining to the moment or situation. This prevents student and athlete information overload and directs their attention to the most important things. For example, among kicking speed, direction, and leg-swinging rhythm, a student learning soccer may need performance feedback about only one, not others. Student and athlete experience levels also determine feedback amounts. For example, feedback about one or two specific performance aspects is enough for volleyball beginners, e.g., "watch the ball," "bend your knees," or "relax your hands." Students having learned basic movement patterns can apply feedback like "smoother and softer," knowing by then that this encompasses planning for ball contact, body positioning, and relaxing the hands. Program feedback should be simpler than parameter feedback: athletes typically find program adjustments harder than parameter adjustments. For example, program feedback for a football quarterback could be "flick your wrist a little more" for basic forward pass timing. Once the quarterback has developed more regular throwing patterns, complex parameter feedback like "add force, release the ball sooner" enables greater throwing distance. Summarizing and averaging feedback are additional ways to prevent information overload.

Studies show skill development does not require greater feedback frequency; practice without external feedback can be more effective than with it. Researchers speculate that this forces learners to attend more to internal feedback and problem solve more independently. Also, overly frequent feedback can engender student or athlete dependency on external feedback. For example, if the teacher or coach tells a baseball outfielder after one throw to keep the ball lower, to follow through more after the next throw, etc., he or she will immediately apply each piece of feedback on the next throw. Such momentary corrections preclude stable performance, preventing players from learning about relationships between their actions and outcomes. Upon external feedback cessation, player performance tends to regress to earlier levels. Teachers and coaches can decrease feedback frequency whenever they observe students or athletes gaining proficiency. This can be early in practice with simpler skills and techniques, and once they show enough consistency with complex skills and techniques. If performance declines, feedback frequency can be raised temporarily until it improves. Feedback quality supersedes quantity. Research finds feedback need not be highly precise for effectiveness; e.g., "a little faster or higher" rather than "0.5 seconds average" or "15 feet high" will suffice. Beginners need only a general idea; more precision is indicated for advanced athletes' fine-tuning.

History and characteristics of aerobic dance

U.S. Air Force exercise physiologist Kenneth Cooper, M.D. and physical therapist Col. Pauline Potts developed and named aerobics. Cooper observed some people with great muscular strength still performed poorly at endurance sports like long-distance running, swimming, and bicycling. He was first to measure ability to utilize oxygen in sustained performance, and to differentiate aerobic capacity from strength, flexibility, etc. He published *Aerobics* in 1968, including research-based walking, running, swimming, and bicycling exercise programs. This book arrived at a historically opportune time, as Americans were becoming increasingly sedentary due to modern conveniences. Once Jane Fonda released her exercise videos using aerobic techniques in 1982, aerobics became popular internationally. Today many gymnasiums and exercise and dance studios offer aerobics classes. With the goal of enhancing all fitness elements—cardiovascular fitness, flexibility, and muscular strength—aerobics exercises combine rhythmic dance-like movements that raise the heart and respiratory rates with strength training and stretching, typically to music with a strong beat. Classes are separated by complexity and intensity level according to student experience (e.g., beginning, intermediate, advanced). Class exercises are led by certified instructors with various specialty areas.

Enabling students to enjoy lifetime activities and recreational pursuits

Some high schools not only include lifetime wellness in their physical education departments, but even require students to complete a year of lifetime wellness courses as well as a year of physical education courses to graduate. Such schools identify their programs' primary goal or objective as ensuring that students become "health-literate" individuals. They define health literacy as characterizing a person who has critical thinking and problem-solving skills, is a self-directed learner, communicates effectively, and is a productive and responsible citizen. Lifetime wellness programs offer students ideas for wisely utilizing their leisure time, helps them acquire useful physical skills while developing positive self-images and self-confidence, and exposes them to a broad range of physical activities in which they will be able to participate throughout their lives. Some schools that espouse lifetime wellness take a holistic approach to health and lifetime physical activities. In other words, they embrace total wellness, encompassing individual physical, mental, emotional, and social well-being. They teach classes that gives students foundations of knowledge about health and wellness practices and issues. Standards and course content can include nutrition, disease prevention and control, substance use and abuse, mental health, safety and first aid, sexuality and family life, personal fitness, and related skills.

Purposes for adventure and outdoor pursuits

Two main purposes for outdoor recreation are: (1) beneficial use, i.e., utilitarian value or social and physical rewards reaped through goal-directed individual or group activity; and (2) pleasurable appreciation, i.e., experiences that enhance perceptual or spiritual development through engagement in the natural world and nature's processes. Some goal-directed outdoor activities include mountain climbing, hill walking, caving (spelunking), canyoning, backpacking, hiking, canoeing, kayaking, and rafting. More general groups of these activities include horseback riding, snow sports, and water sports. While these activities can be emotionally, mentally, and spiritually rewarding, they are primarily physical. The physical and social outdoor setting can meet achievement needs, for testing endurance and stamina, improving or challenging skills, practicing, and excitement or adventure seeking; it can also meet needs for teambuilding and building social connections, risk-taking, survival skills, self-sufficiency, and physical health. Some examples of outdoor experiences that enhance perceptual and spiritual pleasure and appreciation, and may also be physically rewarding, include meditation, aesthetic contemplation, nature study, photography, painting, historical research, archeological research, paleontological research, and ethnography and research into indigenous cultures. People also pursue outdoor activities to relax, enjoy life, and find peace in nature, as alternatives to expensive tourism, and as an educational medium.

Martial arts

Martial arts are standardized combat systems, practiced for various purposes including self-defense, competitions, entertainment, physical fitness, and physical, mental, and spiritual development. They date to over 4,000 years ago in China, and to ancient Greece in Europe. They may be classified by regional origins, e.g., Eastern or Western; historical/traditional or contemporary; intention/application, e.g., sport, choreography, self-defense, military, meditative, fitness, etc.; techniques used, e.g., armed/unarmed; or external/internal in Chinese tradition. Unarmed forms are generally classified as using strikes, grappling, or both. Western boxing, Wing Chun, and Kalaripayattu use punching strikes. Kickboxing, Taekwondo, Savate, and Capoeira use kicking strikes. Karate, Sanshou, and Muay Thai also use strikes. Judo, Sambo, and Hapkido use throwing types of grappling. Aikido, Judo, and Jujitsu use chokehold, submission hold, and joint lock types of grappling. Judo, Sambo, and wrestling use pinning techniques for grappling. Weapon-based martial arts include historical European, kobudo, silat, eskrima, and kalaripayat; single-weapon training martial arts styles like Japanese kendo (sword), kenjutsu, bojutsu (staff), and kyudo (archery); and modern Western martial arts and sports like fencing, singlestick, canne de combat, and archery.

Keeping abreast of and applying current issues and trends

Effective PE teachers must be knowledgeable about how current issues and trends in their field, in education in general, and in wider society influence how their physical education programs will be structured and the learning objectives they will encompass. Teachers must know about the history of physical education and sports and how they have developed and progressed, and the impacts these had and continue to have on teaching. They need to stay informed on an ongoing basis about new research findings and curriculum models. Moreover, they must assess these new developments carefully, and then adapt their teaching practices based on the information and insights they have gained. Good PE teachers stay informed of economic, political, and social issues in their local areas that affect PE, and are aware how their field is affected by these globally, nationally, in their states, and locally. They realize how the learning goals and objectives they develop and their own school and community roles are shaped by these factors. They consider student health issues, obesity, personal wellness, and other needs, and address these by adjusting their teaching practices to promote students' being and becoming productive members of society.

Trend and controversy in accountability

Ever since the 1990s, school accountability has become an increasing trend in education, requiring the establishment of national standards and the use of nationally standardized assessment tests. As in other subjects, it is an issue of debate concerning physical education. People who object to national PE testing do so on the basis that to enjoy physical activity as adults, youth must be able to enjoy it as students. They find that the motivation for lifelong participation in physical activity is not supported by standardized testing. On the other hand, people who agree with national PE testing find that it not only helps students to judge their progress according to national standards for competence in PE skills and physical fitness, but also that PE should be given the same importance and be judged by the same standards and assessments that math, science, language arts, social studies, and other school subjects are.

The National Association for Sport and Physical Education (NASPE) has offered some guidelines in response to differences in public opinion regarding the use of standardized testing to assess PE performance. These guidelines include an operational definition of a person who is physically educated and a set of benchmarks for PE competency at each school grade level. NASPE defines physically educated as being physically fit, being skilled in various physical activities, participating regularly in physical activity, being aware of the benefits of physical activity, valuing the contributions of physical activity to a healthy lifestyle, being respectful of diversity, and being socially responsible in action and behavior. However, the degrees of specificity and direction that are necessary regarding standards and assessments in PE still remain controversial topics. A recent trend in school programs as well as businesses is to use the term "wellness" in place of "health" and "fitness." Although wellness generally represents optimum well-being and health, its definition has been widened to encompass mental, emotional, social, environmental, and spiritual well-being.

Issues challenging education in general

Some recent and current issues that present challenges and cause concern for educators in all subjects and schools in general include lack of adequate resources, lack of support for education from students' parents, overly large class sizes, teacher burnout, student discipline problems, violence, and drug abuse by students. These issues all have an impact on another issue that experts find the most important of all: the concern of educators for all students' well-being and health. These issues have the same impact on PE as on other school subjects. One issue that currently presents the greatest challenge to PE in K-12 schools is the way that curriculum time for PE instruction and activities has been decreased. Not only does this have a direct negative impact on the well-being and health of students, but it also poses a conundrum for educators who are expected to balance academic subjects and accountability requirements with considerations of what is ideal for students' education overall. Ample research shows both the health risks of being sedentary and the physiological and psychological benefits of exercise. Therefore, it is critical to every student's physical, cognitive, and psychological development to provide daily PE.

Identifying instructional goals and objectives

Based on expert PE content knowledge and strong insights into their learning environments, good PE teachers design their lessons thoughtfully. When implementing them, they effectively demonstrate the concepts, pace the progressions involved, and apply teaching strategies to be appropriate to every student. They observe their students' progress and performance carefully, analyze and assess it accurately, and give them timely, positive feedback through applicable teaching opportunities. In designing instruction, PE teachers realize the progressive nature of student motor skill acquisition and sequence units and lessons accordingly. They identify suitable contexts in which to teach specific skills, and combine them with developing related complementary skills. Observing student ability maturation, PE teachers respond to emerging developmental changes. For example, a teacher can design catching lessons that begin with retrieving a rolling ball, progress to learning to control a bouncing ball, and culminate in fielding a flying ball. PE teachers enhance student skill development by analyzing skills on a continuum of task analysis, and focus on critical concepts and components in feedback to inform students. They supply students with opportunities to succeed at appropriately challenging difficulty levels, and with suitable amounts of time for practicing newly learned skills.

<u>Making modifications to instructional goals to address various student variables</u>
PE teachers may initially set certain instructional goals for their students, but then encounter challenges in the forms of variables such as students' physical abilities, student cognitive abilities, different student learning styles, different student developmental levels, and diverse and specific student interests. Good teachers will have the flexibility and judgment to modify the goals to address these and other variables, and the expertise to modify their teaching strategies to be congruent with the new or revised goals. As an example, a teacher who has planned a lesson on throwing and discovers a wide range of skill levels within

the same class might set up a series of learning stations. At one station, students with beginner throwing skills can practice throwing at a stationary target. At another station, students with intermediate throwing skill levels can practice making lead passes. At a third station, students with more advanced levels of throwing skills can practice passing to teammates while they are being defended.

Enabling safety and learning for individual student needs

Effective PE teachers inform themselves of any medical conditions students might have, including those not obvious as visible or identified disabilities, and modify their instructional strategies so that all students learn the same concepts and comparable skills and meet similar learning objectives, but each in ways that address their unique individual needs. As one example, students with Down syndrome, metabolic diseases, birth defects, traumatic injuries, upper respiratory infections, rheumatoid arthritis, and head and neck surgery can all cause a condition known as atlantoaxial instability. This consists of an abnormality in either the bone or the ligament that allows too much movement where the first and second cervical vertebrae (C1 and C2), i.e., the atlas and the axis, are joined. When the spinal cord is also involved, this condition additionally produces neurological symptoms. A student who has this condition would not be able to execute a forward roll in tumbling, gymnastics, or other activities with safety. However, the PE teacher can enable the student to meet a comparable learning objective by performing a log roll instead.

Meeting diverse student needs through varied instructional strategies

PE teachers can avail themselves of various modalities to differentiate their instruction to meet their students' varying needs. For example, some students learn best when they see pictures, diagrams, or visual demonstrations before trying to perform movements themselves; teachers can use visual graphics to teach them. Other students have visual impairments, visual processing disorders, or simply more auditory learning styles; teachers can present them with more spoken, musical, and other sound cues, descriptions, and directions. For students with haptic learning styles, teachers can give them more physical, kinesthetic directions and descriptions. Students with strong reading-writing orientations will benefit when teachers give them descriptions and instructions to read, and have them write or type breakdowns, analyses, or explanations of the skills. PE teachers also develop and use task analyses, whole-to-part instructions, and cue words to explain and present the simpler pieces of more complex skills to help students understand and learn. They use developmentally appropriate metaphors and analogies. For example, they could compare golf putting to an elephant's trunk swinging for younger children, and to a pendulum's action for high school students.

State educational standards

A typical state standard in physical education is for students to understand the rules for a variety of physical activities, including games and sports. Some examples of the kinds of benchmarks that a state education department might specify for this standard are, for third grade: to identify the rules and procedures in specified physical activities, including games; for fifth grade: to demonstrate that they understand the rules that must be followed when participating in specified physical activities, including games; and for high school grades: to demonstrate the rules in complex versions of at least two different categories of movement forms in individual activities, dual activities, cardiorespiratory and aerobic lifetime activities, outdoor activities, team sports, aquatics, self-defense, yoga, martial arts, dance, and strength training and conditioning. For a standard of identifying the rules, procedures, and etiquette in a specified game or physical activity, a typical benchmark for fifth grade might be to demonstrate and explain the rules, procedures, and etiquette to follow when participating in physical activities or games; for eighth grade, to apply safe, effective rules, procedures, and etiquette for specific activities or games;

and for high school, to analyze and apply the safe, effective rules, procedures, and etiquette for specific activities or games.

Analyzing specific game rules

For a high school PE course that teaches a specific sport, e.g., volleyball, the course description might include that students will learn to use the knowledge and skills they acquired in earlier volleyball courses to lead their peers, which includes explaining the rules, the rationale for the rules, and identifying when and how the rules have been violated. Course content might also include for students to apply their knowledge of the game's rules through taking advantage of opportunities for peer coaching and officiating. Learning objectives for such a course could include that upon completing the course, students would be able to analyze and evaluate the rules associated with all course activities, as well as equipment, risks, and safety procedures. Another course learning objective could be that upon completing the course, students would be able to interpret and apply the rules associated with specific activities included in the course. Another objective could be to collaborate with peers in setting rules for discussions and decisions regarding presenting alternative viewpoints, reaching informal consensus, voting on essential issues, setting clear goals and deadlines, and assigning individual roles. Objectives like these would meet PE curriculum standards.

Goal for appropriate elementary school PE programs

NASPE states that the goal of elementary school PE programs that are developmentally and instructionally appropriate is to develop individuals with the confidence, knowledge, and skills to be physically active throughout life. NASPE joins leading child development and medical specialists in recommending that all elementary school-aged children receive a minimum of 150 minutes of quality PE weekly. The association indicates that instructionally appropriate PE practices address the development, changes in movement abilities, and individual differences of children. The design and delivery of elementary school PE programs and lessons must also consider children's past experiences with motor skills, sports, and cognitive and social development. In addition, PE lesson planning and selection of instructional strategies should reflect individual children's ages, physical maturation, fitness levels, and skill levels. Appropriate patterns of PE instruction should also integrate known best practices revealed through both teaching experiences and research studies, to the end of optimizing all children's opportunities to learn and succeed. National, state, and local PE standards should also be reflected in quality PE programs and lessons. PE teachers must evaluate student progress regularly, and adjust their progressions and lessons accordingly.

State education department's model content standards for high school

One example of high school PE model content standards is the California Department of Education's: (1) Students show knowledge and competency regarding motor skills, movement patterns, and strategies necessary for performing various physical activities. (2) Students show knowledge of fitness concepts, principles, and strategies, and attain levels of physical fitness enabling performance and health. (3) Students show they know psychology and sociology concepts, principles, and strategies applicable to learning and executing physical activities. This education department has five model content standards for elementary and middle school PE. For elementary school, it emphasizes movement through time and space, individually and with partners; movement continuity and change; and object manipulation with speed and accuracy through time and space. For middle school, it emphasizes decision making, meeting challenges, problem-solving teamwork, and cooperative goal achievement. Instruction and learning are incremental in grades K-5 for developmental appropriateness, while consolidated and refined in grades 6-8. The rationale is that high school students, capable of higher-order cognition and more sophisticated skill performance, can integrate cumulative knowledge and skills. Hence the five earlier standards are combined into three high school standards, reflecting high school PE's culmination of PE in earlier grades.

Combining teaching styles and various instructional strategies

One analogy from NASPE (in human kinetics) is comparing teaching to cooking: though teachers follow instructional recipes like chefs, they combine these with their own creativity and unique ingredients, whose combinations are influenced by judicious decisions to attain specific results. Teachers must take into account each student's unique aptitudes and abilities, the particular learning environment, the teacher's own instructional strategies and styles, and the teacher's own personality characteristics. Teachers cannot depend on a single teaching method, like chefs cannot depend on one excellent recipe to meet all diners' varying tastes and needs. They both need a repertoire of varied recipes. Before implementing any particular teaching style, the PE teacher must consider additional factors, including the content he or she will be teaching, whether the physical learning environment lends itself to executing particular teaching styles, the time required or allowed for implementing a teaching style, the amount of class time available, personal teacher style, and most of all, the students.

Impact of national demographics on instructional practices in PE

The demographic patterns across American schools are in a state of rapid change. As a result, student populations in our schools are becoming more diverse all the time. This diversity dictates that teachers, including PE teachers, must change their instructional practices to address the challenges presented by populations with increasing diversity. When PE teachers prepare to apply certain teaching styles and instructional strategies, they must first think about whether each style and strategy is congruent with their program objectives, course content, and the developmental levels of their students. They also need to think about which ways are available for them to modify their instruction to enable matching each of their lessons to their teaching styles. While every teaching style produces unique results, no single instructional style has been proven to improve learning for all students. Therefore, PE teachers can make sure to meet all student needs by incorporating a variety of teaching styles. Their primary goal should be to enable every student to experience success in the environment of movement learning. Student achievement defines educational success. If students learned, met lesson objectives, and learned what was intended by the end of a lesson, then the lesson succeeded.

Integration of PE with English Language Arts

<u>Second-grade classroom</u>
One activity combining PE and ELA is "Vocabulary Hot Potato." This meets learning standards to (1) perform fundamental motor and manipulative skills, becoming competent in various physical activities and proficient in a few complex motor and sport activities; (2) recognize safety hazards and respond effectively; and (3) correctly spell words studied earlier. It develops eye-hand coordination and manipulation skills for accurate tossing and catching. Materials needed are vocabulary or spelling lists and a small Nerf, foam, yarn, or wadded paper ball. Teacher assessment is via observation and immediate verbal feedback. Teachers first review correct underhand and overhand throwing techniques previously taught in PE classes with students, including foot opposition and follow-through. Teachers announce one word and toss the ball to a student, who gives the word's first letter and tosses the ball to another student, who supplies the next letter, continuing until the word's correct spelling is complete. The students who spelled the word select a whole-class exercise (e.g., jumping jacks, etc.), with as many repetitions as letters in the spelled word. Repeat with other words. Variations include one student spelling the whole word, another identifying its number of syllables, another using it in a sentence, etc.

Third-grade classroom

"Adverbs on the Move" (Clancy, 2006) combines looking up word meanings in a dictionary and finding synonyms and antonyms in a thesaurus with practicing locomotor movements like walking, jogging or jogging in place, skipping, running, hopping, galloping, jumping, etc. Teachers provide the dictionary, a thesaurus, a list of recently learned adverbs, three-inch-by-five-inch cards, and pencils. Assessment is via observation and student verbal responses. Teachers give students cards, each with an adverb they have recently learned at the top. Each student looks up a synonym and antonym for his or her adverb and writes them below it on his or her card. Students move, carrying their cards softly, quickly, heavily, etc., according to the adverb they received. They stop on a teacher signal, each passing their card to the student next to them. On the teacher's "go" signal, they repeat the movement according to their new adverb. Then the teacher changes the movement and repeats the exercise. Teachers can vary adverbs for non-locomotor movements, e.g., angry, stormy, red, etc., or announce a sentence, have students identify the adverb in it, and then make movements the adverb describes.

Instructing high school students in aquatics

Typically, state learning standards include aquatics as one content area in PE. However, not every school in a state may have a swimming pool in its building. Some solutions for PE departments and teachers include exploring opportunities in the community, such as at YMCAs or YWCAs, community recreation centers, county public swimming pools, or even pools at apartment complexes or private homes whose owners want to help, especially if students in the class live there. Another option is for the school to buy a portable pool if funds are available. If none of these alternatives is available, PE teachers can still teach swim strokes: they write or print task cards on the breathing pattern, kick, arm stroke, and complete combination for each stroke. They assign students to pairs, each with a bench, and give each pair a set of task cards. One student lies on the bench, while the other observes and gives feedback with corrections and reinforcement; then they switch. Each student masters each stroke component, then the complete stroke. An important caution is never to assume that mastering a stroke this way will enable the student to swim in the water safely.

Learning to analyze and apply feedback for complex movement skill performance

A PE teacher can use individual and dual activities to help high school students attend to the feedback they get both from their own proprioception—i.e., their sense of their body's location, orientation, positioning, and movements—and from other students, and to analyze this feedback and apply it to improve their performance of complex movements. For example, the teacher can assign students to pairs. One student executes a golf swing and his or her partner supplies feedback about the correctness of the swinger's form and technique. The first student analyzes both the partner's feedback and his or her own proprioceptive feedback. Together, the partners figure out what the first student must do to improve his or her performance. The performer writes down his or her analysis. To help students achieve and demonstrate independent learning of movement skills, the teacher offers students a choice of movement skills. The teacher instructs students to research their chosen skill's correct technique, and develop learning cues for practicing it. Students must then decide which kind of practice is best for the skill, and then write and implement their own plans for practice.

Physical activity in extreme environments

PE teachers can begin by designing lessons and instructing high school students about extreme environments and some of the physical safety hazards associated with them. For example, the environment of the ocean differs from the swimming environment of a swimming pool or lake because there are waves, undertows, and riptides. Students unfamiliar with these can be thrown by waves or pulled under by currents, and must learn how to address these situations. In the middle of a wave, one cannot see anything and cannot orient to directions like up or down, and even strong swimmers cannot counteract the force of some currents. In the mountains, high altitudes supply less oxygen, making negative impacts on one's breathing ability during physical exertion. Also, at higher altitudes the sun can be very hot during the day and temperatures can plummet to freezing at night. In deserts, high daytime temperatures and lack of water are hazards. In addition to preparing students for activity in extreme environments, teachers can meet learning standards by assigning students to select and research conditions and risks of specific environments, and write research reports about how these would affect physical activity and how to prepare.

High school volleyball activity lesson

A volleyball activity for serving and defending can meet NASPE standards #1.2: setting, spiking, forearm passing, defensive strategies, and officiating; #3.4: aerobic capacity; and #5.6: cooperating and accepting challenges. Once a team's server hits the ball, team defense requires each player to know their base position, defend that space, and respond timely to offensive attacks by the opposing team. A team's first defensive hit should be a pass to enable effective defense-to-offense transition. PE teachers can give these tactical cues: (1) Start in rotational position. This means one setter in front, one in the back row, with no overlapping. (2) Serve the ball. Students should serve using the assigned method, aim at open spaces, and be prepared to move quickly. (3) Transition to base defense. This means upon the serve, players should move from their rotational positions to their base positions. (4) Defend against attack. This means players should watch the ball, call it, and start the sequence passing. After play, teachers can ask students: Did they transition to base defense after the server hit the ball? Why or why not? And did their team defend against attack successfully? If so, how?

Principles to explaining and demonstrating movement and sport skills

According to the SPARK website, PE teachers and coaches have roles during practice of giving students instruction and feedback; monitoring individual student and team performance; giving students motivation, support, and encouragement; assuring student safety; and managing space, time, and equipment involved. To be effective, teachers and coaches should be responsible in character, patient, good listeners, trustworthy, encouraging, and inspiring to students. To optimize student learning, teachers and coaches using designed practice plans should always follow them in the sequence they are written, and consult these plans and any associated content cards or notes regularly for pertinent information (unless or until they are so experienced they know these by heart). To support timely player setup, teachers and coaches should read aloud each task or component of a practice session. Teachers and coaches should "show and tell," i.e., demonstrate movements or actions physically to communicate them. To give players a mental advantage, give them "think-abouts." The 80/20 Rule means although 100 percent of students will learn or understand by doing or practicing a skill, 80 percent grasp the concept through teacher or coach instruction or demonstration, while the other 20 percent will understand through doing. Teachers and coaches also teach fair play, etiquette, and rules in sports.

Teaching a doubles badminton game

Badminton can be taught using doubles teams. In front-to-back formation, one player is responsible for front court, one for mid-court and back court. This formation enables drop and smash shots, making it offensive. Players recover and communicate centrally to their sides to prevent faults and optimize success. Teachers demonstrate while explaining game format. For rally scoring, players must stay in front-to-back formation, finish a 10-hit rally before scoring points, and rotate front and back positions after every point. Rotate the team with more points up after every game. Cues include: "Determine team strategy": students decide if their team is better at offense or defense; "Communicate": call court positions and shots to prevent faults; "Adjust as partner moves": change court positions as partners move to strike; and "Attack/Defend": attack via front-to-back, and defend via side-to-side team formations. Target and trajectory cues include: (Front) A drop shot has low trajectory and front-court target (both near the net); (Back) A smash shot has steep trajectory and mid-court sideline target. Think-abouts: When playing against a team in front-to-back formation, where should your shots land? What is one advantage of front-to-back formation?

In a high school badminton practice plan, racquet types should be selected for maximal student success. The first two practice games can be doubles play, both teams in front-to-back formation: (1) One player serves, starting a rally; players call "Mine" before hitting or returning any shot. Alternate front and back positions with each rally, completing 10 rallies. (2) After serving, play a 10-hit rally; then attempt to score: only a smash or drop shot earns points. Players call as in (1). Play up to 5 points. Switch positions after each point. (3) One team is in front-to-back formation, the other in side-to-side formation; both teams maintain formation throughout the game. Serve, complete a 10-hit rally, and then attempt to score. As in (1) and (2), players call before hitting. Play up to 5 points, rotating player positions following every point. Play four games, rotating team formations after every game. (4) Teams make up, practice, and play their own games, developing rules by varying clear/drive/drop/smash shot types, short/long serve types, front-to-back/side-to-side formation types, space, and scoring methods. Think-abouts include: Which shot was most effective against each doubles formation? Which doubles formation did you like better? Why?

Elements of a high school basketball practice

PE teachers and coaches demonstrate while explaining game format, e.g., five one-minute periods. Play starts or restarts with a pass from the baseline or sideline. Offense only throws after pick and roll, scoring 1 point per basket. Each foul gives the opposing team 1 point. For the first four periods, stay on offense; rotate offense to defense every period. In period five, offense and defense switch every time ball possession changes. Rotate after each game. Offense cues: "Pick": Set a pick or screen on an opponent defending a teammate; the teammate moves past. "Roll": Roll off the screen to the basket, look at the ball-handler, prepare to pass. "Shoot and follow": If open, throw; follow the shot to the basket. If not open, reset. Defense cues: "Match-up": Defend a player similar in size, fitness, and skill level. "Shadow": Stay close to the offensive player you defend no matter where on the court he or she goes. "Box-out-let": On a throw, face the basket, keeping the opponent behind you; rebound and pass. "Communicate": Talk so your teammates always know what is happening. Think-abouts: Did you roll to the basket after every pick? Why or why not? Did you take shots only when open? Why or why not? Which passes worked best with a pick and roll? Why?

Safety considerations for movement activities

Teachers should instruct students in moving safely within general and personal spaces. They must teach skills in the correct order, e.g., stepping into hoops on floors before having to run in and out of them. Games must include skills already taught. Teachers should give activities needing no equipment at the beginning of the school year, and then introduce smaller equipment (hoops, bean bags, etc.) before mobile equipment like utility balls. Teachers should instruct students in floor activities, like balancing when walking on floor lines, before using equipment, like balancing when walking on benches. They should define procedures and rules and give students practice in them, like stop and start signals, looking in the direction they are moving, and safe equipment use, inside the gym before going outside. They must be informed about students with medical conditions, like orthopedic devices or casts, asthma, allergies or anaphylaxis, epilepsy, diabetes, cardiac conditions, etc., that could affect their participation. Pylons, lines, or other markers must be designated away from walls: stages and walls cannot be used as end zones or turning points. Students must always be supervised and never left alone in equipment rooms.

Teachers and coaches must teach students correct, age-appropriate procedures for warming up before movement activities and cooling down afterward. PE teachers have been sued for negligence for neglecting proper warm-ups. For risk management, teachers and coaches must select activities appropriate to students' levels of cognitive development, behavioral patterns, and mental and physical abilities. Teachers and coaches must possess the skills and knowledge for safely teaching and supervising activities according to risk management guidelines. Generally, if an activity is not included in the physical education curriculum or official safety guidelines, teachers and coaches should first determine whether its educational value matches or supersedes its entertainment value, and then submit a proposal to the school board for approval. If approved, officials, teachers, and coaches must identify and minimize inherent risks in the activity. Coaches and teachers must instruct all students in body contact techniques and skills, concussion safety lessons, and head-injury prevention principles (and document the instruction). They must also require helmets and protective equipment as applicable, and ensure that equipment is inspected before activities, practices, and games. For outdoor activities, they must assure parents know safety precautions for extreme weather, temperatures, humidity, smog/air quality, UV rays, frostbite, dehydration, and insects; develop safety protocols and precautions for lightning; and communicate these to students and staff.

Heimlich maneuver and CPR

For choking, quick response is necessary to prevent unconsciousness, even death. For adults and children (procedures for infants differ), perform the Heimlich maneuver. First, remember that panicky victims may unintentionally strike out, and protect yourself. Do NOT perform the Heimlich on someone who is speaking, coughing, or breathing—someone who can do these things is not choking. Stand behind the victim. Wrap your arms around him or her as if hugging. Make a fist with your right hand and put it above the victim's navel. Grasp your right fist with your left hand; thrust in and up forcibly. Repeat thrusting until the victim can breathe. If the victim loses consciousness, begin child CPR for children aged one to eight years, or adult CPR above eight years. Practice universal precautions and use protective equipment if available to avoid contagious and infectious diseases. "Shake and shout," trying to wake the victim. If he or she does not awaken, call 911. If nobody is available, do CPR for two minutes, and then call 911. On children, do two chest compressions per second 30 times and repeat. On adults, do chest compressions at least 100 times a minute, or 30 times in 18 seconds, and repeat.

Practice Test

Practice Questions

1. Which of the following is the smallest of the four muscles in the buttocks?
    a. Gracilis
    b. Gastrocnemius
    c. Gluteus minimus
    d. Tensor fasciae latae

2. What is a definition of body mass index (BMI)?
    a. The ratio of weight to height squared
    b. The ratio of abdominal fat to total fat
    c. The ratio of body fat to muscle cubed
    d. The ratio of total fat to overall weight

3. In the history of research into motor development, which of the following represents the trend from earlier to later findings?
    a. From experience by itself to maturation by itself
    b. From maturation by itself to experience by itself
    c. From maturation to maturation plus experience
    d. From experience to maturation plus experience

4. Related to summation of forces, which is accurate about how body parts move?
    a. The largest body parts are the slowest and move last.
    b. The smallest body parts are the fastest and move first.
    c. The largest body parts are the slowest and move first.
    d. Regardless of speed, all parts move at the same times.

5. Which of the following is true about center of gravity (COG)?
    a. COG is in the same location for each human body.
    b. COG varies according to the body parts' positions.
    c. COG varies among bodies but is constant for each.
    d. COG is the same as center of mass or of pressure.

6. If one skater has longer arms and another has shorter arms, and someone applies equal force to each skater's extended arm, which of these is true about torque?
    a. The skater with longer arms will rotate faster.
    b. The skater with shorter arms will rotate faster.
    c. With equal force, they will turn at equal speed.
    d. Torque involves an axis, not the perpendicular.

7. Relative to spatial awareness, which movement concept involves vertical, horizontal, and circular paths of movement?
    a. Locations and levels
    b. Personal space
    c. Directions
    d. Planes

8. In quality of movement, _____ is bound/interrupted or free/sustained.
    a. flow
    b. effort
    c. speed
    d. rhythm

9. In the movement concept of relationship, which relationship can involve only one body without another body/bodies or object(s)?
    a. The relationship of near and far
    b. The relationship of on or off
    c. Together or with opposition
    d. Symmetrical and asymmetrical

10. When someone bench presses weights to strengthen the arms and upper body, this is an example of which exercise science principle?
    a. Overload
    b. Specificity
    c. Adaptation
    d. Progression

11. Which of the following is an example of the short-term effects of exercise on health?
    a. Exercising releases endorphins, generating euphoria.
    b. Exercising regularly prevents and relieves depression.
    c. Exercising lowers the risk of heart attacks and strokes.
    d. Exercising can reduce one's blood pressure and pulse.

12. Of the following, which most accurately represents an aspect of the relationship between nutrition and fitness?
    a. Exercising regularly and energetically enables you to eat anything you want.
    b. Eating a diet rich in calcium prevents bone density loss, but exercise cannot.
    c. Eating right provides energy for exercise, while exercise can control appetite.
    d. Exercising prevents high blood pressure and cholesterol more than diet does.

13. A part of which body system controls fluid loss, protects deep tissues, and synthesizes vitamin D?
    a. The skeletal system
    b. The muscular system
    c. The lymphatic system
    d. The integumentary system

14. The respiratory system _____ oxygen and _____ carbon dioxide.
    a. inhales; exhales
    b. delivers; expels
    c. creates; absorbs
    d. exhales; inhales

15. In the central nervous system's hierarchy of motor control, which level(s) of the brain produce(s) a motor program?
    a. The highest level
    b. The middle level
    c. The lowest level
    d. All three levels

16. Which of the following is historically accurate about motor development?
    a. It was thoroughly catalogued from the 1930s to the 1940s, progressing less from the 1950s to the1980s.
    b. Due to maturational theory, its description was limited in the 1940s, exploding in the 1950s.
    c. It was described through steady, continuous research from the 1940s through the 1980s.
    d. Researchers lacked the technology to explain it until pioneering work in the 1960s and 1970s.

17. Which statement best characterizes the role of posture in theories of motor development?
    a. As evidence of growing cerebral control, posture was more important to classical theories.
    b. As the biomechanical basis of action, posture is more important to contemporary theories.
    c. For different reasons, posture has been equally important to both earlier and later theories.
    d. In both classical and contemporary theories, posture is a minor part of motor development.

18. Among concepts of movement quality, which one has static and dynamic types?
    a. Flow
    b. Time
    c. Force
    d. Balance

19. Compared to regular baseball, softball has a _____ ball, a _____ infield, _____ innings, and _____ pitch.
    a. smaller; bigger; more; the same
    b. bigger; smaller; fewer; a different
    c. bigger; bigger; fewer; a different
    d. smaller; smaller; more; the same

20. Which of the following is true of soccer as played today?
    a. Each soccer team is composed of nine players.
    b. No player can touch the ball with arms or hands.
    c. Some players can use heads or torsos on the ball.
    d. The Fédération Internationale de Football Association (FIFA) World Cup is an annual soccer event.

21. The frog kick is used in which swimming stroke(s)?
    a. The breaststroke
    b. The butterfly
    c. The crawl
    d. All these

22. Among the following common areas of negligence in physical education, in addition to first aid emergencies, which one can teachers and coaches MOST mitigate by enlisting the help of students?
    a. Instruction
    b. Supervision
    c. Transportation
    d. Class environments

23. Regarding physical education teacher and coach liability compared to classroom teacher liability, which is true?
    a. The sizes of classes are similar in both cases.
    b. Other classes are just as likely to be outdoors.
    c. Other classes travel just as often on field trips, and so on.
    d. Projectiles and water increase liability in physical education classes.

24. Which statement about physical education (PE) class safety and teacher liability is a valid one?
    a. PE classes can include advanced gymnastics safely by having group spotters.
    b. PE classes as well as extracurricular activities can include trampolines safely.
    c. PE teachers must instruct students in calling for and backing away from fly balls.
    d. PE teachers commonly and safely discipline students with strenuous exercise.

25. Which of the following effects on performance is more likely to be caused by student marijuana abuse than student alcohol abuse before physical education classes?
    a. Impaired and low energy
    b. Impaired depth perception
    c. Impaired judgment in general
    d. Impaired physical coordination

26. Of the following effects on student health caused by substance abuse, which one results from the largest number of different substance abuse-related causes?
    a. Death
    b. Organ damage
    c. Avascular necrosis
    d. Human immunodeficiency (HIV) and acquired immune deficiency syndrome (AIDS) transmission

27. Which of these is a typical effect of substance abuse on student behavior?
    a. A shy student becomes more sociable.
    b. An outgoing student becomes withdrawn.
    c. An inhibited student becomes more impulsive.
    d. These are all typical effects of substance abuse.

28. Which kinds of physical education activities are both appropriate for boys and girls to participate in together and are less dependent on team assignment by student skill levels?
    a. Activities that involve participant body contact
    b. Activities that require more upper-body strength
    c. Activities that require agility and lower-body strength
    d. Activities of all these types

29. Regarding individual differences that affect physical education activity performance, which of these sports is most appropriate for the ectomorphic somatotype (body type)?
    a. Wrestling
    b. Gymnastics
    c. Shot-putting
    d. High jump

30. Which of the following reflects a physical education teaching technique that promotes cognitive learning?
    a. Keeping times shorter during instruction and demonstrations
    b. Comparing new movement skills to those previously learned
    c. Using universal language in communicating with all students
    d. Giving all students equal responsibility for their own learning

31. Regarding perceptual-motor abilities, which is a performance skill that would be MOST affected by individual differences in control precision?
    a. Playing quarterback in football
    b. Handling a hockey puck
    c. Dribbling a basketball
    d. Driving a race car

32. Among physical proficiencies that affect individual performance, which type of strength is most involved in the activity of kayaking?
    a. Static strength
    b. Trunk strength
    c. Dynamic strength
    d. Explosive strength

33. In one instructional method to promote psychomotor learning, a physical education teacher clearly explains learning goals and skills to be learned to the students; demonstrates the skills for the students; and provides the students with practice time, frequently and regularly monitoring their progress during practice. This describes which of the following methods?
    a. The contingency or contract method
    b. The command or direct method
    c. The task or reciprocal method
    d. None of these methods

34. Research finds that motor skills training, endurance training, and strength training all share which neuroplasticity effects in common?
    a. New blood vessel formation
    b. Motor map reorganization
    c. Spinal reflex modification
    d. New synapse generation

35. Which development in human manual skills emerges the earliest?
    a. Successfully reaching for objects
    b. Coordinated arm–hand movements
    c. Arm flapping and jerky arm extensions
    d. Changing hand shapes before touching objects

36. Which of the following is a typical characteristic in babies' earliest gait development?
    a. Pointing their toes outward
    b. Walking bending the knees
    c. Keeping arms by their sides
    d. Rolling from the heel to toe

37. One teaching method for managing kindergarten through Grade 12 physical education classes uses three steps to address student noncompliance with class rules. In which of the following sequences should these steps be applied?
    a. An oral warning; a brief time-out; a time-out with written response
    b. A brief time-out; a time-out with written response; an oral warning
    c. A time-out with written response; an oral warning; a brief time-out
    d. A brief time-out; an oral warning; a time-out with written response

38. Which of the following is NOT a common theme many kindergarten through Grade 12 physical education teachers across the United States use to manage their classrooms?
    a. Respect
    b. Cooperation
    c. Doing your best
    d. Speaking out freely

39. Among these class rules that many American kindergarten through Grade 12 physical education (PE) teachers commonly define, which are all applicable to other subjects and classrooms, which one is also more important to PE classes?
    a. Kindness and caring
    b. Following directions
    c. Keeping hands to self
    d. Good sportsmanship

40. Of four factors that affect learning in physical education settings, which one is best exemplified by the physiological and psychological variables that influence individual ability and interest for learning?
    a. Readiness
    b. Motivation
    c. Reinforcement
    d. Individual differences

41. In three stages of motor learning, which of these is characteristic of the associative stage?
    a. Understanding an activity's goal and nature
    b. Making attempts that include major errors
    c. Making fewer and more consistent errors
    d. Effortless automaticity in performance

42. For cooperative learning activities to be more productive than competitive or individual learning activities, one of five necessary elements is positive interdependence among the members of a student group, including student awareness of it. What is accurate about the other four required elements?
　　a. The students occasionally engage in productive, face-to-face interactions.
　　b. The students are accountable for group goals collectively, not individually.
　　c. The students use task-relevant interpersonal and group skills frequently.
　　d. The students process group functioning to sustain current effectiveness.

43. Which of the following external variables that affect physical education activity is more likely to help than hurt performance by its presence?
　　a. Strong outdoor winds
　　b. Advancing technology
　　c. Equipment conditions
　　d. The other participants

44. Concerning the impacts of various resources on student physical education (PE) outcomes, what has research found?
　　a. Class size and student–teacher ratio correlate inversely with activity levels, time, safety, and learning.
　　b. Students receive a higher quantity and quality of PE from teachers who also teach different subjects.
　　c. Student physical activity is the same whether PE curriculum is based on educational standards or not.
　　d. PE facilities and equipment are valuable resources but do not change the amount of student activity.

45. Compared to the amount of time in moderate to vigorous physical activity (MVPA) the Institute of Medicine recommends for children to spend daily, how much do research studies find they actually spend in school physical education classes?
　　a. About one-sixth of what is recommended
　　b. About one-third of what is recommended
　　c. About one-half of what is recommended
　　d. About the same as is recommended

46. Among strategies for increasing internal student motivation for physical activity, which of these is the best example of giving students freedom of choice?
　　a. Providing flexibility for students to adapt activities to their interests
　　b. Changing activity rules, space, and equipment to enable student success
　　c. Matching the specific kinds of activities with the individual students
　　d. Involving students in decision-making processes whenever possible

47. Which of these is an effective strategy for physical education teachers to enhance students' perceived physical competence?
　　a. Specify the number of trials to complete during a certain time period.
　　b. Specify the length of time for practicing but not the number of trials.
　　c. Specify the technical errors students make in instructional feedback.
　　d. Specify a certain activity without varying it to keep students on task.

48. Within the TARGET model, which physical education teaching strategy is an example of the R in the acronym?
    a. Varying the difficulty levels among several different activities
    b. Giving students some responsibility for the choice of activities
    c. Acknowledging process and improvement rather than product
    d. Avoiding peer comparison through rapid and variable grouping

49. Findings of research into physical activity and peer interactions are best reflected by which of these?
    a. Health behavior primarily influences students' peer relationships.
    b. Health behavior and peer relationships have reciprocal influences.
    c. Health behavior is mainly influenced by student peer relationships.
    d. Health behaviors and peer relations have no significant interaction.

50. Regarding appropriate physical education (PE) teaching practices, which statement is MOST valid?
    a. PE teachers must use extrinsic motivations to teach student responsibility for learning.
    b. PE teachers should ignore certain inappropriate student behaviors to extinguish them.
    c. PE teachers do not necessarily need to obtain or renew certification in cardiopulmonary resuscitation (CPR) or automated external defibrillator (AED) use.
    d. PE teachers must regularly and consistently inspect facilities and equipment for safety.

51. Which of these is the MOST appropriate physical education teacher practice to establish productive learning environments for students and promote their responsibility and social skills?
    a. Deliberately designing activities and situations that teach and develop needed skills
    b. Using teachable moments and allowing incidental learning to develop needed skills
    c. Teaching all U.S. team sports to culturally diverse students to develop uniform skills
    d. Allowing highly skilled students to dominate as examples for students of lower skills

52. Which of the following is a recommended strategy for physical education teachers to plan effective class behavior management?
    a. Announce at least ten expectations to the students in oral format.
    b. Enforce expectations occasionally for intermittent reinforcement.
    c. Define expectations in terms of what they want students not to do.
    d. Define expectations in terms of what they want the students to do.

53. Regarding effective ways for physical education (PE) teachers to give instructions to students for the smoothest class operation and best behavior management, which of these is accurate?
    a. PE teachers should tell students only what to do as they cannot follow more directions.
    b. PE teachers should tell students when to do something before telling them what to do.
    c. PE teachers should use the rule of threes by giving three instructional cues at a time.
    d. PE teachers using the 80/20 rule let 80 percent learn by doing and 20 percent learn from teaching.

54. When student disputes develop during physical education classes, how is settling them by rock, paper, scissors viewed?
    a. It is believed to be unprofessional.
    b. It is inappropriate by being childish.
    c. It is effective because it is objective.
    d. It is unfair because it is subjective.

55. According to experts, what is true about the primary functions of nonverbal communication?
    a. Nonverbal communication serves a function of performing social rituals.
    b. Nonverbal communication shows personalities rather than relationships.
    c. Nonverbal communication is used to replace, not help, verbal interaction.
    d. Nonverbal communication is not used like words for expressing feelings.

56. The definition of verbal communication includes which of these formats?
    a. Texting
    b. Sign language
    c. Conversations
    d. All these formats

57. Regarding communication with athletes, which statement is recommended by experts for coaches to consider?
    a. Coaches must not only get athlete attention but also explain, so athletes understand easily.
    b. Coaches must determine if athletes understood them but not whether they believed them.
    c. Coaches must get athletes to understand and believe, not necessarily accept, what they say.
    d. Coaches must disregard athletes' individual and group nonverbal cues for controlling them.

58. Regarding feedback that physical education teachers and coaches give students and athletes, which of the following is an example of prescriptive feedback rather than descriptive feedback?
    a. "You can do this!"
    b. "Follow through!"
    c. "That was great!"
    d. "Way to play ball!"

59. When does physical education instruction not necessarily require giving feedback to students?
    a. When a skill requires specific correction
    b. When a task gets environmental feedback
    c. When a student has experience with a skill
    d. When a teacher demonstration is enough

60. Which of the following is an example of the sandwich approach to giving students and athletes feedback?
    a. Specific skill, general reinforcement, and a different specific skill
    b. General reinforcement, specific skill, and general reinforcement
    c. Positive reinforcement, correction, and positive reinforcement
    d. One correction, positive reinforcement, and another correction

61. When is music useful as a communication medium in physical education?
    a. Dance activities only
    b. Dance and aerobic exercise only
    c. Dance, aerobics, and dribbling basketballs
    d. Dance, aerobics, and many other physical education activities

62. What is MOST accurate about how physical education teachers can use bulletin boards to communicate instructional information to students?
   a. Schools must provide real bulletin boards for physical education teachers to utilize them.
   b. A time-lapse bulletin board accesses student participation and creativity.
   c. A time-lapse bulletin board is a project only the physical education teacher can complete.
   d. Physical education teachers must communicate orally, as students ignore bulletin boards.

63. Relative to video recordings and instructional communication by physical education teachers with students, which statement is correct?
   a. Videos can preserve and repeat ideal demonstrations by teachers and students.
   b. Videos are not as good for teaching body movements as verbal descriptions are.
   c. Videos used by substitute or student teachers are boring in contrast to live action.
   d. Videos lack the variation, making live demonstrations different and thus interesting.

64. According to national physical education (PE) standards, to show respect, which of the following should PE teachers do to address a student's behavior problem?
   a. The teacher describes the student's behavior, why it was disruptive, and solutions for the problem.
   b. The teacher has a classmate describe the behavior, why it was disruptive, and solutions for the problem.
   c. The teacher has the student describe the behavior, why it was disruptive, and solutions for the problem.
   d. The teacher avoids discussing it but provides concrete consequences and solutions for the problem.

65. A physical education teacher writes an entry task on the board before class. How does this relate to teacher communication toward student understanding and ownership of high expectations for themselves?
   a. This is not recommended because the teacher will not be supervising the students for this activity.
   b. This supports high classroom expectations because students can begin the activity independently.
   c. This supports student independence for activities but not student comprehension of expectations.
   d. This is not recommended because the teacher did not structure the learning activity for students.

66. Regarding physical education teacher communication with parents, what is MOST effective related to posting and communicating class rules to students at the beginning of the school year?
   a. Giving rules to students, but not parents, so students feel they can trust teachers
   b. Giving copies of rules to students with instructions to take them home to parents
   c. Sending the rules by postal mail with a cover letter asking parents to review them
   d. E-mailing the rules to the parents with a cover letter asking them to review them

67. Among fundamental movement skills (FMS), which two are both part of the same main category?
   a. Locomotor and manipulative
   b. Manipulative and rotation
   c. Rotation and balance
   d. Balance and stability

68. Which of these locomotor activities is most appropriate for children younger than five years old?
   a. Blob tag
   b. Musical hoops
   c. Follow the leader
   d. Any of these equally

69. In learning how to land during movement activities, which of these is NOT identified as a phase of learning?
    a. Mastery
    b. Discovery
    c. Consolidation
    d. Development

70. When students learn to fall sideways and land using their hands, which of the following should be the last activity they do in a sequence of increasing difficulty?
    a. Falling sideways from kneeling
    b. Rolling sideways down a wedge
    c. Falling, rolling, and standing up
    d. Running, falling, rolling, and standing

71. Which of the following is MOST accurate about giving feedback to students and athletes in physical education or coaching?
    a. External feedback should duplicate internal feedback.
    b. Students request feedback most with advanced skills.
    c. Experts recommend more instead of less feedback.
    d. External feedback should stimulate internal feedback.

72. What has research revealed about feedback in teaching physical education?
    a. Feedback quality is more important than quantity.
    b. Skill development needs more frequent feedback.
    c. Feedback quantity is more important than quality.
    d. Beginners need feedback that is the most precise.

73. Of the following statements, which is true about aerobics?
    a. Aerobics originally focused on the flexibility of the body.
    b. Aerobics originally focused on the strength of the muscles.
    c. Aerobics originally focused on cardiorespiratory endurance.
    d. Aerobics originally focused on one thing as it still does today.

74. Among Japanese martial arts, which one uses a weapon?
    a. Judo
    b. Kendo
    c. Karate
    d. Jujitsu

75. In the debate over standardized physical education tests, which of these is NOT a common argument?
    a. To enjoy physical activity as adults, people must enjoy it during youth.
    b. Standardized testing supports motivation for lifelong physical activity.
    c. Standardized testing allows students to gauge their relative progress.
    d. Standardized testing gives physical education equal importance to all school subjects.

76. Among the most prevalent challenges to kindergarten through Grade 12 physical education, which has recently become even more challenging than the others?
    a. Inadequate resources and parental support
    b. Overly large class sizes and teacher burnout
    c. Violence, student drug abuse, and discipline
    d. Reductions in school curriculum times for physical education

77. A physical education teacher addresses a wide range of skill levels in one class by setting up several learning stations to teach a lesson in throwing. Which station activity represents the highest student skill level?
    a. Throwing lead passes
    b. Throwing at a stationary target
    c. Throwing to teammates while defended
    d. Throwing all these ways equally

78. If a student has the condition of atlantoaxial instability, which of the following activities would be safe for a physical education teacher to assign to the student?
    a. A log roll would be safest for this student.
    b. A forward roll would be better for this student.
    c. No kind of roll should be assigned to this student.
    d. It is irrelevant because atlantoaxial instability is so rare.

79. What amount of quality physical education time most reflects the National Association for Sport and Physical Education (NASPE) recommendation for elementary school students?
    a. A minimum of 15 minutes per day
    b. A maximum of 30 minutes per day
    c. A minimum of 30 minutes per day
    d. A maximum of 60 minutes a week

80. When physical education teachers plan lessons and choose teaching methods, which of the following should these reflect?
    a. Lessons and programs should reflect not only national and state but also local standards.
    b. Lessons and programs should reflect individual child physical maturation more than age.
    c. Lessons and programs should reflect individual child fitness levels more than skill levels.
    d. Lessons and programs should reflect best practices more from research than experience.

81. In light of rapidly increasing diversity in U.S. student populations, which of the following is the best indicator that physical education (PE) is effective?
    a. The PE teacher sticks to a single proven instructional style.
    b. Some students have success in the PE learning experience.
    c. Students learn and meet objectives by the end of a lesson.
    d. The PE teacher's practices are consistent despite changes.

82. Of the following, which elementary school activity best integrates physical education skills with English language arts (ELA) skills within the same lesson?
    a. Students perform movements and then look up adverbs and write synonyms and antonyms.
    b. Students look up and write adverbs, synonyms, and antonyms and then perform movements.
    c. Students identify adverbs in teacher-read sentences and describe movements using adverbs.
    d. Students perform movements in ways described by recently learned adverbs on given cards.

83. How can physical education teachers give aquatics instruction in high schools with no swimming pools?
   a. They can use public or private pools in the community with permission from owners.
   b. They can explore (A), but if these are not available, they can teach swimming with (C).
   c. They can use task cards, teach swim strokes, and have students practice on benches.
   d. They can find no way of teaching swimming if their schools have no swimming pools.

84. A physical education teacher designs a student volleyball activity to meet National Association for Sport and Physical Education (NASPE) standards for setting, spiking, forearm passing, defensive strategies, officiating; aerobic capacity; and cooperating and accepting challenges. Which of the following represents the correct sequence of steps in this activity?
   a. Rotational positions; serve; base positions; defend against attack
   b. Base positions; rotational positions; defend against attack; serve
   c. Serve; base positions; defend against attack; rotational positions
   d. Defend against attack; serve; rotational positions; base positions

85. Of the following, which is a valid principle of physical education (PE) coaching for teaching movement and sport skills to students?
   a. Asking think-about questions gives an advantage to students.
   b. Reading tasks or steps aloud only will delay the setup of players.
   c. PE teachers should alternate practice plan sequence for variety.
   d. PE teachers should either describe or demonstrate but not both.

86. When a physical education teacher gives a defense cue of "Match up" to students during basketball practice, what does this mean?
   a. Students always should pair up with another player on the court for defense.
   b. Students should stay near to offensive players that they defend on the court.
   c. Students should defend players more like them in size than fitness or skill level.
   d. Students should defend players similar to them in size, fitness, and skill level.

87. When is performing the Heimlich maneuver on a student indicated?
   a. The student says he or she is having trouble breathing.
   b. The student is choking and is not able to breathe.
   c. The student has trouble breathing and is coughing.
   d. The Heimlich should not be done until cardiopulmonary resuscitation (CPR) is tried.

88. Compared to naturalistic observations, structured observations are _____ in physical education assessment.
   a. more objective and less subjective
   b. more subjective and less objective
   c. more to see social than motor skills
   d. more realistic regarding behaviors

89. Which of the following methods would be LEAST useful for assessing student performance of physical education skills?
   a. Observational checklists
   b. Rating scales of skill level
   c. Written-response exams
   d. Performance data graphs

90. The Presidential Youth Fitness Program's Fitnessgram has three main categories. Which of the following correctly represents one of these categories?
    a. Muscular strength, endurance, and flexibility
    b. Aerobic capacity, body composition, and strength
    c. Body composition, flexibility, and aerobic capacity
    d. Endurance, aerobic capacity, and muscle strength

91. Which of these describes a function of formative assessments?
    a. They enable teachers to show accountability for adequate yearly progress and similar requirements.
    b. They enable teachers to compare student achievement to population averages.
    c. They enable teachers to adjust instruction in progress to address student needs.
    d. They enable teachers to see if they helped students meet curriculum standards.

92. When using an assessment instrument meant to measure aerobic endurance, physical education teachers find that maximum student repetitions are limited not by their becoming winded but by specific muscle fatigue. After obtaining the same results over repeated administrations, they conclude that this test measures muscular endurance instead. What have they discovered about this test?
    a. The test is neither a reliable nor valid test.
    b. The test is a valid test, but it is not reliable.
    c. The test is a reliable test, but it is not valid.
    d. The test is valid and reliable, but misused.

93. Of the following assessment approaches, which one is traditional rather than alternative?
    a. Students write down their personal fitness plans.
    b. Students perform a series of dance movements.
    c. Students show learning by playing a sports game.
    d. Students label the team's positions on a diagram.

94. Which of the following describes the most appropriate physical education self-assessment activity for kindergarten through Grade 2 students?
    a. Students write entries in journals describing the fitness activities they are doing.
    b. Students pictorially illustrate their activities in each of several fitness categories.
    c. Students keep notebooks of progress notes and give them to teachers regularly.
    d. Students record their progress on index cards they give to teachers at intervals.

95. What do Individuals with Disabilities Education Act (IDEA) regulations for assessing students with disabilities mandate?
    a. Using one standardized, valid, reliable, technically sound instrument
    b. Using multiple instruments that are similar instead of using just one
    c. Using a variety of instruments, all designed for measuring disabilities
    d. Using multiple, varied, valid, reliable, technically sound instruments

96. Regarding indications that a student should be evaluated to determine eligibility for adapted physical education (APE), which of the following (in addition to referral) correctly states a criterion?
    a. The student performs at his or her ability level in group settings but not on an individual basis.
    b. The student's social behaviors impede his or her or others' learning more than half of class time.
    c. The student has scored below average in at least one part of the state physical fitness test.
    d. The student scored at least one standard deviation low on the norm-referenced test used.

97. How should occupational therapists (OTs) help preschoolers with developmental delays to learn fine motor and manipulative skills in schools?
    a. Only OTs, not adapted physical educators (APEs) or classroom teachers, should apply OT strategies.
    b. Both APEs and classroom teachers should use OT methods they learn.
    c. APEs, but not classroom teachers, should use OT methods they learn.
    d. Classroom teachers, but not APEs, should use OT methods they learn.

98. Among the following members of collaborative teams who facilitate education for special needs students, who provides IQ testing and behavior management training?
    a. Administrators
    b. School nurses
    c. Psychologists
    d. Special education teachers

99. Of the following, which accurately reports research findings related to how physical fitness affects academic achievement?
    a. Cardiovascular fitness and body mass index (BMI) correlate positively with test scores in achievement.
    b. More physically fit children react more quickly but not necessarily more accurately.
    c. Children burn more calories during active gaming than teacher-led fitness activities.
    d. Intense exercise is followed by a significant temporary decline in cognitive function.

100. Among the following divisions of biomechanics that involve physics concepts, which one is MOST closely related to Newton's first three laws of motion?
    a. Coplanar vectors
    b. Kinematics
    c. Kinetics
    d. Forces

101. Which of the following biomechanics subjects are based on calculus?
    a. Vector composition and resolution
    b. Differentiation and integration
    c. The parallelogram method
    d. None of these topics

102. Which non-English language is shared in common by some of the terminology in both ballet and ballroom dancing?
    a. French
    b. Italian
    c. Spanish
    d. Russian

103. Among examples of how physical education (PE) teachers can collaborate with other educators, which one applies most to taking advantage of administrator support to improve student motivation and learning?
    a. Reading *A River Runs Through It* to study fly-fishing and character development and relationships
    b. Watching *Footloose* to study dance movements and themes of freedom, rebellion, and repression
    c. Designing a joint PE and Family and Consumer Sciences unit that combines nutrition and exercise
    d. Developing a morning walk/run project together with the principal to help students focus better

104. Which statement is most reflective of the benefits of engaging parents in student physical education experiences?
    a. Parents can enrich learning with different knowledge and experience than teachers have.
    b. Teachers learn about student interests and motivations from students, not their parents.
    c. Teachers will not learn what parents want and hope for their children by involving them.
    d. Family knowledge is not something teachers can access by collaborating with the parents.

105. What is true about how teachers can engage community members and groups in physical education (PE) programs?
    a. It would be inappropriate to solicit funds from local health agencies to buy sports equipment.
    b. Local trophy companies are in business to make money and will not donate for school events.
    c. Local governments lack departments that could talk to students about community resources.
    d. When PE teachers plan Olympics-themed events, they may find volunteers from local colleges.

106. What is MOST accurate about different physical activities that teachers can encourage students to engage in before and after school?
    a. All schools have cheerleaders established for their athletic teams.
    b. Teachers encouraging students to bicycle will find no help online.
    c. Teachers should avoid advising canoeing because it is dangerous.
    d. Students who like art, self-expression, and music can try dancing.

107. For a student who has joint problems but wants to be physically active, which is the best extracurricular activity?
    a. Skiing
    b. Swimming
    c. Skateboarding
    d. Playing soccer

108. As an event that promotes opportunities for physical activity, which of the following is a characteristic of National Dance Day?
    a. Its events revolve around a single headquarters.
    b. Its activities are limited to certain dance classes.
    c. Its instruction includes nonambulatory persons.
    d. Its dance routines are all for beginning dancers.

109. Which of these characterizes teachers' reflections that best inform their physical education instruction?
    a. They reflect not only on themselves but also on students and class elements.
    b. They reflect on student personalities and behaviors, not school demographics.
    c. They reflect only on emotional and social influences to student performance.
    d. They reflect on each student's abilities and needs rather than class dynamics.

110. A physical education teacher has included an objective for student heart rates to reach a target range when they play a sport. The teacher discovers the majority of students did not reach that target. Which teacher response to this discovery is the best example of using reflection to inform instruction?
    a. The teacher decides students were not playing hard enough and gives them a pep talk.
    b. The teacher experiments with having the students play the next game at faster speeds.
    c. The teacher changes the rules of the game so all students will participate more actively.
    d. The teacher might do either (B) or (C) or even both of these but is less likely to use (A).

111. As employed by effective physical education teachers, what is reflection?
    a. An exercise they engage in periodically to review their effectiveness
    b. A process they utilize to support their curriculum planning and design
    c. A tool that they depend upon for adjusting curriculum and instruction
    d. A process they rely on continually to improve all elements of teaching

112. Among professional development activities a physical education teacher can pursue, which of these would MOST directly enrich the students' learning experiences?
    a. Obtaining an advanced certification in physical education or some related discipline
    b. Obtaining certification for an activity that many students want to do
    c. Obtaining a position on a national, state, or local physical education committee
    d. Obtaining invitations to present papers at workshops and conferences

113. Professional development at its best accomplishes which of these?
    a. Improves primarily the teacher's own knowledge and skills
    b. Improves both a teacher's and his or her colleagues' expertise
    c. Improves primarily the expertise of the teacher's colleagues
    d. Improves teaching practices primarily at the classroom level

114. What do professional growth and educational interactions enable physical education teachers to do?
    a. To learn more, stay current, partner, and improve learning communities
    b. To develop their own self-confidence rather than inspire others' initiative
    c. To perform the functions of role modeling more than those of advocating
    d. To demonstrate achievement taking priority before professional integrity

115. What advantages does Fitbit technology include for physical education teachers and students?
    a. Weight control but not sleep quality
    b. Self-monitoring but not competition
    c. Fashion appeal as well as motivation
    d. Stand-alone fitness progress tracking

116. The MyFitnessPal, Endomondo, and Fitbit digital fitness apps all share what in common?
    a. Sync
    b. Recipes
    c. Audio feedback
    d. Social networking

117. According to experiences reported by physical education teachers, what are some characteristics of technology in applications such as GradeBookPro?
    a. Apps like this enable physical education teachers to use most of their time for teaching.
    b. Apps like this reduce final grade disputes by consolidating student data.
    c. Apps like this can exponentially speed up the task of taking attendance.
    d. Apps like this streamline all these and a great many more teacher tasks.

118. What have physical education teachers found about using apps like Coach's Eye, iCoachview, and so on with their students?
    a. Student enthusiasm helps them appreciate constructive criticism.
    b. Students typically cannot use apps after only brief demonstration.
    c. Students are uncomfortable seeing their performance postgame.
    d. Students experience delayed feedback when teachers play videos.

119. What is true about technology tools that let schools and teachers use electronic records?
    a. They are more efficient but only for maintaining records.
    b. They permit faster, easier access but afford less security.
    c. They not only keep records but also produce new records.
    d. They are not subject to paper confidentiality regulations.

120. Which of the following activities represents a physical education teacher's using technology to enhance his or her professional development?
    a. Spending more time on scoring tests instead of time on interpreting them
    b. Recording, playing back, and analyzing teaching practices for improvement
    c. Searching online for research resources with their field's latest innovations
    d. Using programs to organize and deliver information to students and others

Answers and Explanations

1. **D:** The gracilis (A) is an inner thigh muscle that runs between the pubic bone and the tibia (shin bone). The gastrocnemius (B) is a muscle in the lower leg. The gluteus minimus (C) is the third of the four buttocks muscles: The gluteus maximus is the largest; the gluteus medius is the second largest; the gluteus minimus the third largest. The tensor fasciae latae (D) is the fourth and smallest.

2. **A:** Body mass index (BMI) is the ratio of weight to height squared, which shows the relationship between a person's weight and height. It is not the ratio of abdominal to total fat (B), fat to muscle (C), or fat to weight (D). Healthy BMIs are generally between 18.5 and 24.9. Below 18.5 is considered underweight, and 25 to 29.9 is considered overweight (with a few exceptions; e.g., some people with very high muscle mass rather than fat may have higher BMIs). A BMI of 30 or above is considered obese.

3. **C:** Earlier researchers attributed motor development to genetically determined maturation, not experience alone, (A) and (D). Later research findings show that a combination and interaction of maturation and experience are responsible for motor development. Thus, the trend has not been away from maturation alone toward experience alone (B) but toward growth and development combined with learning and their interactions.

4. **C:** Summation of forces refers to producing the maximum possible force from any movement using multiple muscles. Adding up the forces generated by each individual muscle yields the total force or summation of forces. Related to this, the order of use is that the largest body parts are slowest, and being stronger and hence the initiators of power, they move first; the smallest body parts are fastest, and being in charge of coordination and refinement, they move last. Thus, the largest, slowest parts do not move last (A), and the smallest, fastest parts do not move first (B). Therefore, (D) is also incorrect.

5. **B:** Center of gravity (COG) is not in the same location in every human body (A); neither is it always in a certain location of every individual body (C). Rather, it shifts corresponding to changes in the positions of the body parts (B). COG is not precisely the same as center of mass, but their difference is negligible, so for all practical purposes they are considered synonymous; however, center of gravity or mass is not the same as center of pressure (D).

6. **A:** Torque equals force times its perpendicular distance from the axis of rotation. Thus, (D) is incorrect. The greater the perpendicular distance between the axis and the force, the greater the torque. Thus, the skater with longer arms will rotate faster because that skater's arms have a longer perpendicular distance from the body, that is, axis of rotation. The skater with shorter arms will rotate slower, not faster (B). Hence, with equal force applied, they will not both rotate at equal speeds (C).

7. **D:** In spatial awareness, locations and levels (A) of the body or body parts can be high, middle, or low. Personal space (B) refers to the space immediately surrounding an individual person, as opposed to general space, which refers to the total space available or playing area. Directions (C) of movement in space include forward, backward, up, down, and sideways. Planes of movement in space include vertical, horizontal, and circular paths (D).

8. **A:** In quality of movement, the flow of movement can be bound, that is, interrupted, or free, that is, sustained. Effort (B), or the amount of force in a body movement, can be strong, medium, light, or other increments within each of these. Speed (C) of movement can be quick, slow, or any degree in between these. Rhythm (D) of body movement can be constant, accelerating, or decelerating.

9. B: The relationship of on or off means engaged in a movement activity (on) or in suspension of a movement activity (off), which may involve multiple bodies but also can involve only a single body. The relationship of near or far (A) must involve a body plus another body or an object as it refers to the distance between them. The relationship of moving together or with opposition (C) necessarily involves two or more bodies. The relationship of symmetrical or asymmetrical (D) movement involves a body plus one or more other bodies or objects: If they have corresponding points or proportions, their relationship is symmetrical; if they do not have these, their relationship is asymmetrical.

10. B: In exercise science, the principle of specificity means that, to improve certain body parts, muscles, or sports movements and techniques, one must exercise those specific parts, muscles, or movements and techniques. Exercising the lower body will not strengthen the upper body or vice versa. Specificity also means that one must practice football skills, for example, to improve in football rather than only exercising for general body conditioning: The latter may be required for and benefit playing football but will not improve specific football skills; only practicing those skills specifically will. The principle of overload (A) means extra or unaccustomed stimuli are required to make the body respond beyond its normal levels. If the question had said someone bench presses more weight than usual to make the upper body stronger, this would illustrate overload as well as specificity. The principle of adaptation (C) means the body adjusts to processes and demands, making activities easier over time and eventually requiring variation for continuing progress. The principle of progression (D) means individuals must progress at certain rates natural to them to achieve results and avoid injuries.

11. A: When we exercise, our bodies access their stored glycogen supplies for energy; glycogen depletion triggers the release of endorphins, hormones that generate feelings of euphoria. These feelings of well-being are short-term effects of exercise. The prevention and relief of depression through regular exercise are long-term effects. So are lower risks of heart attacks and strokes (C), which result from consistent aerobic exercise over time. While a short-term effect of exercise is an immediate increase in blood circulation, a reduction of blood pressure and pulse (D) can be a long-term effect of exercising regularly for at least a few months.

12. C: Good nutrition provides the body with more energy, which enables and motivates people to exercise. Reciprocally, getting regular exercise can help to control the appetite and prevent overeating. Exercising does not mean you can eat anything you want (A). Both calcium and other nutrients in the diet and weight-bearing exercise can prevent loss of bone density and osteoporosis (B). A combination of exercise and a nutritious diet, not one or the other, prevents high blood pressure, high cholesterol (D), diabetes, and other diseases that unhealthy lifestyles often contribute to or cause.

13. D: The skin is a part of the integumentary system, along with the hair, nails, nerves, and glands. The skin controls fluid loss, protects deep tissues, and synthesizes vitamin D. The skeletal system (A) gives the body its bony supporting structure, protects vital organs, collaborates with muscles in body movement, stores calcium, and produces red blood cells. The muscular system (B) maintains posture, collaborates with the bones in body movement, uses energy, and generates heat. The lymphatic system (C) retrieves fluids leaked from capillaries and contains white blood cells, and parts of it support parts of the immune system.

14. B: Our respiratory systems inhale air, of which oxygen is one component. From that inhaled air, the respiratory system delivers oxygen to the body. Through gas exchange, it then expels carbon dioxide (CO_2) from the body as we exhale. The respiratory system obtains oxygen from the air we inhale; it does not create it, and it expels CO_2 rather than absorbing it (C). We do not use our respiratory systems to exhale oxygen or inhale CO_2 (D).

15. B: The highest level (A) of the brain contains command neurons that initiate the intention to produce body movement and send the message to the middle level. The mid-level neurons (B) in the sensorimotor cortex of the cerebral cortex, the basal ganglia of the subcortical nuclei, the cerebellum, and the brain stem produce a motor program by determining necessary postures and movements and coordinating these with information about body posture and surroundings that they receive from eye, vestibular, skin, joint, and muscular receptors. They send this program to the lowest level (C) of the motor neurons and interneurons, which determine muscle tension and joint angles. Therefore, (D) is incorrect.

16. A: Pioneers in the study of motor development, including Arnold Gesell and Myrtle McGraw, achieved extensive, thorough catalogues of the stages and milestones of motor development during the 1930s and 1940s. However, from the 1950s to the 1980s, there was little further progress in the field as scientists assumed everything had been covered. Thus, (B), (C), and (D) are incorrect. During the 1980s, further research was stimulated when new technologies and methods, pioneered by Nicholai Bernstein's dynamic systems concept, Esther Thelen's extension of it, and James and Eleanor Gibson's modern motor skills theory emphasizing perceptual-motor learning, shifted scientific perspectives away from the former emphasis on neuromuscular maturation as the explanation for motor development and toward more complex interactions of perceptual information, adaptive learning of movement control, and peripheral factors with maturation.

17. C: Posture has played an equally significant role in classical and contemporary theories of motor development. In classical theories attributing motor skill development to neuromuscular maturation, increasingly vertical posture was evidence of babies' progress as their cerebral cortices developed more control over their abilities to overcome gravitational pull. In contemporary theories attributing motor development to dynamic systems and relationships between perceptions and actions, posture became the stable biomechanical basis for action and was evidence of learning about new perception–action systems. Hence, posture was not more important to either classical theories (A) or contemporary theories (B). Neither did these theories regard its role in motor development as minor (D).

18. D: Balance includes static balance, that is, the ability to balance while remaining stationary, and dynamic balance, that is, the ability to balance while shifting the weight as in walking, climbing, dancing, and so on. Flow (A) involves combining different movements and movement sequences in a smooth, continuous manner and performing movements within limited times and spaces. Time (B) involves distinguishing among various speeds and being able to increase and decrease movement speeds. Force (C) involves producing the amount of tension or effort required for various movements and modifying these as necessary.

19. B: Compared to regular baseball, softball has a bigger ball, a smaller infield, fewer innings, and a different pitch. Softballs are 11 to 12 inches around, whereas baseballs are 8 to 9 inches around. Softball infields have their bases 60 feet apart, whereas baseball infields have their bases 90 feet apart. Regulation softball games consist of seven innings, whereas regulation baseball games consist of nine innings. Softball requires underhand pitching, whereas baseball typically uses overhand pitching.

20. C: In today's soccer, outfielders are allowed to contact the ball with their heads or torsos. Soccer teams consist of 11 players, not 9 (A). Soccer goalies can touch the ball with their arms or hands within their penalty areas, while it is in play (B). The Fédération Internationale de Football Association (FIFA) World Cup is held every four years, not every year (D).

21. A: The breaststroke uses the frog kick. The frog kick is also used in self-contained underwater breathing apparatus (SCUBA) diving and can be used for treading water. The butterfly (B) stroke uses the dolphin kick. The crawl (C) typically uses the flutter kick. Therefore, (D) is incorrect.

22. B: Physical education (PE) instructors can address negligence in instruction (A) by ensuring they teach students the correct procedures and protocols for safety and for equipment setup, use, and takedown and ensuring students understand and practice how to execute sport and movement activities beforehand. Because PE classes often are large and getting larger, they can address negligence best in supervision (B) by ensuring they continually and actively supervise students throughout all activities and enlisting students to practice peer supervision in addition to supplement teacher supervision. In transportation (C), teachers and coaches are liable outside of school and must obtain written parental consent; follow all school policies, practices, and procedures; and supervise student behavior on buses. In class environments (D), teachers and coaches must be alert for possible dangerous conditions, which can vary daily, and space students to limit hazards.

23. D: Physical education (PE) classes are generally larger than regular classes (A), increasing PE teacher liability. PE classes are also more likely to include outdoor as well as indoor activities than regular classes (B), so PE teachers must not only cover larger areas but also address areas with different physical characteristics. While regular classes may travel for field trips, PE classes travel much more often (C) to away games, meets, and other activities outside of school. Two more liability factors in PE classes are sports equipment: baseballs and bats, footballs, tennis balls and racquets, golf balls and clubs, discus, shot-puts, javelins, and so on can become or propel projectiles at high speeds, risking student injury; and swimming classes include the presence of water, risking slips, falls, and drowning.

24. C: When physical education (PE) classes involve a baseball, for example, injuries are much more likely when fielding teams include 30 or more students instead of only 9 as in regulation games. Teachers must instruct students wanting to field fly balls to call for them and other students to back away from them. Experts with legal and PE experience warn teachers to limit any gymnastics to only basic vaulting and tumbling and these only with individual spotters (A). Most average students cannot support their bodies or hang by their arms, making falls likely; falling from inverted positions risks spinal damage, paralysis, and death. Experts additionally warn PE teachers never to include trampolines in PE classes and also not in extracurricular activities (B) like gymnastics, cheerleading, and so on unless school insurance includes trampoline accidents, which are often not covered or incur excessive premiums. PE teachers should never discipline students using strenuous exercise (D), which is unsafe.

25. B: Abusing marijuana before physical education (PE) classes is more likely to cause impaired depth perception, which interferes with student ability to judge distances accurately in team sports, track and field, and so on. Both alcohol and marijuana abuse before PE classes are likely to impair and lower student energy (A). Alcohol abuse before PE classes is more likely to cause generally impaired judgment (C). Both alcohol and marijuana abuse before PE classes are likely to impair physical coordination (D).

26. A: Student substance abuse can cause death through auto accidents from driving under the influence, drug overdoses, homicide, suicide, drug-induced illnesses, human immunodeficiency (HIV) and acquired immune deficiency syndrome (AIDS), and so on. Organ damage (B) is primarily caused by substance abuse itself. Avascular necrosis (C), that is, loss of blood supply to a joint, is caused by abusing anabolic steroids to enhance performance or by abusing alcohol. HIV/AIDS transmission (D) is caused by sharing needles to inject drugs, by engaging in unprotected sex under the influence of substances, and from mothers to babies by abusing drugs during pregnancy or childbirth.

27. D: Alcohol, cocaine, Prozac, and other substances temporarily can reduce inhibitions so that students who are usually shy or introverted behave more sociably around peers (A). When students see substance use as a solution to being socially awkward and unpopular, they repeat it, which can lead to addiction. Conversely, students who were normally extroverted often withdraw socially when they become addicted

to substances (B). Students who normally demonstrate self-control often behave more impulsively under the influence of substances (C).

28. C: Activities that require agility and lower-body strength, which do not involve body contact (A), are most appropriate for coed participation and are less dependent on team assignment by student skill levels. For activities that require more upper-body strength (B), it is more important for physical education teachers to assign teams according to individual student skill levels to prevent injuries. Therefore, (D) is incorrect.

29. D: Ectomorphs have long, narrow, thin body shapes with little muscle or fat. The high jump (D) and long-distance running are examples of appropriate sports for this somatotype. Wrestling (A) and shot-putting (C) are more suitable for endomorphic body types, which tend to be pear-shaped with more fat on the torso and limbs but small wrists and ankles. Gymnastics (B) is more appropriate for mesomorphs, who tend to have triangular shapes and strong limbs with more muscle and less fat.

30. B: When physical education (PE) teachers help students to identify the similarities between new movement skills and those they learned previously, this promotes cognitive learning by helping students to transfer their existing knowledge. Other things PE teachers can do to promote cognitive learning include allowing slightly longer times for instruction and demonstrations (A) to enable student memorization of new skills and cues; varying their language to communicate appropriately for individual student vocabulary, cognitive level, processing ability, and comprehension (C); and giving students with greater capabilities more responsibility for their own learning (D) to promote their conceptual thinking.

31. B: Handling a hockey puck is an example of a performance skill that would be affected most by individual differences in the perceptual-motor ability of control precision. Football quarterbacking (A) is an example of a performance skill that would be affected most by individual differences in the perceptual-motor abilities of response orientation or choice reaction time. Dribbling a basketball (C) is an example of a performance skill that would be affected most by individual differences in the perceptual-motor ability of manual dexterity. Driving a race car (D) is an example of a performance skill that would be affected most by individual differences in the perceptual-motor ability of rate control.

32. C: Kayaking is an activity that most involves the physical proficiency of dynamic strength. Static strength (A) is most involved in an activity like weight lifting. Trunk strength (B) is most involved in an activity like pole-vaulting. Explosive strength (D) is involved most in an activity like the standing long jump.

33. B: This is a description of the command or direct method, which uses teacher-centered task instruction to promote psychomotor learning. The contingency or contract method (A) is a behavioral approach that uses specified rewards that are contingent on student task completion to reinforce psychomotor behaviors. The task or reciprocal method (C) uses stations whereby student learning of specific psychomotor tasks is integrated into the learning setup. Because (B) is correct, (D) is incorrect.

34. C: Research studies find that motor skills, endurance, and strength training all modify the spinal reflexes according to the specific behaviors each task requires. New blood vessels are formed (A) through endurance training but not motor skills or strength training. Motor maps are reorganized (B) through motor skills training but not endurance or strength training. New synapses are generated (D) through motor skills and strength training but not endurance training.

35. B: Human babies actually display coordinated arm–hand movements in the womb before birth, such as moving their thumbs to their mouths. The amniotic fluid provides buoyancy to make this easier. After

birth, gravity makes arm and hand movements harder for newborns, who initially exhibit arm flapping and jerky arm extensions (C) before progressing to successfully reaching for objects (A) around four to five months old. At this age, they only adjust their hand shapes to object shapes after touching them. They develop the ability to use visual information to change their hand shapes before touching objects (D) around the age of eight months.

36. A: In the earliest stages of their gait development, babies typically walk with their legs wide apart, toes pointing outward. They keep their legs straight rather than bending their knees (B). They do not let their arms swing in opposition as adults do, but they do not keep their arms by their sides (C) either. Rather, they tend to bend them upward at the elbows with the palms of their hands facing the ceiling. They do not roll from the heel to toe (D) of the foot as adults do. Instead, they either set each foot down flat all at once, or some babies walk on their toes. From first steps to toddling to adultlike walking, children go through marked yet gradual gait changes until around the age of seven years.

37. A: These steps are sequenced in order of ascending severity: First, the teacher gives the noncompliant student an oral warning that he or she is not following class rules. If the student fails to comply, second, the teacher gives the student a brief time-out from class to refocus his or her attention. If the student is still not complying upon returning, third, the teacher assigns another time-out wherein the student must write a response, for example, identifying the rules he or she broke and what he or she will do now to follow the class rules.

38. D: Among many kindergarten through Grade 12 physical education (PE) teachers across the United States surveyed about their class rules, themes that commonly and frequently recurred included that students should show respect (A) for themselves, others, the PE equipment, and the environment; that they should cooperate (B) with one another and their teachers; that they should try or do their best (C); and that they should be good listeners, not talking when teachers or classmates are talking and knowing when to talk, look, listen, and be quiet. Keeping eyes and ears open and mouth closed, and so on rather than speaking out freely (D) was not mentioned by any of the teachers surveyed.

39. D: While all of these class rules used by many American kindergarten through Grade 12 physical education (PE) teachers apply equally well to other subjects and classrooms, good sportsmanship—though also important in other classrooms in terms of treating others fairly in general, using teamwork in collaborative activities, and being good winners and losers whenever competition is involved—is even more important in PE classes, which more frequently and regularly involve competitive activities and team sports or games. Choices (A) and (B) are equally applicable to any classroom. Keeping one's hands to oneself (C), as well as one's feet and objects, applies more in PE classes due to their more physical nature but also can become an issue in other classrooms. However, sportsmanship is the most important rule for PE classes.

40. A: Physiological and psychological variables that influence individual ability and interest for learning are examples of the factor of readiness for learning. Examples of the factor of motivation (B) are internal conditions of needs and drives that are required for individuals to initiate goal-directed activities. Examples of the factor of reinforcement (C) are positive or negative events and behaviors that make an individual more likely to repeat the same behavior in response to a stimulus. Examples of the factor of individual differences (D) are student abilities, backgrounds, intelligence, personalities, and learning styles.

41. C: In the first, cognitive stage of motor learning, learners understand the activity's goal and nature (A) and make initial attempts to perform it that include major errors (B). In the second, associative stage, learners engage in practice to master the timing of the skill, and they make fewer errors that are more

consistent in nature (C). In the third, autonomous stage, learners perform the activity effortlessly and automatically (D), enabling them to redirect their attention to other aspects of the skill.

42. C: In effective cooperative learning activities, the students engage in productive, face-to-face interactions frequently and substantially, not occasionally (A). They are accountable and responsible for their group goals not only collectively but also personally and individually (B). They frequently do apply their interpersonal and small-group skills that pertain to their specific cooperative learning activity (C). They regularly, frequently conduct group processing of how their group currently functions in order to improve their group's future effectiveness, not simply to sustain its current effectiveness (D).

43. B: More advanced computer and video technology is more likely to help than harm physical education (PE) activity performance by enabling improved feedback and analysis. Strong winds affecting outdoor activities (A) either can help or hurt performance: For example, wind can interfere with tennis performance but improve sailing performance. The condition of equipment (C) can help performance when it is better but hurt performance when it malfunctions or fails. The other participants (D), for example, teammates or opponents, can help individual and team performance when they perform well but harm performance when they perform poorly.

44. A: Researchers have found that smaller class sizes and student–teacher ratios correlate with larger quantities of activity time, activity level, safety, and learning for students, whereas larger class sizes and student–teacher ratios correlate with smaller quantities of student activity times, levels, safety, and learning—that is, an inverse correlation. Studies show that students receive more and better physical education (PE) from teachers who teach only PE rather than dividing their teaching time and attention between PE and other subjects (B). Researchers are coming to increasing consensus that standards-based PE curriculum results in greater student physical activity (C). Well-maintained, safe, appropriate, and aesthetically appealing PE facilities and equipment also are found to increase and improve student activity (D).

45. A: The Institute of Medicine recommendation is for children to spend an hour a day in moderate to vigorous physical activity (MVPA). But studies show that, in actual schools, physical education (PE) classes last about 23 minutes a day, with only 10 of those minutes spent in MVPA. In other words, children get about one-sixth the MVPA that is recommended from school PE classes. Researchers conclude that not only must children be physically active outside of PE classes, but also schools must increase how much children are active during PE class times.

46. D: Involving the students in decision-making processes whenever possible is an example of the motivational strategy of giving students the freedom to choose among physical education (PE) activities. Another example of this strategy is giving students choices among more than one activity. Providing flexibility for students to adapt PE activities to their individual interests (A) and needs is an example of the motivational strategy of modifying activities and skills. Another example of this strategy is changing the rules, space, or equipment in an activity to facilitate student success (B). Matching the specific kinds of activities with individual students (C) is an example of the motivational strategy of giving ideal challenges to every student. Another example of this strategy is letting students select among materials or equipment to use in certain activities.

47. B: To enhance students' perceived physical competence, it is better for physical education (PE) teachers not to specify how many trials to complete during a certain time period (A) but rather to specify the time period for practicing without requiring any specific number of trials (B). This allows students to focus not on how many times they complete the actions but rather on perfecting their technique. Rather than emphasizing technical errors they make (C), it is better to emphasize which things students do well

technically, providing positive reinforcement that increases their motivation to practice. Varying assigned activities is more effective to minimize off-task student behavior than not varying them (D).

48. C: TARGET stands for task, authority, recognition, grouping, evaluation, and timing. Varying difficulty levels (A) refers to task. Giving students some responsibility for choice of activities (B) refers to authority. Acknowledging process and improvement rather than product (C) and outcome refers to recognition. Avoiding peer comparison through strategies that get students to form groups quickly and switch groups frequently (D) refers to grouping.

49. B: Research into physical activity and peer interactions consistently finds that health behavior and peer relationships influence one another reciprocally. Health behavior does not primarily influence peer relationships (A); neither do peer relationships mainly influence health behavior (C). Rather, their interactions are mutual. Therefore, it is not true that health behavior and peer relationships in students have no significant interaction (D).

50. D: Physical education (PE) teachers must always conduct regular safety inspections of facilities and equipment on a consistent basis. Rather than using extrinsic motivations (A) like external punishments or rewards, PE teachers are advised to enhance intrinsic student motivations to be responsible for learning. When student behaviors are inappropriate, PE teachers should not ignore them (B) but address them immediately. PE teachers do need to obtain and regularly renew certification in cardiopulmonary resuscitation (CPR) and automated external defibrillator (AED) use (C).

51. A: The most appropriate practice for physical education (PE) teachers to create productive environments and promote student responsibility and social skills is to design activities and situations deliberately for teaching and developing those skills rather than only taking advantage of teachable moments or allowing incidental learning to develop them (B). To support all students equally, PE teachers should include culturally diverse activities rather than only teaching U.S. team sports (C). Rather than letting highly skilled students dominate (D), PE teachers should provide challenges and encouragement equally to students of all developmental levels, ability levels, and disabilities.

52. D: For effective class behavior management plans, physical education (PE) teachers should define their expectations positively in terms of what they want the students to do, not negatively in terms of what they want them not to do (C). They should limit expectations to five at most, as students will be unable to remember more than that, and put them in writing, not orally (A), posted visibly in locker rooms and on classroom bulletin boards. They also should enforce their stated expectations consistently, not just occasionally (B).

53. B: Physical education (PE) teachers should not just tell students what to do (A) because they will stop listening to further instructions to follow the first one. For example, if the teacher says, "Each team pick up a ball," they will immediately do that and stop paying attention. Instead, PE teachers should tell students when before telling them what, for example, "When I say 'go,' each team pick up a ball." This way, students will keep paying attention while they wait for the teacher to give them the prompt before acting. The rule of threes does not mean giving three cues at a time (C); it means using the number three uniformly to help students remember, for example, three passes, three feet, three minutes, three seconds, and so on. The 80/20 rule does not mean 80 percent learn by doing and 20 percent from teaching (D) but the opposite: PE teachers should teach a concept until 80 percent of the class understands it because, during subsequent practice, the other 20 percent will learn by doing to understand it.

54. C: Experts recommend the rock, paper, scissors method for physical (PE) teachers to settle student disputes during classes because it is random and hence objective rather than subjective, which would be

unfair (D). These experts do not consider this method to be unprofessional (A), inappropriate, or childish (B). Using a random method ensures they are not treating any student preferentially in their decisions.

55. A: According to social psychologists, nonverbal communication has these primary functions: performing social rituals (A) like greetings, farewells, and so on; revealing personalities as well as interpersonal relationships (B); supporting verbal interactions (C); and expressing feelings (D).

56. D: All these formats are included in the definition of verbal communication: sending and receiving text messages (A); communicating among the Deaf using sign language (B); spoken conversations (C), both in person and over the phone; writing and reading e-mails; speaking on and listening to radio and TV programs, Skype, online videos and vlogs; and writing and reading on paper.

57. A: Experts advise coaches that they must first determine whether they have athletes' attention before communicating with them successfully, and second, whether they are explaining in a way that athletes can understand easily. Third, coaches must determine whether the athletes have in fact understood what they said, and fourth, whether the athletes believed what they told them (B). Fifth, coaches must determine whether their athletes have accepted what they told them (C) as well as understanding and believing it. To control a team or group of athletes, coaches also must be sensitive to the nonverbal cues they give (D), while the coaches are talking. These cues communicate whether the athletes are puzzled, confused, disbelieving, bored, resentful, disrespectful, and so on toward a coach and what he or she is saying.

58. B: "Follow through!" is an example of prescriptive feedback, which is specific. It specifies an instruction that corrects or improves what the student or athlete is doing or needs to do. In this example, it tells the student or athlete that, when batting, kicking, throwing, and so on, he or she must follow the movement through for it to be effective rather than stopping it abruptly upon contact or release. The other examples are all descriptive feedback, which is general. It gives students or athletes positive social reinforcement by encouraging or praising their performance in general but does not specify exactly what it was that they did well or need to do better or differently.

59. A: While feedback is important in physical education (PE) instruction, knowing when and when not to provide feedback is equally important to effective teaching. PE teachers need to give feedback to give students specific corrections to incorrectly performed techniques, for example. However, when a task furnishes inherent environmental feedback (B),—for example, a student throws a basketball, and it goes through the hoop—additional feedback may be unnecessary. When a student already has enough experience with a skill (C), sometimes PE teachers need not give them feedback. Also, when a teacher's demonstration enables students to see easily how to perform a skill correctly (D), they may need little or no additional feedback.

60. C: The sandwich approach consists of first giving the student or athlete positive reinforcement for something he or she did well, identifying one thing to correct or improve, and then giving positive reinforcement for something else he or she did well. By sandwiching the correction between two pieces of praise, the physical education (PE) teacher or coach makes it feel more acceptable and less critical of the student or athlete. This technique does not sandwich one piece of positive reinforcement between two corrections (D) but vice versa. The congruent feedback technique involves giving general reinforcement followed by specifying the skill being reinforced; for example, "Good job following through." This not only gives the student or athlete praise but specifies what he or she did well. Repeating the general reinforcement after specifying the skill (B) is not necessary. While teachers or coaches might also specify the skill and follow it with praise—for example "You followed through; good job!"—this is not followed by a different specific skill (A).

61. D: Music obviously is used along with choreography and performing dance movements, and it increases student motivation, control, endurance, and enjoyment during aerobic exercise (B). But it also is helpful in a wide range of other physical education (PE) activities. For instance, PE teachers can help students gain control over the speeds, rhythms, and evenness with which they can dribble basketballs (C) by having them practice in time to recorded music. They can play music for students to practice repeated chest passes and bounce passes with basketballs; this enables students to practice for longer times as well as control their speeds and intervals. Teachers can use music with different tempi for warm-up and cool-down exercises. Also, they can assign students to complete as many of a given action as possible while music continues to play.

62. B: A time-lapse bulletin board can begin with the physical education (PE) teacher labeling a board's theme (e.g., balance, strength, speed, teamwork, sportsmanship, a certain sport, etc.) posting about a dozen pictures to provide examples and ideas for students and get them started. The teacher then assigns students to bring in pictures—drawings, photos, diagrams, art, and so on that they have found or made—that apply to the board's identified theme. Over time, student contributions fill the board with pictures, which students can view, discuss, and use as illustrations to help them understand aspects of a learning unit or topic. PE teachers need not even have schools provide (A) or have to buy their own real bulletin boards; they simply can create a board by hanging large pieces of paper, poster board, or fabric on the wall. This project is completed by students, not just teachers (C). Students do not ignore such boards (D), especially when they contain their own and classmates' contributions.

63. A: Video recording technology has many advantages for physical education (PE) teachers in communicating instructional information to students. When a teacher demonstrates a technique or movement with outstanding expertise, this can be captured and preserved on video and repeated for many future demonstrations. This eliminates the possibility that another time the teacher is having a bad day and does not demonstrate as well. Body movements are much better demonstrated visually than described verbally (B): Students can see what to do and how rather than having to imagine it. Videos of the regular PE teacher's demonstration also help substitute and student teachers who cannot demonstrate, or demonstrate very differently, which can confuse students. Videos provide consistency and continuity, not boredom (C). To learn body movements, they must be repeated exactly the same way each time to form muscle memory; thus, variation is not interesting (D) but detracts from learning. Variation can be interesting when a dancer improvises from one performance to another but not for students to learn new movements.

64. C: The National Board for Professional Teaching Standards (NBPTS) include creating an environment of respect and rapport with students. The board provides an example for addressing student problem behaviors of having the misbehaving student describe his or her behavior, state what made it disruptive, and identify solutions for the problem. This standard's example does not advise for the teacher to do these things (A): The student must do them for ownership, responsibility, and understanding of his or her behavior. Neither should the teacher ask a classmate (B) to do them for the same reasons. The standard does not recommend giving concrete consequences and solutions instead of discussing the problem (D).

65. B: When the teacher writes a task on the board that students can begin upon entry to physical education (PE) class, this supports high expectations for students to take responsibility for classroom procedures and routines. While it encourages their independence in starting the activity, this does not mean the teacher will not be supervising them (A) thereafter. This teacher practice not only supports student independence in initiating activities; it also helps them comprehend their learning objectives and expectations (C) by the teacher's structuring the learning activities (D) he or she has provided for them.

66. D: It is not a good idea to keep class rules from parents in a misguided attempt to gain student trust (A). Parents need to be informed of the rules, so they know what is expected of their children and can make sure their children understand the rules. Teachers also protect themselves by informing parents of rules in advance: In the event of student behavior problems, injuries, or disputes, parents cannot subsequently deny knowledge or accuse teachers of not informing them. Giving the students copies of the rules to take home to parents (B) often means the parents never receive them. Postal mail (C) is much slower when today's technology enables almost instant transmission of e-mails (D), eliminating the potential for events to occur before parents receive the information.

67. C: The three main categories of fundamental movement skills (FMS) are locomotor (A), manipulative, (A and, (B), and stability (D). Within the main category of stability are included the subcategories of rotation, (B) and (C), and balance, (C) and (D). Activities like spinning, twirling, rocking, bending, and turning demonstrate rotation. Balance can involve both stationary and movement activities. Both rotation and balance are components of stability. Locomotor skills involve activities like walking, running, and so on. Manipulative skills include activities like throwing, catching, hitting, batting, kicking, and transporting objects.

68. B: Musical hoops is played like musical chairs, except children must jump into hoops instead of sitting on chairs when the music stops. This is appropriate for younger children. Freeze tag or blob tag (A) is more appropriate for children older than 5 years, up to 12 years old. Children must try to tag others while holding hands with those in their blob. This demands higher levels of coordination than younger children have. Follow the leader (C) is better as a warm-up activity for children age 5 to 12 years, as younger children can have difficulty with leading and following and with the variations in leaders and locomotor skills that teachers can use with older children. Therefore, (D) is incorrect.

69. A: Mastery is not one of the three phases of learning identified in landing skills. The three learning phases are: (1) discovery (B). In this phase, children do not yet demonstrate any stable base of support, land flat-footed with little knee bending, and explore how to land. (2) Development (D): in this phase, children show stable support bases. They learn to appreciate the value of shock absorption, bending their knees after their heels touch ground. They rotate forward upon landing and are more consistent about landing in order from toes to ball of foot to heel. They are able to land from various distances and heights. (3) Consolidation (C): in this phase, children demonstrate wide, stable bases of support; can land during unpredictable or changing circumstances; can land safely with control; use their hips, knees, and ankles to absorb shock; and land with confidence.

70. D: When learning to fall sideways and land on the hands, students should first learn to fall sideways from a kneeling position (A). Then they can practice rolling sideways down a wedge (B) to simulate falling down an incline. Then they learn while moving to fall, roll sideways, stand up (C), and keep moving. They begin this exercise from a walking speed and gradually increase to jogging then running (D). Thereafter, they can practice this activity with dodging. After mastering these activities, students can try in pairs to pull each other off balance and take turns tipping each other sideways from an all-fours position.

71. D: Experts advise physical education (PE) teachers and coaches that external feedback should not duplicate internal feedback (A). Rather, external feedback should replace missing internal feedback, as when a student asks the teacher why he or she keeps repeating the same technical error. Students do not request feedback most with advanced skills (B) but earlier in learning new skills. Experts recommend that lesser feedback is preferable to more feedback, not vice versa (C): As one author at Kinetics.com put it, "When in doubt, be quiet." To support the problem-solving skills necessary in learning, PE teachers and coaches help most by giving external feedback that directs students or athletes to focus on sources of

internal feedback, for example, body parts, positions, movements, and relationships to inform their learning processes.

72. A: Research finds that a higher quality of physical education (PE) teaching feedback is more important than a higher quantity (C). Studies show that skill development does not need more frequent feedback (B); in fact, practice can be more effective without feedback than with it. Researchers theorize that learners are forced to do more independent problem solving and attend more to internal feedback when they are not given external feedback. They also find that students and athletes become dependent on external feedback when they receive too much of it, regressing when it is withdrawn. Beginners need less precise feedback (D), while more advanced athletes need more precision to refine their skills.

73. C: When Cooper and Potts developed and named aerobics in the late 1960s, it originally focused on the ability of the heart and lungs to use oxygen in sustained physical activity. Cooper was the first to differentiate aerobic capacity from body flexibility (A) and muscular strength (B) and to notice that some people who were very flexible or very strong still did not have good endurance for running, biking, or swimming long distances. Although aerobics initially focused on cardiorespiratory endurance exclusively, today's aerobics classes combine all the elements of fitness (D), incorporating stretching for flexibility and strength training for the muscles along with movements that raise heart and breathing rates for cardiovascular fitness in their exercises.

74. B: Judo (A) is a Japanese martial art that uses throwing types of grappling. Kendo (B) is a Japanese martial art that uses a sword. Karate (C) is a Japanese martial art that uses strikes, mainly with the hands, though the legs are secondarily involved. Jujitsu (D) is a Japanese martial art that uses grappling holds. Of these four, Kendo is the only weapon-based martial art; the other three are unarmed.

75. B: Common arguments in the debate over standardized physical education (PE) tests include these: Opponents of standardized PE testing say people must enjoy physical activity in their youth to enjoy it in adulthood (A), and they argue that standardized testing does not support motivation to engage in lifelong physical activity. Proponents of standardized PE testing say that test scores enable students to gauge their progress relative (C) to national standards and student averages. Additionally, they argue that national standards and assessments accord PE the same importance as all other school subjects (D) that it deserves.

76. D: Recently, the issue that has become the greatest challenge to kindergarten to Grade 12 (K–12) school physical education (PE) is that time in school curricula for PE classes and activities has been reduced significantly to make time for other academic classes. Inadequate resources and parental support (A); overly large class sizes and teacher burnout (B); and violence, student drug abuse, and discipline problems (C) are also challenges to K–12 PE, but these are also equal challenges to other school subjects and to education in general.

77. C: Throwing at a stationary target (B) represents a beginner level of throwing skill. Throwing lead passes (A) represents an intermediate level of throwing skill. Throwing to teammates while being defended (C) by another player represents an advanced level of throwing skill. Therefore, these do not all represent similar levels of throwing skill (D).

78. A: Atlantoaxial instability consists of excessive movement at the junction of the atlas, or first cervical vertebra (C1), and axis, or second cervical vertebra (C2), due to bone or ligament abnormality. It includes neurological symptoms when the spinal cord also is involved. This condition would make it unsafe for a student to perform a forward roll (B). However, to meet a learning objective, a physical education teacher could substitute a log roll, which would be safe for a student with this condition (A). Therefore, it is

incorrect that no kind of roll should be assigned (C). Atlantoaxial instability is not necessarily that rare (D): It is caused by Down syndrome, a number of metabolic diseases, birth defects, traumatic spinal injuries, upper respiratory infections, rheumatoid arthritis, and surgeries to the head or neck. With so many different etiologies, the chances for a student to have this condition are not so remote.

79. C: National Association for Sport and Physical Education (NASPE) recommends that elementary school students should receive a minimum of 150 minutes per week of quality PE time in schools, meaning that somewhat more than this would not be too much. Thirty minutes per day most reflects the recommendation of 150 minutes per week as school is in session five days per week. A minimum of 15 minutes per day (A) is not enough. A maximum of 30 minutes per day (B) implies that more than this is bad, which does not reflect the NASPE recommendation. A maximum of 60 minutes for an entire week (D) is also far too little: This would break down to only 12 minutes daily, or two 30-minute classes per week, or three 20-minute sessions, four 15-minute sessions, and so on.

80. A: Physical education (PE) teachers should plan their lessons and programs and choose their teaching methods to reflect national, state, and local PE standards; the physical maturation and age of each individual child equally (B); the fitness levels and skill levels of each individual child equally (C); and the best instructional practices identified equally through research studies and teaching experience (D).

81. C: With U.S. populations and hence student populations rapidly becoming increasingly diverse, all teachers, including physical education (PE) teachers, must change their practices to adapt to these changes rather than simply continuing to do the same thing regardless (D). No single teaching style is proven to enhance all students' learning (A), so PE teachers are most likely to meet all student needs by using a variety of styles. The measure of educational effectiveness is the success of all students, not just some (B). If all of the students learn and meet the targeted learning objectives by the end of a lesson (C), this indicates that the PE teacher's educational efforts have succeeded.

82. D: Teachers can give students cards with adverbs they recently learned, have them look up synonyms and antonyms for these, and write them on the cards. The teacher then directs the students to perform movements in ways described by the adverbs on their cards. The teacher then has students pass their cards to classmates and repeat the activity with new words. This lesson integrates physical education (PE) and English language arts (ELA) skills. Performing movements and then working with words separately or vice versa, (A) and (B), do not integrate PE and ELA skills together into the same activity. Describing movements using the adverbs (C) makes a mental connection between words and movement, but the students are not actually performing any body movements; they are only describing them verbally, so this is an ELA activity rather than an integrated PE and ELA activity.

83. B: In high schools that do not have swimming pools, physical education (PE) teachers can look for opportunities such as pools at community recreation centers, county public pools, YMCA or YWCA pools, or privately owned pools, especially by parents and families of their students and ask for permission to use them. Another option at some schools having sufficient funds is to buy portable pools. If none of these is possible, PE teachers can teach swim strokes; make and give students task cards with written directions and diagrams of each stroke, kick, and breathing pattern and combination; and pair students to take turns, with one practicing on a bench and the other watching and giving feedback. Thus, it is not true that there is no way to teach swimming without a pool (D). However, PE teachers also should not assume it is safe for students to swim in water after mastering strokes on benches only; they will need supervised lessons and practice to transfer the skills.

84. A: The first step in the volleyball activity is for students to assume rotational positions, that is, with one setter in front and one in the back row, without overlapping. The second step is for a student to serve

the ball. In the third step, following the serve, students move from their rotational positions to their base positions. The fourth step is for players to defend against attack by watching, calling, and passing the ball.

85. A: When physical education (PE) teachers pose think-about questions to students, for example, asking them what the pros and cons are of certain playing formations, positions, or strategies or where they should be aiming their shots, and so on, they give the students a mental advantage by getting them to consider, analyze, and then plan their playing strategies. Thinking about what they just did in one practice session enables them to plan ahead for the next one and improve their game. When PE teachers read aloud the tasks or steps of a practice session, they ensure that player setup is timely rather than delayed (B). They should not alternate the sequence of practice plans (C) but always follow them in the sequence they are written. PE teachers should both verbally describe and physically demonstrate movements or actions, not do only one or the other (D).

86. D: "Match up" as a defense cue in basketball means that students should defend other players who are as similar to them in size, fitness, and skill level as possible—not just in size (C). This cue does not mean to pair up with another player (A). Staying near to the offensive players they are defending wherever they move on the court (B) is indicated to students with a cue of "Shadow" rather than "Match up."

87. B: The Heimlich maneuver should be performed only on someone who is choking and cannot breathe. This means the person cannot speak, so the Heimlich maneuver should not be performed on a student who says he or she is having trouble breathing (A). Someone who is choking and cannot breathe also cannot cough, so the Heimlich maneuver should not be performed on a student who is coughing (C), which means he or she can breathe. The Heimlich maneuver should be done first if someone is choking; cardiopulmonary resuscitation (CPR) should be started after that if the victim loses consciousness (D).

88. A: Structured observations involve informing both teacher and student of the observation and applying specific criteria for evaluating student performance in physical education (PE) assessment. Naturalistic observations involve not informing students of the observation to capture typical student behavior, such as during their daily practice in regular PE classes. Though naturalistic observations are more realistic regarding behaviors than structured observations, not vice versa (D), they have been criticized for being more subjective, whereas structured observations are more objective, not vice versa (B). Structured observations are equally good for assessing social skills, motor skills (C), and movement skills.

89. C: Tests on which students must write answers are least useful for assessing their performance of physical education skills, which typically must be physically demonstrated. Observational checklists (A) are more useful as teachers can watch students perform the skills to be assessed and mark whether they can do them or not or mark the degree to which they have mastered them. Rating scales of skill level (B) are more useful as teachers can observe student skill performance and then rate the level of mastery or skill they have attained on a scale with degrees between most and least. Graphs of performance data (D) are more useful as teachers can record numbers of successful demonstrations per session, and so on as points and connect these to form a line or curve showing progress over time. Graphs also can include a line indicating a criterion for reference, so performance points can be seen as above, below, and at this line.

90. A: The three main categories assessed by the Fitnessgram are: (1) aerobic capacity; (2) body composition; and (3) muscular strength, endurance, and flexibility. (A) correctly represents the three components of the third category. (B) lists categories (1) and (2) plus one component of category (3). (C) lists category (2), one component of category (3), and category (1) in that order. (D) lists one component of category (3), category (1), and another component of category (3) in that order.

91. C: Formative assessments measure student progress during the instructional process. They enable teachers to use the assessment results to inform ongoing instruction and adjust it to meet their students' particular needs and strengths, for example, making their pace faster or slower according to student learning rates; spending more or less time on different skills or areas according to which students have already mastered or are struggling with more; or replacing teaching methods that are ineffective for some students with different ones. Showing accountability (A), comparing student achievement to state or national population averages (B), and assessing whether instruction has helped students meet curriculum standards (D) are all functions of summative assessments rather than formative assessments.

92. C: According to the description, the test is reliable, meaning that it gives the same results every time it is administered, but it is not valid, meaning that it does not measure what it was intended to measure. Therefore, it is not correct that the test is neither reliable nor valid (A). It is not true that the test is valid but not reliable (B) but, rather, vice versa. The test is not both valid and reliable, and it is not simply misused (D); it is actually not valid because it does not test what it means or claims to test but assesses something else instead.

93. D: Labeling a diagram is an example of a traditional assessment approach. Other traditional approaches include short-answer, constructed-response, and fill-in-the-blank written questions; written matching tests or worksheets; and written multiple-choice or true–false questions. Writing down a personal fitness plan (A) is an example of a written alternative assessment. Additional examples include research papers, essays, stories, poems, anecdotes, journals, logs, checklists, rating scales, brochures, advertisements, rubrics, performance records, newspapers, magazines, projects, pre-assessment inventories, surveys, questionnaires, interviews, editorials, and reflections. Performing dance movements (B) and playing sports games (C) are examples of alternative performance task assessments. Additional examples include locomotor or gymnastics routines, officiating games, making fitness assessments or oral reports, teaching lessons, warm-up routines, showcases, debates, skits, role-plays, or interviews.

94. B: Physical education (PE) teachers can provide kindergarten through Grade 2 (K–) students with log sheets with a prepared left column and an empty right column. The left side uses simple statements like "I have a strong heart," "I have strong muscles," "I can do movements over and over again," and "I can stretch," accompanied by graphic pictures (a heart, a bicep, a figure with arrows indicating repeated movement, and a figure with arrows or lines depicting stretching) to represent cardiovascular endurance, muscular strength, muscular endurance, and flexibility, respectively. In the blank right side, children make drawings or cut and paste pictures illustrating their activities (e.g., running, lifting, dancing, stretches, etc.) in each category. Teachers can guide this activity and collect the products to get assessment information. Writing journal entries (A), notes (C), or cards (D) is inappropriate for students with the limited writing skills of K–2 levels, as is independently turning in records regularly (C) or periodically (D) on a schedule at these ages.

95. D: Individuals with Disabilities Education Act (IDEA) regulations mandate that students with disabilities should be assessed using multiple instruments rather than just one (A). While these instruments should be valid, reliable, and technically sound, they may or may not be standardized: If a formal standardized test does not allow a disabled student to demonstrate individual strengths and needs, it may be inappropriate. While multiple instruments are required, they should be varied rather than all similar (B). The assessment instruments should not only measure disabilities (C) but also abilities.

96. B: In addition to referrals, criteria indicating that a student should be evaluated to determine eligibility for adapted physical education (APE) include that the student performs below his or her ability

level in group settings (A); has social behaviors that interfere with his or her or others' learning more than one-third of class time (B); has scored below average in two or more parts of the state physical fitness test used by the school district (C); and scored 1.5 or more standard deviations below the norm on the norm-referenced test used (D) by the school or district.

97. B: As one example of how educators can and should collaborate to meet student needs, both adapted physical educators (APEs) and classroom teachers are advised by experts to use the instructional methods they learn from occupational therapists (OTs) to help preschoolers with developmental delays to learn fine motor and manipulative skills. These strategies are not limited to implementation by OTs only (A), APEs but not classroom teachers (C), or classroom teachers but not APEs (D). All three disciplines should use them to meet these children's needs.

98. C: Psychologists provide IQ testing and behavior management programs, training, and implementation as well as mental status examinations, therapy, and counseling. Administrators (A) do not. They supervise faculty and staff; help with curriculum development, programs, and initiatives; manage school facilities; plan and manage school budgets; and have many other duties. School nurses (B) provide physical health services, not mental health or psychological services. Special education teachers (D) provide specialized instruction in a variety of areas to students with disabilities who require special education services; write and coordinate implementation of individual education plans (IEPs), and have many other duties, but they do not conduct IQ testing, mental health status examinations, or psychological evaluations used to determine eligibility for special education services; psychologists or behavior specialists do.

99. A: Large-scale state research has found that student cardiovascular fitness achievement and healthy body mass index (BMI) scores correlate positively with student scores on the state academic achievement test of knowledge and skills. Other research has found that children who are more physically fit demonstrate not only quicker reaction times but also more accurate responses (B). Another investigation found that children burn more calories and take nearly twice as many steps during teacher-led fitness activities as during active gaming, not vice versa (C). Other studies show that intense exercise is followed by improvement in cognitive function (D).

100. C: Kinetics is the division of biomechanics that studies the forces causing motion. Newton's First Law of Inertia, Second Law of Momentum, and Third Law of Reaction are most closely related to kinetics. Coplanar vectors (A) belong in the biomechanics division of vector algebra. Kinematics (B) is the biomechanics division that describes motion. Kinematics involves physics concepts including mass, center of gravity, inertia, displacement, linear and angular motion, linear and angular velocity, and acceleration. The biomechanics division of forces (D) involves concepts including center of pressure; force line; resultant force; muscular forces, joint forces, joint reaction forces, ground reaction forces, resisting forces, inertial forces, and gravitational forces; and fulcrums, levers, rotation, couples, equilibrium, weight, friction, and mechanical advantage.

101. B: Differentiation is a calculus technique for finding a quantity's rate of change, used in biomechanics to get derivatives of curves or functions like velocity, acceleration, and jerk, which are derivatives of displacement. Integration is a calculus technique to determine the area between an x-axis and a curve, used in biomechanics to obtain integrals like velocity as an integral of acceleration, displacement as an integral of velocity, and work as an integral of power. Composition and resolution of vectors (A) in biomechanics are ways of combining coplanar and concurrent vector quantities by using vector algebra, not calculus. The parallelogram method (C) is a method for resolving vectors in different directions in biomechanics that is based on geometry, not calculus: The parallelogram is a geometric shape. Because (B) is correct, (D) is incorrect.

102. A: Other than terms that have been translated into English for use by English-speaking people, a great deal of ballet terminology is in French because, historically, the dance form was popularized in France. While ballroom dance uses many Spanish (C) terms, especially related to Latin ballroom styles and techniques, ballroom also incorporates many French terms taken from ballet to describe steps also taken from ballet, for example, the passé step, chainé turns, pirouettes, and so on. Italian (B) is not shared in common by ballet and ballroom dance. Although ballet technique was highly developed in Russia later in its history after its early popularization in France, and Russia remains a stellar center of the ballet discipline today, ballet does not use Russian (D) terms, and neither does ballroom dance.

103. D: Working together with the principal to develop an exercise program that benefits student learning by enhancing the environment is an example of using administrator support and collaboration. (A) is an example of collaborating with an English language arts (ELA) teacher by using a novel to study a sport for the physical education (PE) component and character development and relationships for the ELA component. (B) is also an example of how to collaborate with an ELA teacher by watching a movie, studying its dance movements for the PE component and its themes for the ELA component. (C) is an example of collaborating with a Family and Consumer Sciences teacher by combining nutrition with exercise—a very natural and valuable combination as good nutrition and physical activity interact and mutually support one another in healthy lifestyles.

104. A: Teachers have expertise in the subject areas they teach and often in other areas as well, but parents who work in various occupations can enrich student education further by contributing their knowledge and experience in additional areas when physical education teachers invite them to collaborate. For example, a parent who is a cardiologist can talk to students about how choices in physical activity, nutrition, and weight management affect the heart. While teachers learn about their students' interests and motivations directly from the students through relationships and conversations with them, they also can learn additional information from their parents (B). Moreover, teachers can learn about parental expectations and aspirations for their children by involving them (C). Another benefit of engaging parents in their children's physical education is that teachers not only access family knowledge (D); they also have opportunities to communicate their recognition and respect for it, strengthening their relationships with students, parents, and families.

105. D: When physical education (PE) teachers want to hold events with Olympics themes for students, their local colleges are good places for them to find students willing to volunteer their time and work to help. PE teachers whose schools are short on funds for sports equipment can solicit financial assistance from local health and wellness agencies, which is not inappropriate (A) as these organizations may be able and often want to help. PE teachers also can ask local trophy companies to donate some of their products—and even refreshments as well—to student athletic events; these businesses frequently welcome the good public relations and advertising they can get by helping out schools (B). Local governments do have a department where PE teachers can recruit representatives to present to students about the use of community resources (C): their county and city Parks and Recreation Departments.

106. D: Dancing is a way to engage in physical activity before and after school that incorporates artistry, self-expression, and music. Teachers can encourage students with these interests to try some style of dancing to get enjoyable physical activity. Not all schools have cheerleaders for their athletic sports teams (A). Therefore, in schools that do not, teachers can encourage and help interested students to organize competitive cheer teams as a form of physical activity. Teachers encouraging students to bicycle for physical fitness, learning, sightseeing, adventure, and fun can find plenty of resources on the Internet (B) that offer biking supplies, information, and opportunities. Teachers should not avoid advising able and interested students to try canoeing for fear of danger (C): It provides an outdoor physical activity that

combines physical fitness, safety skills, wilderness survival skills, adventure, and interaction with nature. Trained, experienced instructors and guides are available to teach and supervise learners and ensure their safe experiences.

107. B: Of the activities named, swimming is ideal for students with joint problems because it puts no weight or stress on the joints. The buoyancy of the body in water keeps weight and impact off the joints. Students can be active and get exercise without aggravating joint conditions or pain. Skiing (A) requires a lot of knee bending and turning, hip swiveling, and bearing weight on the joints, so it is not compatible with joint problems. Skateboarding (C) also involves much knee bending and turning, as well as jumping and landing, and would be hard on joint problems. Playing soccer (D) requires running and kicking, again putting too much impact on the joints. These other sports also are done on the ground and subject to gravity, whereas swimming relieves the joints of weight.

108. C: National Dance Day (NDD), the brainchild of TV show *So You Think You Can Dance (SYTYCD)* creator, producer, and judge Nigel Lythgoe, is hosted by the Dizzy Feet Foundation charity, which Lythgoe and movie director, producer, choreographer, and *SYTYCD* guest judge Adam Shankman cofounded. This national day was made official by Congresswoman Eleanor Holmes Norton (D–D.C.). Its events are held jointly in Los Angeles, California; Washington, D.C.; and New York, New York; giving it multiple locations (A). Americans also are invited to hold events in their communities nationwide on NDD. NDD encourages creative applications like flash mobs, dance-a-thons, charitable dance events, fund-raising to support access to dance for youth, and whatever ideas people have (B). It incorporates video instruction, including a video choreographed and demonstrated by Lythgoe, while seated for nonambulatory persons (C). NDD videos also include both beginner and advanced dance routines (D).

109. A: Effective physical education (PE) teachers who are skilled in reflection engage not only in productive self-reflection but also in reflection about their students and about every element of their classes. They reflect about individual student personalities, behaviors, and dispositions as well as about the demographics of their schools (B) and how these affect class composition, student needs and interests, and interpersonal student interactions. In addition to emotional and social factors that influence student performance, reflective PE teachers also reflect about environmental, physical, and cognitive factors that affect their performance (C). They reflect not only on student abilities and needs, but also on classroom dynamics (D), and consider all of these in context. This reflection about every aspect of each class enables PE teachers to plan and deliver culturally sensitive, personally meaningful, and outcome-oriented lessons for their students.

110. D: A teacher using reflection to inform instruction is less likely to use (A) as placing the responsibility for meeting the objective entirely with the students betrays a lack of reflection. Reflective teachers evaluate how students respond to their instruction, analyze their own design and implementation of lessons, evaluate the results, and determine how they can change what they do to promote the best outcomes for their students. Thus, the teacher using reflection might see whether having the students play the next game faster (B) will increase their heart rates to the target range, or change the game rules to enhance more active participation by all students (C), or even both of these.

111. D: Effective physical education teachers do not use reflection periodically (A), or only for planning and designing curriculum (B), or only for adjusting the curriculum and instruction (C) after planning and designing. Rather, they utilize reflection continuously every day to improve all aspects of their teaching (D). They use reflection to incorporate their students' interests and needs and their own interests as well. They use it to consider teaching resources and interdisciplinary opportunities. They also use it to consider their own strengths and weaknesses as teachers and how they can supplement their instructional practices to take advantage of the strengths and compensate for the weaknesses.

112. B: These are all examples of good ways that physical education teachers can pursue professional development. However, if a teacher finds out that many students are interested in a certain activity, then obtains certification to teach that activity, that would most directly enrich their learning experiences. At the same time, this also would expand the teacher's expertise and enrich the school's curriculum.

113. B: The best professional development not only improves a teacher's own expertise (A) and that of the teacher's colleagues (C) but both mutually as well as enabling physical education teachers to promote their own discipline. It enables teachers to improve instruction not only at the classroom level (D) but also at schoolwide and districtwide levels.

114. A: By pursuing and achieving professional growth and participating in professional educational interactions, physical education teachers are able to learn more information and skills; stay up-to-date on current research; collaborate with colleagues and exchange ideas with them; and improve their learning communities' quality. They not only develop their own self-confidence; they also inspire initiative in others (B). They function as both role models and advocates (C). They demonstrate not only achievement but also professional integrity (D), both in their own disciplines and beyond in their wider educational communities.

115. C: Fitbit devices can help physical education teachers to support and increase student motivation and also include a line of designer fashion accessories. They can be used for both controlling weight and monitoring sleep quality (A). Students can self-monitor their own progress using Fitbit devices; they also can use them to challenge and compete with friends (B). They are not just stand-alone progress trackers (D); they also sync wirelessly with mobile smartphones and tablets and with charts, graphs, and badges available online for documenting improvements and gaining insights about physical fitness.

116. A: MyFitnessPal is an app that features healthy recipes (B) and an extensive food database, whereby users can enter meals to calculate caloric and nutritional content. The Endomondo Sports Tracker features Audio Coach feedback (C) on user exercise performance. Endomondo and Fitbit both include social networking (D) capabilities for sharing fitness motivation, goals, progress, support, and reinforcement with friends. One thing these apps share in common is that they all sync (A) with each other as well as with other apps, devices, and online tools. MyFitnessPal and Endomondo sync with heart-rate monitors as well as with each other and Fitbit.

117. D: Physical education teachers report that apps like Apple's GradeBookPro enable them to spend much more of their class time actually teaching by reducing the time it takes them to perform administrative tasks like taking attendance (C); using standard or weighted grading systems; and displaying assignment, absence, percentage, and other student data all on one page, making disputes at the end of the course or year less likely (B). This app and similar ones enable teachers to create reports and assignments easily; e-mail current attendance and grade status to students; send copies of assignments across classes; quickly take and attach student photos to files, helping them learn students' names sooner; record grades with far greater speed and ease; and overall, streamline and make more efficient all of the tasks that used to be cumbersome, even irrelevant, yet are necessary.

118. A: Physical education (PE) teachers find that their students are enthusiastic about apps that allow them to view their and classmates or teammates' athletic performance. This enthusiasm makes it easier for teachers to create positive learning environments wherein students are more appreciative of constructive criticism and more motivated to improve their performance. PE teachers find that, after only a brief demonstration, students can easily use them (B) for recording one another, viewing the recordings, and giving each other feedback. Teachers find student athletes really enjoy watching their

performance postgame (C) in the locker room. They can much more easily identify which strategies and tactics they used were most and least effective through this viewing. Also, when PE teachers use apps to record video and they play it back, students get much more immediate feedback (D).

119. C: Technology tools are more efficient and not just for keeping electronic records (A): They also can produce new records; for example, advanced programs and applications can compute statistical analyses of many kinds of educational data, like student enrollment, attendance, teacher–student ratios, athletic performance, parent involvement, statistics on competitive sports teams, community standing, progress relative to accountability measures, and comparisons of current years to past years. Today's technology tools not only maintain more accurate records and perform calculations to produce new records; they provide more organized and legible documents, enable quicker and easier access, and yet are also more secure (B) than paper records. Electronic records are subject to the same confidentiality regulations as paper records (D).

120. B: When a physical education (PE) teacher records video of his or her own teaching practices, plays it back, and analyzes those practices to improve them, this represents using technology to enhance professional development. Technology enables PE teachers to spend less time on scoring tests and more on interpreting them, not vice versa (A). With automated test scoring, they have more time to interpret test results to inform the lessons they plan and the instruction they give. When a PE teacher searches online for research resources containing the field's latest innovations (C), this represents the teacher's using technology to locate resources. When a PE teacher uses programs (e.g., Microsoft Word, Excel, Power Point, etc.) to organize and deliver information to students and others (D), like other teachers, parents, and attendees, to professional conferences and conventions, this represents using technology to present information.

Secret Key #1 - Time is Your Greatest Enemy

Pace Yourself

Wear a watch. At the beginning of the test, check the time (or start a chronometer on your watch to count the minutes), and check the time after every few questions to make sure you are "on schedule."

If you are forced to speed up, do it efficiently. Usually one or more answer choices can be eliminated without too much difficulty. Above all, don't panic. Don't speed up and just begin guessing at random choices. By pacing yourself, and continually monitoring your progress against your watch, you will always know exactly how far ahead or behind you are with your available time. If you find that you are one minute behind on the test, don't skip one question without spending any time on it, just to catch back up. Take 15 fewer seconds on the next four questions, and after four questions you'll have caught back up. Once you catch back up, you can continue working each problem at your normal pace.

Furthermore, don't dwell on the problems that you were rushed on. If a problem was taking up too much time and you made a hurried guess, it must be difficult. The difficult questions are the ones you are most likely to miss anyway, so it isn't a big loss. It is better to end with more time than you need than to run out of time.

Lastly, sometimes it is beneficial to slow down if you are constantly getting ahead of time. You are always more likely to catch a careless mistake by working more slowly than quickly, and among very high-scoring test takers (those who are likely to have lots of time left over), careless errors affect the score more than mastery of material.

Secret Key #2 - Guessing is not Guesswork

You probably know that guessing is a good idea. Unlike other standardized tests, there is no penalty for getting a wrong answer. Even if you have no idea about a question, you still have a 20-25% chance of getting it right.

Most test takers do not understand the impact that proper guessing can have on their score. Unless you score extremely high, guessing will significantly contribute to your final score.

Monkeys Take the Test

What most test takers don't realize is that to insure that 20-25% chance, you have to guess randomly. If you put 20 monkeys in a room to take this test, assuming they answered once per question and behaved themselves, on average they would get 20-25% of the questions correct. Put 20 test takers in the room, and the average will be much lower among guessed questions. Why?

1. The test writers intentionally write deceptive answer choices that "look" right. A test taker has no idea about a question, so he picks the "best looking" answer, which is often wrong. The monkey has no idea what looks good and what doesn't, so it will consistently be right about 20-25% of the time.

2. Test takers will eliminate answer choices from the guessing pool based on a hunch or intuition. Simple but correct answers often get excluded, leaving a 0% chance of being correct. The monkey has no clue, and often gets lucky with the best choice.

This is why the process of elimination endorsed by most test courses is flawed and detrimental to your performance. Test takers don't guess; they make an ignorant stab in the dark that is usually worse than random.

$5 Challenge

Let me introduce one of the most valuable ideas of this course—the $5 challenge:
- *You only mark your "best guess" if you are willing to bet $5 on it.*
- *You only eliminate choices from guessing if you are willing to bet $5 on it.*

Why $5? Five dollars is an amount of money that is small yet not insignificant, and can really add up fast (20 questions could cost you $100). Likewise, each answer choice on one question of the test will have a small impact on your overall score, but it can really add up to a lot of points in the end.

The process of elimination IS valuable. The following shows your chance of guessing it right:

If you eliminate wrong answer choices until only this many remain:	Chance of getting it correct:
1	100%
2	50%
3	33%

However, if you accidentally eliminate the right answer or go on a hunch for an incorrect answer, your chances drop dramatically—to 0%. By guessing among all the answer choices, you are GUARANTEED to have a shot at the right answer.

That's why the $5 test is so valuable. If you give up the advantage and safety of a pure guess, it had better be worth the risk.

What we still haven't covered is how to be sure that whatever guess you make is truly random. Here's the easiest way:
- *Always pick the first answer choice among those remaining.*

Such a technique means that you have decided, **before you see a single test question**, exactly how you are going to guess, and since the order of choices tells you nothing about which one is correct, this guessing technique is perfectly random.

This section is not meant to scare you away from making educated guesses or eliminating choices; you just need to define when a choice is worth eliminating. The $5 test, along with a pre-defined random guessing strategy, is the best way to make sure you reap all of the benefits of guessing.

Secret Key #3 - Practice Smarter, Not Harder

Many test takers delay the test preparation process because they dread the awful amounts of practice time they think necessary to succeed on the test. We have refined an effective method that will take you only a fraction of the time.

There are a number of "obstacles" in the path to success. Among these are answering questions, finishing in time, and mastering test-taking strategies. All must be executed on the day of the test at peak performance, or your score will suffer. The test is a mental marathon that has a large impact on your future.

Just like a marathon runner, it is important to work your way up to the full challenge. So first you just worry about questions, and then time, and finally strategy:

Success Strategy

1. Find a good source for practice tests.
2. If you are willing to make a larger time investment, consider using more than one study guide. Often the different approaches of multiple authors will help you "get" difficult concepts.
3. Take a practice test with no time constraints, with all study helps, "open book." Take your time with questions and focus on applying strategies.
4. Take a practice test with time constraints, with all guides, "open book."
5. Take a final practice test without open material and with time limits.

If you have time to take more practice tests, just repeat step 5. By gradually exposing yourself to the full rigors of the test environment, you will condition your mind to the stress of test day and maximize your success.

Secret Key #4 - Prepare, Don't Procrastinate

Let me state an obvious fact: if you take the test three times, you will probably get three different scores. This is due to the way you feel on test day, the level of preparedness you have, and the version of the test you see. Despite the test writers' claims to the contrary, some versions of the test WILL be easier for you than others.

Since your future depends so much on your score, you should maximize your chances of success. In order to maximize the likelihood of success, you've got to prepare in advance. This means taking practice tests and spending time learning the information and test taking strategies you will need to succeed.

Never go take the actual test as a "practice" test, expecting that you can just take it again if you need to. Take all the practice tests you can on your own, but when you go to take the official test, be prepared, be focused, and do your best the first time!

Secret Key #5 - Test Yourself

Everyone knows that time is money. There is no need to spend too much of your time or too little of your time preparing for the test. You should only spend as much of your precious time preparing as is necessary for you to get the score you need.

Once you have taken a practice test under real conditions of time constraints, then you will know if you are ready for the test or not.

If you have scored extremely high the first time that you take the practice test, then there is not much point in spending countless hours studying. You are already there.

Benchmark your abilities by retaking practice tests and seeing how much you have improved. Once you consistently score high enough to guarantee success, then you are ready.

If you have scored well below where you need, then knuckle down and begin studying in earnest. Check your improvement regularly through the use of practice tests under real conditions. Above all, don't worry, panic, or give up. The key is perseverance!

Then, when you go to take the test, remain confident and remember how well you did on the practice tests. If you can score high enough on a practice test, then you can do the same on the real thing.

General Strategies

The most important thing you can do is to ignore your fears and jump into the test immediately. Do not be overwhelmed by any strange-sounding terms. You have to jump into the test like jumping into a pool—all at once is the easiest way.

Make Predictions

As you read and understand the question, try to guess what the answer will be. Remember that several of the answer choices are wrong, and once you begin reading them, your mind will immediately become cluttered with answer choices designed to throw you off. Your mind is typically the most focused immediately after you have read the question and digested its contents. If you can, try to predict what the correct answer will be. You may be surprised at what you can predict.

Quickly scan the choices and see if your prediction is in the listed answer choices. If it is, then you can be quite confident that you have the right answer. It still won't hurt to check the other answer choices, but most of the time, you've got it!

Answer the Question

It may seem obvious to only pick answer choices that answer the question, but the test writers can create some excellent answer choices that are wrong. Don't pick an answer just because it sounds right, or you believe it to be true. It MUST answer the question. Once you've made your selection, always go back and check it against the question and make sure that you didn't misread the question and that the answer choice does answer the question posed.

Benchmark

After you read the first answer choice, decide if you think it sounds correct or not. If it doesn't, move on to the next answer choice. If it does, mentally mark that answer choice. This doesn't mean that you've definitely selected it as your answer choice, it just means that it's the best you've seen thus far. Go ahead and read the next choice. If the next choice is worse than the one you've already selected, keep going to the next answer choice. If the next choice is better than the choice you've already selected, mentally mark the new answer choice as your best guess.

The first answer choice that you select becomes your standard. Every other answer choice must be benchmarked against that standard. That choice is correct until proven otherwise by another answer choice beating it out. Once you've decided that no other answer choice seems as good, do one final check to ensure that your answer choice answers the question posed.

Valid Information

Don't discount any of the information provided in the question. Every piece of information may be necessary to determine the correct answer. None of the information in the question is there to throw you off (while the answer choices will certainly have information to throw you off). If two seemingly unrelated topics are discussed, don't ignore either. You can be confident there is a relationship, or it wouldn't be included in the question, and you are probably going to have to determine what is that relationship to find the answer.

Avoid "Fact Traps"

Don't get distracted by a choice that is factually true. Your search is for the answer that answers the question. Stay focused and don't fall for an answer that is true but irrelevant. Always go back to the question and make sure you're choosing an answer that actually answers the question and is not just a true statement. An answer can be factually correct, but it MUST answer the question asked. Additionally, two answers can both be seemingly correct, so be sure to read all of the answer choices, and make sure that you get the one that BEST answers the question.

Milk the Question

Some of the questions may throw you completely off. They might deal with a subject you have not been exposed to, or one that you haven't reviewed in years. While your lack of knowledge about the subject will be a hindrance, the question itself can give you many clues that will help you find the correct answer. Read the question carefully and look for clues. Watch particularly for adjectives and nouns describing difficult terms or words that you don't recognize. Regardless of whether you completely understand a word or not, replacing it with a synonym, either provided or one you more familiar with, may help you to understand what the questions are asking. Rather than wracking your mind about specific detailed information concerning a difficult term or word, try to use mental substitutes that are easier to understand.

The Trap of Familiarity

Don't just choose a word because you recognize it. On difficult questions, you may not recognize a number of words in the answer choices. The test writers don't put "make-believe" words on the test, so don't think that just because you only recognize all the words in one answer choice that that answer choice must be correct. If you only recognize words in one answer choice, then focus on that one. Is it correct? Try your best to determine if it is correct. If it is, that's great. If not, eliminate it. Each word and answer choice you eliminate increases your chances of getting the question correct, even if you then have to guess among the unfamiliar choices.

Eliminate Answers

Eliminate choices as soon as you realize they are wrong. But be careful! Make sure you consider all of the possible answer choices. Just because one appears right, doesn't mean that the next one won't be even better! The test writers will usually put more than one good answer choice for every question, so read all of them. Don't worry if you are stuck between two that seem right. By getting down to just two remaining possible choices, your odds are now 50/50. Rather than wasting too much time, play the odds. You are guessing, but guessing wisely because you've been able to knock out some of the answer choices that you know are wrong. If you are eliminating choices and realize that the last answer choice you are left with is also obviously wrong, don't panic. Start over and consider each choice again. There may easily be something that you missed the first time and will realize on the second pass.

Tough Questions

If you are stumped on a problem or it appears too hard or too difficult, don't waste time. Move on! Remember though, if you can quickly check for obviously incorrect answer choices, your chances of guessing correctly are greatly improved. Before you completely give up, at least try to knock out a couple of possible answers. Eliminate what you can and then guess at the remaining answer choices before moving on.

Brainstorm

If you get stuck on a difficult question, spend a few seconds quickly brainstorming. Run through the complete list of possible answer choices. Look at each choice and ask yourself, "Could this answer the question satisfactorily?" Go through each answer choice and consider it independently of the others. By systematically going through all possibilities, you may find something that you would otherwise overlook. Remember though that when you get stuck, it's important to try to keep moving.

Read Carefully

Understand the problem. Read the question and answer choices carefully. Don't miss the question because you misread the terms. You have plenty of time to read each question thoroughly and make sure you understand what is being asked. Yet a happy medium must be attained, so don't waste too much time. You must read carefully, but efficiently.

Face Value

When in doubt, use common sense. Always accept the situation in the problem at face value. Don't read too much into it. These problems will not require you to make huge leaps of logic. The test writers aren't trying to throw you off with a cheap trick. If you have to go beyond creativity and make a leap of logic in order to have an answer choice answer the question, then you should look at the other answer choices. Don't overcomplicate the problem by creating theoretical relationships or explanations that will warp time or space. These are normal problems rooted in reality. It's just that the applicable relationship or explanation may not be readily apparent and you have to figure things out. Use your common sense to interpret anything that isn't clear.

Prefixes

If you're having trouble with a word in the question or answer choices, try dissecting it. Take advantage of every clue that the word might include. Prefixes and suffixes can be a huge help. Usually they allow you to determine a basic meaning. Pre- means before, post- means after, pro - is positive, de- is negative. From these prefixes and suffixes, you can get an idea of the general meaning of the word and try to put it into context. Beware though of any traps. Just because con- is the opposite of pro-, doesn't necessarily mean congress is the opposite of progress!

Hedge Phrases

Watch out for critical hedge phrases, led off with words such as "likely," "may," "can," "sometimes," "often," "almost," "mostly," "usually," "generally," "rarely," and "sometimes." Question writers insert these hedge phrases to cover every possibility. Often an answer choice will be wrong simply because it leaves no room for exception. Unless the situation calls for them, avoid answer choices that have definitive words like "exactly," and "always."

Switchback Words

Stay alert for "switchbacks." These are the words and phrases frequently used to alert you to shifts in thought. The most common switchback word is "but." Others include "although," "however," "nevertheless," "on the other hand," "even though," "while," "in spite of," "despite," and "regardless of."

New Information

Correct answer choices will rarely have completely new information included. Answer choices typically are straightforward reflections of the material asked about and will directly relate to the question. If a new piece of information is included in an answer choice that doesn't even seem to relate to the topic being asked about, then that answer choice is likely incorrect. All of the information needed to answer the question is usually provided for you in the question. You should not have to make guesses that are unsupported or choose answer choices that require unknown information that cannot be reasoned from what is given.

Time Management

On technical questions, don't get lost on the technical terms. Don't spend too much time on any one question. If you don't know what a term means, then odds are you aren't going to get much further since you don't have a dictionary. You should be able to immediately recognize whether or not you know a term. If you don't, work with the other clues that you have—the other answer choices and terms provided—but don't waste too much time trying to figure out a difficult term that you don't know.

Contextual Clues

Look for contextual clues. An answer can be right but not the correct answer. The contextual clues will help you find the answer that is most right and is correct. Understand the context in which a phrase or statement is made. This will help you make important distinctions.

Don't Panic

Panicking will not answer any questions for you; therefore, it isn't helpful. When you first see the question, if your mind goes blank, take a deep breath. Force yourself to mechanically go through the steps of solving the problem using the strategies you've learned.

Pace Yourself

Don't get clock fever. It's easy to be overwhelmed when you're looking at a page full of questions, your mind is full of random thoughts and feeling confused, and the clock is ticking down faster than you would like. Calm down and maintain the pace that you have set for yourself. As long as you are on track by monitoring your pace, you are guaranteed to have enough time for yourself. When you get to the last few minutes of the test, it may seem like you won't have enough time left, but if you only have as many questions as you should have left at that point, then you're right on track!

Answer Selection

The best way to pick an answer choice is to eliminate all of those that are wrong, until only one is left and confirm that is the correct answer. Sometimes though, an answer choice may immediately look right. Be careful! Take a second to make sure that the other choices are not equally obvious. Don't make a hasty mistake. There are only two times that you should stop before checking other answers. First is when you are positive that the answer choice you have selected is correct. Second is when time is almost out and you have to make a quick guess!

Check Your Work

Since you will probably not know every term listed and the answer to every question, it is important that you get credit for the ones that you do know. Don't miss any questions through careless mistakes. If at all possible, try to take a second to look back over your answer selection and make sure you've selected the correct answer choice and haven't made a costly careless mistake (such as marking an answer choice that you didn't mean to mark). The time it takes for this quick double check should more than pay for itself in caught mistakes.

Beware of Directly Quoted Answers

Sometimes an answer choice will repeat word for word a portion of the question or reference section. However, beware of such exact duplication. It may be a trap! More than likely, the correct choice will paraphrase or summarize a point, rather than being exactly the same wording.

Slang

Scientific sounding answers are better than slang ones. An answer choice that begins "To compare the outcomes…" is much more likely to be correct than one that begins "Because some people insisted…"

Extreme Statements

Avoid wild answers that throw out highly controversial ideas that are proclaimed as established fact. An answer choice that states the "process should used in certain situations, if…" is much more likely to be correct than one that states the "process should be discontinued completely." The first is a calm rational statement and doesn't even make a definitive, uncompromising stance, using a hedge word "if" to provide wiggle room, whereas the second choice is a radical idea and far more extreme.

Answer Choice Families

When you have two or more answer choices that are direct opposites or parallels, one of them is usually the correct answer. For instance, if one answer choice states "x increases" and another answer choice states "x decreases" or "y increases," then those two or three answer choices are very similar in construction and fall into the same family of answer choices. A family of answer choices consists of two or three answer choices, very similar in construction, but often with directly opposite meanings. Usually the correct answer choice will be in that family of answer choices. The "odd man out" or answer choice that doesn't seem to fit the parallel construction of the other answer choices is more likely to be incorrect.

Special Report: How to Overcome Test Anxiety

The very nature of tests caters to some level of anxiety, nervousness, or tension, just as we feel for any important event that occurs in our lives. A little bit of anxiety or nervousness can be a good thing. It helps us with motivation, and makes achievement just that much sweeter. However, too much anxiety can be a problem, especially if it hinders our ability to function and perform.

"Test anxiety," is the term that refers to the emotional reactions that some test-takers experience when faced with a test or exam. Having a fear of testing and exams is based upon a rational fear, since the test-taker's performance can shape the course of an academic career. Nevertheless, experiencing excessive fear of examinations will only interfere with the test-taker's ability to perform and chance to be successful.

There are a large variety of causes that can contribute to the development and sensation of test anxiety. These include, but are not limited to, lack of preparation and worrying about issues surrounding the test.

Lack of Preparation

Lack of preparation can be identified by the following behaviors or situations:
- Not scheduling enough time to study, and therefore cramming the night before the test or exam
- Managing time poorly, to create the sensation that there is not enough time to do everything
- Failing to organize the text information in advance, so that the study material consists of the entire text and not simply the pertinent information
- Poor overall studying habits

Worrying, on the other hand, can be related to both the test taker, or many other factors around him/her that will be affected by the results of the test. These include worrying about:
- Previous performances on similar exams, or exams in general
- How friends and other students are achieving
- The negative consequences that will result from a poor grade or failure

There are three primary elements to test anxiety. Physical components, which involve the same typical bodily reactions as those to acute anxiety (to be discussed below). Emotional factors have to do with fear or panic. Mental or cognitive issues concerning attention spans and memory abilities.

Physical Signals

There are many different symptoms of test anxiety, and these are not limited to mental and emotional strain. Frequently there are a range of physical signals that will let a test taker know that he/she is suffering from test anxiety. These bodily changes can include the following:
- Perspiring
- Sweaty palms
- Wet, trembling hands

- Nausea
- Dry mouth
- A knot in the stomach
- Headache
- Faintness
- Muscle tension
- Aching shoulders, back and neck
- Rapid heart beat
- Feeling too hot/cold

To recognize the sensation of test anxiety, a test-taker should monitor him/herself for the following sensations:
- The physical distress symptoms as listed above
- Emotional sensitivity, expressing emotional feelings such as the need to cry or laugh too much, or a sensation of anger or helplessness
- A decreased ability to think, causing the test-taker to blank out or have racing thoughts that are hard to organize or control.

Though most students will feel some level of anxiety when faced with a test or exam, the majority can cope with that anxiety and maintain it at a manageable level. However, those who cannot are faced with a very real and very serious condition, which can and should be controlled for the immeasurable benefit of this sufferer.

Naturally, these sensations lead to negative results for the testing experience. The most common effects of test anxiety have to do with nervousness and mental blocking.

Nervousness

Nervousness can appear in several different levels:
- The test-taker's difficulty, or even inability to read and understand the questions on the test
- The difficulty or inability to organize thoughts to a coherent form
- The difficulty or inability to recall key words and concepts relating to the testing questions (especially essays)
- The receipt of poor grades on a test, though the test material was well known by the test taker

Conversely, a person may also experience mental blocking, which involves:
- Blanking out on test questions
- Only remembering the correct answers to the questions when the test has already finished.

Fortunately for test anxiety sufferers, beating these feelings, to a large degree, has to do with proper preparation. When a test taker has a feeling of preparedness, then anxiety will be dramatically lessened.

The first step to resolving anxiety issues is to distinguish which of the two types of anxiety are being suffered. If the anxiety is a direct result of a lack of preparation, this should be considered a normal reaction, and the anxiety level (as opposed to the test results) shouldn't be anything to worry about. However, if, when adequately prepared, the test-taker still panics, blanks out, or seems to overreact, this is not a fully rational reaction. While this can be considered normal too, there are many ways to combat and overcome these effects.

Remember that anxiety cannot be entirely eliminated, however, there are ways to minimize it, to make the anxiety easier to manage. Preparation is one of the best ways to minimize test anxiety. Therefore the following techniques are wise in order to best fight off any anxiety that may want to build.

To begin with, try to avoid cramming before a test, whenever it is possible. By trying to memorize an entire term's worth of information in one day, you'll be shocking your system, and not giving yourself a very good chance to absorb the information. This is an easy path to anxiety, so for those who suffer from test anxiety, cramming should not even be considered an option.

Instead of cramming, work throughout the semester to combine all of the material which is presented throughout the semester, and work on it gradually as the course goes by, making sure to master the main concepts first, leaving minor details for a week or so before the test.

To study for the upcoming exam, be sure to pose questions that may be on the examination, to gauge the ability to answer them by integrating the ideas from your texts, notes and lectures, as well as any supplementary readings.

If it is truly impossible to cover all of the information that was covered in that particular term, concentrate on the most important portions, that can be covered very well. Learn these concepts as best as possible, so that when the test comes, a goal can be made to use these concepts as presentations of your knowledge.

In addition to study habits, changes in attitude are critical to beating a struggle with test anxiety. In fact, an improvement of the perspective over the entire test-taking experience can actually help a test taker to enjoy studying and therefore improve the overall experience. Be certain not to overemphasize the significance of the grade - know that the result of the test is neither a reflection of self worth, nor is it a measure of intelligence; one grade will not predict a person's future success.

To improve an overall testing outlook, the following steps should be tried:
- Keeping in mind that the most reasonable expectation for taking a test is to expect to try to demonstrate as much of what you know as you possibly can.
- Reminding ourselves that a test is only one test; this is not the only one, and there will be others.
- The thought of thinking of oneself in an irrational, all-or-nothing term should be avoided at all costs.
- A reward should be designated for after the test, so there's something to look forward to. Whether it be going to a movie, going out to eat, or simply visiting friends, schedule it in advance, and do it no matter what result is expected on the exam.

Test-takers should also keep in mind that the basics are some of the most important things, even beyond anti-anxiety techniques and studying. Never neglect the basic social, emotional and biological needs, in order to try to absorb information. In order to best achieve, these three factors must be held as just as important as the studying itself.

Study Steps

Remember the following important steps for studying:
- Maintain healthy nutrition and exercise habits. Continue both your recreational activities and social pass times. These both contribute to your physical and emotional well being.
- Be certain to get a good amount of sleep, especially the night before the test, because when you're overtired you are not able to perform to the best of your best ability.
- Keep the studying pace to a moderate level by taking breaks when they are needed, and varying the work whenever possible, to keep the mind fresh instead of getting bored.
- When enough studying has been done that all the material that can be learned has been learned, and the test taker is prepared for the test, stop studying and do something relaxing such as listening to music, watching a movie, or taking a warm bubble bath.

There are also many other techniques to minimize the uneasiness or apprehension that is experienced along with test anxiety before, during, or even after the examination. In fact, there are a great deal of things that can be done to stop anxiety from interfering with lifestyle and performance. Again, remember that anxiety will not be eliminated entirely, and it shouldn't be. Otherwise that "up" feeling for exams would not exist, and most of us depend on that sensation to perform better than usual. However, this anxiety has to be at a level that is manageable.

Of course, as we have just discussed, being prepared for the exam is half the battle right away. Attending all classes, finding out what knowledge will be expected on the exam, and knowing the exam schedules are easy steps to lowering anxiety. Keeping up with work will remove the need to cram, and efficient study habits will eliminate wasted time. Studying should be done in an ideal location for concentration, so that it is simple to become interested in the material and give it complete attention. A method such as SQ3R (Survey, Question, Read, Recite, Review) is a wonderful key to follow to make sure that the study habits are as effective as possible, especially in the case of learning from a textbook. Flashcards are great techniques for memorization. Learning to take good notes will mean that notes will be full of useful information, so that less sifting will need to be done to seek out what is pertinent for studying. Reviewing notes after class and then again on occasion will keep the information fresh in the mind. From notes that have been taken summary sheets and outlines can be made for simpler reviewing.

A study group can also be a very motivational and helpful place to study, as there will be a sharing of ideas, all of the minds can work together, to make sure that everyone understands, and the studying will be made more interesting because it will be a social occasion.

Basically, though, as long as the test-taker remains organized and self confident, with efficient study habits, less time will need to be spent studying, and higher grades will be achieved.

To become self confident, there are many useful steps. The first of these is "self talk." It has been shown through extensive research, that self-talk for students who suffer from test anxiety, should be well monitored, in order to make sure that it contributes to self confidence as opposed to sinking the student. Frequently the self talk of test-anxious students is negative or self-defeating, thinking that everyone else is smarter and faster, that they always mess up, and that if they don't do well, they'll fail the entire course. It is important to decreasing anxiety that awareness is made of self talk. Try writing any negative self thoughts and then disputing them with a positive statement instead. Begin self-encouragement as though it was a friend speaking. Repeat positive statements to help reprogram the mind to believing in successes instead of failures.

Helpful Techniques

Other extremely helpful techniques include:
- Self-visualization of doing well and reaching goals
- While aiming for an "A" level of understanding, don't try to "overprotect" by setting your expectations lower. This will only convince the mind to stop studying in order to meet the lower expectations.
- Don't make comparisons with the results or habits of other students. These are individual factors, and different things work for different people, causing different results.
- Strive to become an expert in learning what works well, and what can be done in order to improve. Consider collecting this data in a journal.
- Create rewards for after studying instead of doing things before studying that will only turn into avoidance behaviors.
- Make a practice of relaxing - by using methods such as progressive relaxation, self-hypnosis, guided imagery, etc - in order to make relaxation an automatic sensation.
- Work on creating a state of relaxed concentration so that concentrating will take on the focus of the mind, so that none will be wasted on worrying.
- Take good care of the physical self by eating well and getting enough sleep.
- Plan in time for exercise and stick to this plan.

Beyond these techniques, there are other methods to be used before, during and after the test that will help the test-taker perform well in addition to overcoming anxiety.

Before the exam comes the academic preparation. This involves establishing a study schedule and beginning at least one week before the actual date of the test. By doing this, the anxiety of not having enough time to study for the test will be automatically eliminated. Moreover, this will make the studying a much more effective experience, ensuring that the learning will be an easier process. This relieves much undue pressure on the test-taker.

Summary sheets, note cards, and flash cards with the main concepts and examples of these main concepts should be prepared in advance of the actual studying time. A topic should never be eliminated from this process. By omitting a topic because it isn't expected to be on the test is only setting up the test-taker for anxiety should it actually appear on the exam. Utilize the course syllabus for laying out the topics that should be studied. Carefully go over the notes that were made in class, paying special attention to any of the issues that the professor took special care to emphasize while lecturing in class. In the textbooks, use the chapter review, or if possible, the chapter tests, to begin your review.

It may even be possible to ask the instructor what information will be covered on the exam, or what the format of the exam will be (for example, multiple choice, essay, free form, true-false). Additionally, see if it is possible to find out how many questions will be on the test. If a review sheet or sample test has been offered by the professor, make good use of it, above anything else, for the preparation for the test. Another great resource for getting to know the examination is reviewing tests from previous semesters. Use these tests to review, and aim to achieve a 100% score on each of the possible topics. With a few exceptions, the goal that you set for yourself is the highest one that you will reach.

Take all of the questions that were assigned as homework, and rework them to any other possible course material. The more problems reworked, the more skill and confidence will form as a result.

When forming the solution to a problem, write out each of the steps. Don't simply do head work. By doing as many steps on paper as possible, much clarification and therefore confidence will be formed. Do this with as many homework problems as possible, before checking the answers. By checking the answer after each problem, a reinforcement will exist, that will not be on the exam. Study situations should be as exam-like as possible, to prime the test-taker's system for the experience. By waiting to check the answers at the end, a psychological advantage will be formed, to decrease the stress factor.

Another fantastic reason for not cramming is the avoidance of confusion in concepts, especially when it comes to mathematics. 8-10 hours of study will become one hundred percent more effective if it is spread out over a week or at least several days, instead of doing it all in one sitting. Recognize that the human brain requires time in order to assimilate new material, so frequent breaks and a span of study time over several days will be much more beneficial.

Additionally, don't study right up until the point of the exam. Studying should stop a minimum of one hour before the exam begins. This allows the brain to rest and put things in their proper order. This will also provide the time to become as relaxed as possible when going into the examination room. The test-taker will also have time to eat well and eat sensibly. Know that the brain needs food as much as the rest of the body. With enough food and enough sleep, as well as a relaxed attitude, the body and the mind are primed for success.

Avoid any anxious classmates who are talking about the exam. These students only spread anxiety, and are not worth sharing the anxious sentimentalities.

Before the test also involves creating a positive attitude, so mental preparation should also be a point of concentration. There are many keys to creating a positive attitude. Should fears become rushing in, make a visualization of taking the exam, doing well, and seeing an A written on the paper. Write out a list of affirmations that will bring a feeling of confidence, such as "I am doing well in my English class," "I studied well and know my material," "I enjoy this class." Even if the affirmations aren't believed at first, it sends a positive message to the subconscious which will result in an alteration of the overall belief system, which is the system that creates reality.

If a sensation of panic begins, work with the fear and imagine the very worst! Work through the entire scenario of not passing the test, failing the entire course, and dropping out of school, followed by not getting a job, and pushing a shopping cart through the dark alley where you'll live. This will place things into perspective! Then, practice deep breathing and create a visualization of the opposite situation - achieving an "A" on the exam, passing the entire course, receiving the degree at a graduation ceremony.

On the day of the test, there are many things to be done to ensure the best results, as well as the most calm outlook. The following stages are suggested in order to maximize test-taking potential:
- Begin the examination day with a moderate breakfast, and avoid any coffee or beverages with caffeine if the test taker is prone to jitters. Even people who are used to managing caffeine can feel jittery or light-headed when it is taken on a test day.
- Attempt to do something that is relaxing before the examination begins. As last minute cramming clouds the mastering of overall concepts, it is better to use this time to create a calming outlook.
- Be certain to arrive at the test location well in advance, in order to provide time to select a location that is away from doors, windows and other distractions, as well as giving enough time to relax before the test begins.

- Keep away from anxiety generating classmates who will upset the sensation of stability and relaxation that is being attempted before the exam.
- Should the waiting period before the exam begins cause anxiety, create a self-distraction by reading a light magazine or something else that is relaxing and simple.

During the exam itself, read the entire exam from beginning to end, and find out how much time should be allotted to each individual problem. Once writing the exam, should more time be taken for a problem, it should be abandoned, in order to begin another problem. If there is time at the end, the unfinished problem can always be returned to and completed.

Read the instructions very carefully - twice - so that unpleasant surprises won't follow during or after the exam has ended.

When writing the exam, pretend that the situation is actually simply the completion of homework within a library, or at home. This will assist in forming a relaxed atmosphere, and will allow the brain extra focus for the complex thinking function.

Begin the exam with all of the questions with which the most confidence is felt. This will build the confidence level regarding the entire exam and will begin a quality momentum. This will also create encouragement for trying the problems where uncertainty resides.

Going with the "gut instinct" is always the way to go when solving a problem. Second guessing should be avoided at all costs. Have confidence in the ability to do well.

For essay questions, create an outline in advance that will keep the mind organized and make certain that all of the points are remembered. For multiple choice, read every answer, even if the correct one has been spotted - a better one may exist.

Continue at a pace that is reasonable and not rushed, in order to be able to work carefully. Provide enough time to go over the answers at the end, to check for small errors that can be corrected.

Should a feeling of panic begin, breathe deeply, and think of the feeling of the body releasing sand through its pores. Visualize a calm, peaceful place, and include all of the sights, sounds and sensations of this image. Continue the deep breathing, and take a few minutes to continue this with closed eyes. When all is well again, return to the test.

If a "blanking" occurs for a certain question, skip it and move on to the next question. There will be time to return to the other question later. Get everything done that can be done, first, to guarantee all the grades that can be compiled, and to build all of the confidence possible. Then return to the weaker questions to build the marks from there.

Remember, one's own reality can be created, so as long as the belief is there, success will follow. And remember: anxiety can happen later, right now, there's an exam to be written!

After the examination is complete, whether there is a feeling for a good grade or a bad grade, don't dwell on the exam, and be certain to follow through on the reward that was promised…and enjoy it! Don't dwell on any mistakes that have been made, as there is nothing that can be done at this point anyway.

Additionally, don't begin to study for the next test right away. Do something relaxing for a while, and let the mind relax and prepare itself to begin absorbing information again.

From the results of the exam - both the grade and the entire experience, be certain to learn from what has gone on. Perfect studying habits and work some more on confidence in order to make the next examination experience even better than the last one.

Learn to avoid places where openings occurred for laziness, procrastination and day dreaming.

Use the time between this exam and the next one to better learn to relax, even learning to relax on cue, so that any anxiety can be controlled during the next exam. Learn how to relax the body. Slouch in your chair if that helps. Tighten and then relax all of the different muscle groups, one group at a time, beginning with the feet and then working all the way up to the neck and face. This will ultimately relax the muscles more than they were to begin with. Learn how to breathe deeply and comfortably, and focus on this breathing going in and out as a relaxing thought. With every exhale, repeat the word "relax."

As common as test anxiety is, it is very possible to overcome it. Make yourself one of the test-takers who overcome this frustrating hindrance.

Additional Bonus Material

Due to our efforts to try to keep this book to a manageable length, we've created a link that will give you access to all of your additional bonus material.

Please visit http://www.mometrix.com/bonus948/iltsphysicaled to access the information.